150 Ways
Teens Can Make a Difference

The Peterson's H.S. Series
Books by, for, and about teens

War and Peace in the Persian Gulf:
What Teenagers Want to Know
(A "Peterson's H.S." Special Report)

Greetings from High School
Teenspeak About Life and Acing High School

150 Ways Teens Can Make a Difference
Strategies for Making a Genuine Contribution

150 Ways
Teens Can Make a Difference

by Marian Salzman and Teresa Reisgies
with Maribel Becker and Ann O'Reilly
and

Dan Altman, Maya Beasley, Sarah Beatty, Jongnic Bontemps, John Boris,
Suzanne Doran, John Gaghan, Nicole Gaghan, Sylvia Heredia, Jean Hoffman,
Jane Odiseos, Chris Pennisi, David Portny, and Melissa Wagner

Peterson's Guides
Princeton, New Jersey

Most references to students reflect the 1990–91 school year.

Library of Congress Cataloging-in-Publication Data

Salzman, Marian, 1959–
    150 ways teens can make a difference / by Marian Salzman and Teresa Reisgies with Ann O'Reilly ... [et al.].
        p.   cm. — (The Peterson's H.S. series)
    Includes index.
    Summary: Teenagers discuss the rewarding and sometimes frustrating experiences of being a volunteer, including their commitment and accomplishments, parental support, and how they incorporate volunteer activities into their busy high school schedules.
    ISBN 1-56079-093-8 : $7.95
    1. Voluntarism—United States—Juvenile literature.
[1. Voluntarism.] I. Reisgies, Teresa, 1966– . II. Title.
III. Series.
HN90.V64S25   1991
302'.14—dc20   91-2965

Cover and text design by Frierson + Mee Associates, Inc.

Printed in the United States of America

10 9 8 7 6 5 4 3 2 1

Table of Contents

Dedication

Here's to hoping that the nineties is the decade of giving back and that today's teenage realists will prove that caring can make a difference, for once and for all.

Acknowledgments

Special thanks to the following schools for their cooperation:
Abbeville High School, Abbeville, Alabama; Aiken Preparatory School, Aiken, South Carolina; Allentown High School, Allentown, New Jersey; Apollo High School, St. Cloud, Minnesota; Apple Valley High School, Rosemount, Minnesota; Arts High School, Newark, New Jersey; The Asheville School, Asheville, North Carolina; Ashley Hall School, Charleston, South Carolina; Augusta Preparatory School, Augusta, Georgia; Bailey Magnet School, Jackson, Mississippi; Bancroft School, Worcester, Massachusetts; Bay High School, Bay Village, Ohio; Beachwood High School, Beachwood, Ohio; Bergen School, Jersey City, New Jersey; Berwick Academy, South Berwick, Maine; The Bishop's School, La Jolla, California; The Blake School, Minneapolis, Minnesota; Bordentown Regional High School, Bordentown, New Jersey; Brandon Hall School, Atlanta, Georgia; The Brearley School, New York, New York; Breck School, Minneapolis, Minnesota; Brick Township High School, Brick, New Jersey; Bridgewater-Raritan High School East, Martinsville, New Jersey; Brimhall School, Minneapolis, Minnesota; The Brimmer and May School, Chestnut Hill, Massachusetts; Bronx High School of Science, New York, New York; Brooklyn Friends School, Brooklyn, New York; Brooks Academy, North Andover, Massachusetts; Brunswick School, Greenwich, Connecticut; Byram Hills Senior High School, Armonk, New York; The Calhoun School, New York, New York; The Cambridge School, Weston, Massachusetts; Canton High School, Canton, Massachusetts; Cathedral High School, New Ulm, Minnesota; The Cathedral Schools of St. Mary and St. Paul, Garden City, New York; Central Regional High School, Bayville, New Jersey; Chaminade High School, Mineola, New York; Chapin School, Princeton, New Jersey; Cherry Hill High School East, Cherry Hill, New Jersey; Cherry Hill High School West, Cherry Hill, New Jersey; Clearfield High School, Clearfield, Utah; Cohasset Senior High School, Cohasset, Massachusetts; The Charles River School, Dover, Massachusetts; The Collegiate School, New York, New York; Columbia Grammar and Preparatory School, New York, New York; Convent of the Sacred Heart, Greenwich, Connecticut; Convent of the Sacred Heart, New York, New York; Convent of the Visitation School, St. Paul, Minnesota; Coon Rapids Senior High School, Coon Rapids, Minnesota; Cranbrook Kingswood School, Bloomfield Hills, Michigan; Dana Hall School, Wellesley, Massachusetts; David Douglas High School, Portland, Oregon; The Daycroft School, Greenwich, Connecticut; Dedham Country Day School, Dedham, Massachusetts; Delano High School, Delano, Minnesota; Delphian School, Sheridan, Oregon; The Derryfield School, Manchester, New Hampshire; Division Avenue High School, Levittown, New York; The Donoho School, Anniston, Alabama; Dwight-Englewood School, Englewood, New Jersey; Edgemont High School, Scarsdale, New York; Egg Harbor Township High School, Pleasantville, New Jersey; Eldorado High School, Las Vegas, Nevada; Elisabeth Irwin High School, New York, New York; Ewing High School, Trenton, New Jersey; The Fieldston School, Bronx, New York; Forest Ridge School, Bellevue, Washington; Fort Worth Country Day School, Fort Worth, Texas; Franklin County High School, Winchester, Tennessee; Friends Academy, Locust Valley, New York; Friends Seminary, New York, New York; Garden City Middle School, Garden City, New York; Gainesville High School, Gainesville, Florida; Glen Cove High School, Glen Cove, New York; Gould Academy, Bethel, Maine; Grapevine High School, Grapevine, Texas; Greens Farms Academy, Greens Farms, New York; Greenhills School, Ann Arbor, Michigan; Greensboro Day School, Greensboro, North Carolina; Greenvale School, Glen Head, New York; Greenwich Academy, Greenwich, Connecticut; Greenwich High School, Greenwich, Connecti-

cut; Grosse Pointe South High School, Grosse Pointe, Michigan; Haddonfield Memorial High School, Haddonfield, New Jersey; Hammonton High School, Hammonton, New Jersey; Hanover Park High School, East Hanover, New Jersey; Hartford Union High School, Hartford, Wisconsin; Herricks Senior High School, New Hyde Park, New York; Hicksville High School, Hicksville, New York; The Hewitt School, New York, New York; Holmdel High School, Holmdel, New Jersey; Horace Mann School, Bronx, New York; The Hun School of Princeton, Princeton, New Jersey; Huntsville High School, Huntsville, Alabama; Immaculate Heart High School, Tucson, Arizona; Jericho Senior High School, Jericho, New York; Jesuit College Preparatory School, Dallas, Texas; John F. Kennedy High School, Plainview, New York; Kahuku High School, Kahuku, Hawaii; Kellenberg High School, Uniondale, New York; Kent Denver School, Englewood, Colorado; Kent Place School, Summit, New Jersey; King & Low-Heywood Thomas School, Stamford, Connecticut; The Kinkaid School, Houston, Texas; La Jolla Country Day School, La Jolla, California; Lake Forest Academy, Lake Forest, Illinois; The Lawrenceville School, Lawrenceville, New Jersey; Livingston High School, Livingston, New Jersey; The Loomis Chaffee School, Windsor, Connecticut; Loyola School, New York, New York; Lynbrook Senior High School, Lynbrook, New York; Malcolm X. Shabazz High School, Newark, New Jersey; Manhasset Senior High School, Manhasset, New York; The Marvelwoods School, Cornwall, Connecticut; The Masters School, West Simsbury, Connecticut; The Masters School/Dobbs, Dobbs Ferry, New York; Maui High School, Maui, Hawaii; McCluer Senior High School, Florissant, Missouri; Mid-Pacific Institute, Honolulu, Hawaii; Millburn Senior High School, Millburn, New Jersey; Milton Academy, Milton, Massachusetts; The Montgomery Academy, Montgomery, Alabama; Moorestown Friends School, Moorestown, New Jersey; Moravian Academy, Bethlehem, Pennsylvania; The Morristown-Beard School, Morristown, New Jersey; Moses Brown School, Providence, Rhode Island; Mounds Park Academy, St. Paul, Minnesota; Mount St. Joseph Academy, Rutland, Vermont; Mountain Home Senior High School, Mountain Home, Idaho; Nampa Christian High School, Nampa, Idaho; Naperville North High School, Naperville, Illinois; Newark Academy, Livingston, New Jersey; Norcross High School, Norcross, Georgia; The Norfolk Academy, Norfolk, Virginia; Notre Dame High School, Fairfield, Connecticut; Notre Dame High School, West Haven, Connecticut; North Shore High School, Glen Cove, New York; Nottingham High School, Trenton, New Jersey; Oceanside High School, Oceanside, New York; The Packer Collegiate Institute, Brooklyn, New York; The Peddie School, Hightstown, New Jersey; The Pennington School, Pennington, New Jersey; Phillips Academy, Andover, Massachusetts; Pine Crest School, Fort Lauderdale, Florida; Pine Ridge School, Williston, Vermont; Pingree School, South Hamilton, Massachusets; The Pingry School, Martinsville, New Jersey; Pitman High School, Pitman, New Jersey; Portledge School, Locust Valley, New York; The Princeton Day School, Princeton, New Jersey; Princeton High School, Princeton, New Jersey; Providence Day School, Charlotte, North Carolina; Provo Senior High School, Provo, Utah; Ravenscroft School, Raleigh, North Carolina; T. F. Riggs High School, Pierre, South Dakota; Rippowam Cisque School, Bedford, New York; Rippowam High School, Stamford, Connecticut; Riverdale Country School, Bronx, New York; Robert Louis Stevenson High School, Pebble Beach, California; Roland Park Country School, Baltimore, Maryland; Roncalli High School, Aberdeen, South Dakota; Roslyn High School, Roslyn Heights, New York; Roycemore School, Evanston, Illinois; Rye High School, Rye, New York; Sacred Heart Academy, Hempstead, New York; Sacred Heart School, Atherton, California; Saint Agnes High School, St. Paul, Minnesota; Saint Andrew's School of Boca Raton, Boca Raton, Florida; Sandia Preparatory School,

Albuquerque, New Mexico; Sayville High School, Sayville, New York; School of the Holy Child, Rye, New York; Science High School, Newark, New Jersey; Shawnee Mission East High School, Shawnee Mission, Kansas; Somerville High School, Somerville, New Jersey; South High School, Omaha, Nebraska; Southfield School, Shreveport, Louisiana; Southwest High School, Minneapolis, Minnesota; St. Albans School, Washington, D.C.; St. Andrew's Episcopal School, Bethesda, Maryland; St. Croix Lutheran High School, St. Paul, Minnesota; St. Francis Preparatory School, Fresh Meadows, New York; St. Hilda's and St. Hugh's School, New York, New York; St. John's Preparatory School, Collegeville, Minnesota; St. Thomas Academy, St. Paul, Minnesota; St. Stephen's School, Alexandria, Virginia; The Summit School, Winston-Salem, North Carolina; Tabor Academy, Marion, Massachusetts; Trenton Central High School, Trenton, New Jersey; Trinity Valley School, Fort Worth, Texas; Tilton School, Tilton, New Hampshire; Tower Hill School, Wilmington, Delaware; Trumbull High School, Trumbull, Connecticut; Upper Dublin High School, Fort Washington, Pennsylvania; United Nations International School, New York, New York; Wardlaw-Hartridge School, Edison, New Jersey; Wasatch Academy, Mt. Pleasant, Utah; Washburn Senior High School, Minneapolis, Minnesota; The Webb School, Bell Buckle, Tennessee; Whitby School, Greenwich, Connecticut; William Chrisman Senior High School, Independence, Missouri; William H. Hall High School, West Hartford, Connecticut; The Wilson School, Mountain Lakes, New Jersey; Wilton High School, Wilton, Connecticut; Wilmington Friends School, Wilmington, Delaware; Woodmere Academy, Woodmere, New York; Woodstock Union High School, Woodstock, Vermont; Wooster School, Danbury, Connecticut; and York Preparatory School, New York, New York.

And special thanks to Donna Zaccaro, Terry Barnett, Cindy Lane Fazio, and Cordelia Richards of The Bedford Kent Group; to Gary Goldstein and his colleagues at The Whitney Group; to Rick Salomon and Lori Phillipson of Christy & Viener; to the staff at Peterson's; and to Carol Cone and Linda Berlinghoff of Cone Communications.

Finally, thanks to the people who are Esprit de Corps, including Bruce Katz, Susie Tompkins, Isaac Stein, Neil Kraft, Gaynor Strachen, and Cat Doran.

How—and Why—to Use This Book

So you're going to volunteer. Congratulations! You've joined the ranks of Americans who donate more than 2 billion hours per year to volunteer work. Of those 2 billion hours, young people contribute about 250 million. Their causes cover every human concern: health, education, the arts, recreation, the environment, youth, business, politics, animal rights, and public service, to name just a few. What keeps these young volunteers coming back for more? It's plain and simple: Working for something you really believe in makes you feel good.

For some of you, this volunteer experience will be the first "job" you've ever had. As with most jobs, you'll have to search a bit to find the one that will keep you coming back for more. But whatever your goals, whatever your interests, remember that you can find your niche in the world of service work. This book will steer you toward the job that is right for you. After all, the happier you are with your volunteer job, the more you'll be giving back to your cause.

Use this book as both a source of ideas and a guide to volunteer employment. In Part I, glance over the personal accounts of kids from across the country to see what they say about the volunteer work they do. Find out about their motivations and about the pros and cons of their jobs. Read about the way these young people feel at the end of a service stint and about what volunteering has done for their sense of worth. Then take a look at the list of some of the organizations that accept young volunteers. Though many of the organizations listed are located in major cities, such as Washington, DC, and New York, most of them will be able to provide you with information about what you can do in your area. (Also see the state-by-state listings that begin on page 109.)

If you're not sure how you'd best fit into the world of community service, take a look at the case studies in Part II. Here you'll find profiles of teenagers who have successfully matched their volunteer activities with their personalities and interests. Whether you're shy, outgoing, ultracommitted, or just casually interested, this section will give you a feel for the types of activities that might suit you best and will help you summarize the experiences for yourself.

The third section of *150 Ways Teens Can Make a Difference* is a state-by-state listing of some of the not-for-profit organizations that encourage teenage volunteers. Unless you plan to spend a summer volunteering for an organization in a distant city, you'll most likely want to get involved with a group close to home. Those of you who don't live in or near a city may not find an organization on the list convenient to you. If you're interested in the work of an organization, call anyway. A chapter may be located near you.

Once you have decided where you'd like to volunteer, call to schedule a meeting with the volunteer coordinator or another member of the staff. Don't be shy. Keep in mind that you have a valuable resource to offer the organization: your time and energy. Once you're there, ask to see the entire facility and to meet the staff and volunteers. Your first impressions are important: Do you like the people working there? Do they seem happy with their work? Are they friendly? Don't hesitate to ask any questions that come to mind. What is the organization's mission, and how do volunteers help to achieve its goals? What will be expected of you? If you don't think the organization or position is right for you, say so. Having your questions answered up front will help ensure that your volunteer experience is rewarding and satisfying.

The Power of One: Changing the World, One Step at a Time

"Basketball can serve as a kind of metaphor
for ultimate cooperation. It is a sport where
success, as symbolized by the champions, requires
that the dictates of community prevail over
selfish personal impulses."
Senator Bill Bradley (D., N.J.)

During October, November, and December 1990, the authors of this book traveled to town meetings in many areas. We sat with teenagers and listened carefully to what's on your minds. You also wrote to us, eloquently, about how deeply you care about the world, about making it a better place for all of us to live in. What follows are just a few of the responses to our questions that touched us, responses we believe to be representative of the ideals and concerns all caring people share.

Question: If you could make a difference in your school, your community, or society, what would it be?

"I would change people's ignorance. That can fall under many subcategories, such as racism, sexism, ageism, and all the other isms. Also, ignorance comes from not learning, so we need better worldwide education. Ignorance isn't knowing/reacting to animal cruelty and pollution. We can change it by giving people knowledge

so they can make changes in themselves and the world." Fiona Inion Hahn, a tenth grader at International Studies Academy, San Francisco, California

"*I would change the gangs out on the street by opening up more recreational places and set up group counseling for underprivileged students. This would help them to see society in a new, improved way. That would be a start to a better society.*" Jalquetta Thomas, an eleventh grader at Lillie B. Williamson High School, Mobile, Alabama

"*I would change how people treat other people, animals, and nature. I would try to set an example by getting my friends and myself involved in projects in our community.*" Danielle Butler, a ninth grader at Cabrini High School, New Orleans, Louisiana

"*I live in a small town where there are hardly any minorities. I would be interested in starting a program that would educate the town about different cultures and races so that they could see that every human being should have equal rights.*" Susanna Marie Hohmann, a tenth grader at Greenhills School, Ann Arbor, Michigan

"*I would eliminate all prejudices that many people hold toward different races and sexes by giving people insight into the people they are prejudiced against.*" Lauren Williford, a ninth grader at Biloxi High School, Biloxi, Mississippi.

"*I would like to start a drive where everyone gets to know each other and break the barriers that people put up.*" Rob Maras, a tenth grader at Immaculate Heart High School, Tucson, Arizona

"*Although this sounds very idealistic, I would love to see the homeless off the streets. If everyone had to contribute a little of their salaries to centers for the homeless, there would be more opportunities for these people to live under roofs and eat.*" Stephanie Miller, an eleventh grader at Crystal Springs Uplands School, Hillsborough, California

"*I would like to take a more active part in interacting with children, by going into the lower schools.*" Jennifer Anstead, a tenth grader at Cohasset Junior/Senior High School, Cohasset, Massachusetts

"*I would make people stop feeling hate for one another by showing them that we are all humans, each just as imperfect as the rest.*" Doug Mangin, an eleventh grader at Biloxi High School, Biloxi, Mississippi

"I'd undertake just about anything to help teach people about the problems of the world, because I've known many of these problems on a personal level and I want to let others know that they're all serious problems." Lyric Walker, an eleventh grader at Monroe Catholic High School, Fairbanks, Alaska

"I would instill within people the idea that freedom is a choice. It is a choice between being ruled by God or a strong government. That is the difference between a free nation and a dictatorship. Freedom can be lost. I'd tell people with a national campaign—speeches, rallies, advertisements, etc." Meilan King, a twelfth grader at Skyline High School, Idaho Falls, Idaho

"I would like to see our school begin a small literacy program. I think our students could help those who can't read. Of course, a professional supervisor would be needed." Amanda Michelle Mors, an eleventh grader at The Montgomery Academy, Montgomery, Alabama

"I would make all the people in the world speak one language so people can understand each other easily. You could have countries open themselves up on tourism so other cultures are learned, making people less ignorant." Noel Mingoa, an eleventh grader at Galileo High School, San Francisco, California

"What I would change first is the judicial system. Too many people are committing crimes and not receiving due punishment. In my school, I have friends who drive drunk and end up doing five hours of community service. They don't care. I would, and might, write a book on why this is a problem." Tara Clare Russell, a twelfth grader at Skyline High School, Idaho Falls, Idaho

"I'd abolish hatred. It's such an ugly, putrid emotion. Everyone in the world would be a lot better off if they let go of their hate. Think about it: abolishing hatred would abolish war; no nuclear weapons, no racial tension, no riots. How nice it would be." Heather Robinson, a twelfth grader at Lowell High School, San Francisco, California

"I would want people to look beyond skin color, social class, and age and start looking at the people inside. I would start a camp and invite people from all over the world to it for one month at a time.

The people would live and relate with one another." Ashley King, an eleventh grader at Episcopal High School, Houston, Texas

"I would convert this country's medical system into a government-run, free-to-the-citizens type deal. There are too many poor people dying from lack of care and too many people getting filthy rich off of minor ailments." Benjamin Lewis Bretz, a twelfth grader at Skyline High School, Idaho Falls, Idaho

"The first thing I would change is the growing population of home-less people on the streets. We could use the money that we use to send a space shuttle to space. It doesn't make sense that we spend billions of dollars on sending people to the moon, when a block away people are living on the streets." Roxana Pitcher, a tenth grader at Cabrini High School, New Orleans, Louisiana

"Discrimination—age, sex, race, mentally retarded, etc. If the world could push aside the deep-laid conditioning of being superior to another person, cooperation would be achieved more easily. This could only come about by the people dismissing these feelings by themselves. Someone could help this along by exposing the shame to the people." Kevin Woods, an eleventh grader at Billings Senior High School, Billings, Montana

"If I could change one thing about society it would be the lack of people who care and give their time. I would change this by making a law requiring everybody to participate in a certain amount of community service per year." Robin Kathleen Hensarling, a twelfth grader at Mirabeau B. Lamar Senior High School, Houston, Texas

"I'd like to take time with young adults—kids—who aren't as fortu-nate as me, and tell them to stay off drugs and be kind to others. Stop the violence!" Anyana Morris, an eleventh grader at Gainesville High School, Gainesville, Florida

"I would like to help organize food or clothing drives and work at a soup kitchen, and I would especially like to work with handicapped or disturbed children or adolescents." Laura Peltonen, a tenth grader at The Derryfield School, Manchester, New Hampshire

"If I could change one thing about the world or society, I would wish to help develop cures for such fatal diseases as AIDS, cancer, etc. My plan in going about making this change is to become a scientist or

physician." Man-Ku Leung, a ninth grader at Saint Ignatius College Preparatory, San Francisco, California

In researching this book and others in the "Peterson's H.S." series, we met with more than 2,000 high school students and heard from at least 10,000 more. We spent weeks reading surveys and reviewing transcripts of the tapes we made of your comments, and then we asked some of you to participate more closely in creating this book. Fourteen teenagers were invited to join us for a rigorous review of the manuscript. These coauthors are credited on the title page.

In our conversations with all of the members of our teenage network, clear patterns emerged. We found that your generation is realistic about the problems confronting us in the nineties and that you have a keen understanding of the need to address these problems right away. Our meetings with our coauthors helped us to understand better the level of commitment today's teens have made to community service, and they gave us a clearer idea of the juggling act it takes to incorporate community service into an already busy high school schedule.

Support from friends and families has been extremely important to all the teenage volunteers with whom we spoke. After all, grasping the concept of the "power of one" isn't easy. It's difficult to comprehend how a single person—a teenager, no less—can have any effect on the seemingly insurmountable problems facing our world in the 1990s. But just as the actions of millions of individuals have contributed to the sorry state our planet and society are in, so too can the actions of millions of individuals contribute to the healing of our world.

For a very, very long time in the face of progress and growth, the fundamental needs of our planet and its people took a back seat to "progress" and growth. Progress meant competition for the newer, the better, and the improved, whatever the cost to the air, the water, the animals, and the people. There's no sense in pointing fingers of blame. In some way, all of us are responsible. And that's the point. We've pushed our world closer to its breaking point—but now it's time to turn back.

What you do with your life—how you choose to live it—has an impact not only on those around you but also on the planet as a whole. The fact that you're reading this book seems to indicate that you've already decided to make that impact a positive one. We hope that the information contained within these pages will help and inspire you to fully explore the power of one.

It's also important to caution you about one possible downside to volunteerism. Don't concentrate on making a difference to the exclusion of everything else. Colleges are unlikely to admit volunteers who can't master geometry; future employers value real-life experience that one can get on a volunteer job, but this is still no substitute for the real McCoy: English, history, math, and so on. Still, since it has been our experience that you get as much out of volunteering as you put into it, by doing something that positively affects your world, you positively affect your own life.

Go do it!

Marian Salzman
Teresa Reisgies

Part I
The Causes
Protecting Our Planet
Conservation and the Environment

"We are totally destroying the Earth. The ozone layer is deteriorating simply from what human beings are doing to it."
Holly Ebbert, a twelfth grader at Coral Gables Senior High School, Coral Gables, Florida

"This year, 1990, the year I leave my teenage years behind, I realize that nothing else matters but this: We must heal our planet if we're to survive. There's a lot packed into our teenage years. It all seems to come at us so fast—we are developing physically and taking on much more responsibility at home. We're dealing with our school workload, peer pressure, the continual 'What are you gonna be when you grow up?' question. And with so much going on, it was quite a relief to think that our elected officials would take care of all of those major planetary concerns while we were just to concentrate on growing up. It's obvious now that not only was no one taking care of our home as we trusted, but that people were, and still are, perpetuating this planetary destruction. I'm amazed at how the earth itself is letting us know in so many ways that there has been a gross injustice done by humankind . . . but with the help of all of you, I look forward to the years ahead of us when our generation can work together to create a happy, healthy, clean, and loving environment."

River Phoenix, as quoted in Seventeen, *April 1990*

At every high school we've visited, and at most summer camps, the first thing we notice when we head to the cafeteria is the recycling cans. Two or three years ago you would have never seen teenage vigilantes turning one another in for the crime of using styrofoam or buying munchies with excessive packaging. But times have sure changed—and for the better.

1 Work at your town's recycling center.

"I volunteer at a recycling center at around 8 a.m. on Saturdays. We wear goggles and gloves while sorting through the recycling bins: aluminum, tin, three different colors of glass, mixed paper and cardboard, and newspaper. When people dropped off the materials during the week, they would just sort of dump them there—if it had rained, it would all be soggy. Some people didn't even care enough to wash out the milk, and it could get really messy." *Kori Bell, ninth grade, Roland Park Country School, Roland Park, Maryland*

2 Volunteer for a project at the wildlife commission.

"I work for the Fish and Game Service, a branch of the Parks and Wildlife Commission. The projects available for volunteers range from a wild turkey project that they're trying to get established, to hanging platforms on trees so that the geese have a place to rest. The Fish and Game Service will provide you with, or at least help you to get, the things you need, such as materials and gear, and will allow you access to all of their resources. Volunteers are supervised by a professional in the area in which they've chosen to work." *Stephen Boren, twelfth grade, Boise High School, Boise, Idaho*

3 Lobby for an environmental group.

"I spent my summer volunteering for MASSPIRG [Massachusetts Public Interest Research Group], which at the time was dealing with the specific issue of the Recycling Initiative. The initiative would put environmental standards on all packaging in the Commonwealth of Massachusetts. For the first part of the summer, I went door to door and asked people if they would help out with either a financial contribution or by pressuring their representatives. My parents didn't really like me canvassing too much; they thought it was unsafe. So we compromised, and for the second half of the summer I worked in the main offices.

"The way I saw it, when I was canvassing, if I knocked on ten doors, even if I let one person know that there was a problem, I felt that I had accomplished something. I felt that I changed a lot of lives and that I was really contributing to the environment. A lot of times, people don't want to listen, and you just can't let them get you down. If you canvass, take a conservative attitude. If you go around dressed like a freak, you won't get too far." *Julie Goodman, eleventh grade, Canton High School, Canton, Massachusetts*

4 Teach environmental awareness to younger students.

"I am involved in a group called 'Outdoor School.' It is a program offered to sixth graders to learn about water, soil, plants, and animals. Participating as a counselor requires patience, cooperation, good disciplinary techniques, and a sense of humor. It's hard work, but I enjoy it because I'm teaching kids about how precious our Earth is." *Cindy Nguyen, eleventh grade, David Douglas High School, Portland, Oregon*

5 Run a recycling program in your school.

"When I was a junior, I volunteered to be the first director of a new recycling program at my high school. By the end of the year, we had moved from recycling just white paper to recycling colored paper, aluminum, and glass as well. We've adopted two whales. We also own three acres of rain forest and are planning a mug sale for the faculty to discourage the daily waste of paper cups. Not only has this had a positive effect on me, but I know that I have had a large effect on my peers.

"Despite the great success of the program, many days I found myself doing the job of several volunteers. Unfortunately, as with any responsibility, there is much frustration involved. But it's important to remember that whatever you choose to do is important, no matter how insignificant you may think it is." *Joanna Silver, twelfth grade, Livingston High School, Livingston, New Jersey*

More ideas:

6   Cut back on your driving (carpool!).

7   Use unleaded gas.

8   Use compact fluorescents instead of conventional light bulbs.

9   Plant trees.

10   Eat less red meat.

11   Cut down on the use of the air conditioner in your car.

12   Take a quick shower instead of a bath.

13   Buy products packaged in paper, aluminum, and glass rather than plastic and foam.

14   Write to elected officials. Expressing your opinions to policymakers by letter or telephone is a right you should exercise. If you call, ask to speak with a staffer who deals with environmental issues. Question him or her as to what your elected official is doing about protecting the environment. And don't think that what you say won't get anywhere—politicians rely on their staffers to keep them updated on public opinion. If you're not sure who your local elected officials are, refer to the government section of your local phone book.

Or, go for the top:

President George Bush
The White House
1600 Pennsylvania Avenue, NW
Washington, DC 20500
(202) 456-1414

James Baker
Secretary of State
U.S. State Department
2201 C Street, NW
Washington, DC 20520
(202) 647-4000

Edward Madigan
Secretary of Agriculture
U.S. Department of Agriculture
14th Street & Independence
   Avenue, SW
Washington, DC 20250
(202) 447-3631

FACT

We create between 300 million and 400 million tons of hazardous waste each year. (*International Register of Potentially Toxic Chemicals*, 1990)

FACT

In Brazil and Costa Rica alone, it is estimated that in the next quarter century 1.2 million animal and plant species are at risk of being forever wiped from the face of our planet. (Rain Forest Foundation, 1990)

FACT

Forty-nine million acres of rain forest are destroyed or degraded every year, the equivalent of one and a half football fields every second. (*Seventeen*, April 1990)

How You Can Help

For more information on what you can do to protect the environment, contact:

American Forestry Association
1319 18th Street, NW
Washington, DC 20036
(202) 467-5810
1-800-368-5748

Center for Environmental Education
624 9th Street, NW
Washington, DC 20001
(202) 737-3600

Children of the Green Earth
Box 95219
Seattle, WA 98145
(206) 525-4002

Defenders of Wildlife
1244 19th Street, NW
Washington, DC 20036
(202) 659-9510

Earthwatch
680 Mount Auburn Street

Box 403
Watertown, MA 02172
(617) 926-8200

Environmental Action Foundation
1525 New Hampshire Avenue, NW
Washington, DC 20036
(202) 745-4871

Environmental Defense Fund
257 Park Avenue South

150 Ways

New York, NY 10010
(212) 505-2100

Forest Service
U.S. Department of
    Agriculture
Box 96090
Washington, DC 20013
(202) 535-0927

Friends of the Earth
1629 K Street, NW
Washington, DC 20006
(202) 295-2600

Greenpeace USA
1436 U Street, NW
Washington, DC 20036
(202) 466-2823

**International Tree
Project**
DC 2 - Room 1103,
    United Nations
New York, NY 10017
(212) 754-3123

**National Audubon
Society**
950 Third Avenue

New York, NY 10022
(212) 832-3200

**National Clean Air
Coalition**
40 West 20th Street, 11th
    Floor
New York, NY 10011
(212) 727-4400

**National Coalition
Against Misuse of
Pesticides**
701 E Street, SE
Washington, DC 20003
(202) 543-5450

National Park Service
19th & C Streets, NW
Washington, DC 20240
(202) 343-7394

**National Recycling
Coalition**
1101 30th Street, NW,
    Suite 305
Washington, DC 20007
(202) 625-6406

**The Nature
Conservancy**
1815 North Lynn Street
Arlington, VA 22209
(703) 841-5300

New Alchemy Institute
237 Hatchville Road
East Falmouth, MA 02536
(617) 563-2655

The Sierra Club
730 Polk Street
San Francisco, CA 94109
(415) 776-2211

**Student Conservation
Association, Inc.**
P.O. Box 550
Charlestown, NH 03603
(603) 826-5206

**Students
Environmental Action
Coalition**
P.O. Box 1168
Chapel Hill, NC 27514
(919) 967-4600

Hotline

National Response Center Hotline (for reporting accidents):
1-800-424-8802

If you're interested in learning more about protecting the environment, note that the Public Broadcasting System (PBS) has published the *Resource Compendium*. It includes the names and addresses of organizations, books, and videos, as well as ideas for classroom and community projects. The guide is available for $10 from:

> Resource Compendium
> PBS Elementary/Secondary Service
> 1320 Braddock Place
> Alexandria, VA 22314
> (703) 739-5038

Recommended Reading

50 Simple Things You Can Do to Save the Earth by The EarthWorks Group, EarthWorks Press, Berkeley, California

How to Make the World a Better Place by Jeffrey Hollender, Quill/ William Morrow, 1990

The Rainforest Book by Scott Lewis, Living Planet Press, 1990

The Recycler's Handbook by The EarthWorks Group, EarthWorks Press, Berkeley, California

Teens for Tots
Child Care

"I am extremely concerned about the future of our children. Day-care centers are getting overpopulated, and companies just aren't providing the child-care facilities they should for working parents."
Wendy Maynes, a twelfth grader at Lincoln Senior High School, Sioux Falls, South Dakota

"Children are the most vulnerable members of our society. Too many are battered, abused, molested, rejected or abandoned. Too many spend their childhoods in 'legal limbo,' being shunted among foster homes and institutions like packages. Too many end up involved with drugs or prostitution, living lives of dependency or lives of crime.

"What are we to do about the fact that some three-year-olds have already lived in so many foster homes they call every woman they meet 'Mommy'? Or about an eleven-year-old girl abandoned by her mother with the parting advice that she should earn her money 'on her back'? What about a ten-year-old boy given up at birth by his parents but never adopted, who was labeled retarded although he was, in fact, gifted? He was shuffled around from institution to institution and finally stabbed himself in protest over transfer to yet another institution. And a thirteen-year-old girl whose mother was murdered and whose father beat her repeatedly? Or a disabled child who needs a special program to reach his potential but is, instead, shuffled between bureaucracies rather than receiving the services he needs. The sad stories may seem endless or insolvable, but, in fact, there is much that can be done."

Excerpted from material printed by Legal Services for Children, Inc., the nation's first free and comprehensive law firm just for children, San Francisco, California

As we've traveled around the country talking to teens, we were repeatedly impressed by students' compassion for younger kids. One guy in Princeton, New Jersey, sticks in our minds. He volunteers for an after-school "latchkey" program—where teens befriend elementary school children whose parents are at work when they finish their school day. He was a totally hip and cool guy and there were tears in his eyes when he told us something like, "Sometimes I think about how much I wish I could trade places with the kids in the after-school program. I mean I have this great house and great parents and money and everything. And some of these kids are so lonely. I just want them to have the kind of happy life I had growing up in this town. And it's not possible. And it's also not fair. I volunteer at the Mercer Street Program so that I can give what I can to make the kids' days happier. When they smile at me, well . . . ."

15 Organize a fun event for abused kids.

"I helped organize a carnival for abused children who live in a home. We set up a really great fair at my school. There were different games, and it was unbelievable because my 'buddy' just clung to me. He still keeps in touch with me. When I see him, he jumps on me and kisses and hugs me. The kids got a little wild, but I think it was just because they weren't sure how to act because they were having so much fun all of a sudden."
Brian Klugman, tenth grade, Germantown Academy, Huntingdon Valley, Pennsylvania

16 Educate children about staying safe.

"I go into the first and third grades through a program in my high school called 'Kid-Ability.' We teach the children about 'bad' and 'good' touches by grown-ups, especially by a parent or other family member or by a family friend. We educate the students in a vocabulary that they will understand and that won't scare them. The message is that once they are able to identify a 'good' and a 'bad' touch, they should immediately tell another adult or a friend if they're ever touched in a 'bad' way. And they should not be ashamed. We also talk to them about getting into strangers' cars, drugs, and accepting candy from strangers. The kids love the program." *Maria Stafford, twelfth grade, Omaha South High School, Omaha, Nebraska*

17 Look after "latchkey" children.

"'Latchkey' children are those whose parents work and are not home to supervise them after school. I volunteer at the Mercer Street Friends Center in Trenton, working with such children. We play games, conduct art projects, and talk with them. It gives me a special feeling to watch as they become attached to us. Every time we return to the after-school program, the smiles on the faces of both the latchkey kids and the high school kids are a perfect way to prove that this program is a success." *David Long, twelfth grade, Princeton High School, Princeton, New Jersey*

18 Work at a center for abused children.

"Once a week I go to a center for abused children to play with and help the kids in any way I can. Some of the kids have already been rehabilitated, so there aren't any blatant physical signs of abuse. In working with the kids, we are asked not to say anything to them about their past, unless they bring it up themselves. Some kids have been burned with frying pans, hit, or verbally abused." *Christina Costantino, eighth grade, Aiken Preparatory School, Aiken, South Carolina*

More ideas:

19 **Take care of babies born with the AIDS virus.**

20 **Become a Big Brother or Big Sister.**

21 **Help build a playground for less-privileged kids.**

22 **Volunteer for child care at a center for teenage mothers.**

FACT

After accidents, child abuse is the largest killer of all children between the ages of one and five. (Kempe Children's Foundation, 1990)

FACT

Forty thousand children die every day because of a lack of food, shelter, or primary health care. The U.S. ranks a dismal fourteenth in the world in terms of infant mortality rates, yet has cut its spending on family health care. (Child Welfare League of America, 1990)

FACT

Eighty-five percent of our country's prison inmates were abused as young children. (Childhelp USA, 1990)

How You Can Help

For more information on what you can do to help children, contact:

Action for Children's Television
20 University Road
Cambridge, MA 01238
(617) 876-6620

American Association for Protecting Children
63 Inverness Drive East
Englewood, CO 80112
(303) 792-9900

Big Brothers/Big Sisters of America
230 North 13th Street
Philadelphia, PA 19107
(215) 567-7000

Boys and Girls Clubs of America
771 First Avenue
New York, NY 10017
(212) 351-5900

Child Find, Inc.
P.O. Box 277
New Paltz, NY 12561
1-800-I AM LOST
(426-5678)

Child Welfare League of America
440 1st Street, NW, Suite 310
Washington, DC 20001
(202) 638-2952

Clearinghouse on Child Abuse and Neglect
P.O. Box 1182
Washington, DC 20013
(703) 821-2086

Defense for Children International—USA
210 Forsyth Street
New York, NY 10002
(212) 353-0951

Foster Parents Plan
Department 113
155 Plan Way
Warwick, RI 02886
1-800-556-7918, Ext. 212

International Society for Prevention of Child Abuse and Neglect
1205 Oneida Street
Denver, CO 80220
(303) 321-3963

Legal Services for Children
1254 Market Street, 3rd Floor
San Francisco, CA 94102
(415) 552-8035

National Collaboration for Youth
1319 F Street, NW, Suite 601
Washington, DC 20004
(202) 347-2080

National Committee for Prevention of Child Abuse
332 South Michigan Avenue
Suite 1600
Chicago, IL 60604
(312) 663-3520

Save the Children Federation, Inc.
54 Wilton Road
Westport, CT 06880
(203) 226-7272

Other branches:

10351 Santa Monica Boulevard
Suite 302
Los Angeles, CA 90025
(213) 277-7608

1875 Century Park East
Los Angeles, CA 90067
(213) 555-1191

540 North Michigan Avenue
Chicago, IL 60611
(312) 670-2379

1360 Post Oak Boulevard
Houston, TX 77056
(713) 963-9390

3384 Peachtree Road NE
Atlanta, GA 30326
(404) 233-9429

Village of Childhelp
P.O. Box 247
Beaumont, CA 92223
(714) 845-3155

"In My Little Town"
Community Service

"In the eternal words of the Horace Mann, for whom my school is named, 'Be afraid to die until you have done one good deed for humanity.'"
Neil Potischman, a twelfth grader at Horace Mann School,
Bronx, New York

"We are not the sum of our possessions. They are not the measure of our lives. In our hearts we know what matters. We cannot hope only to leave our children a bigger car, a bigger bank account. We must hope to give them a sense of what it means to be a loyal friend, a loving parent, a citizen who leaves his home, his neighborhood, and town better than he found it.

"And what do we want the men and women who work with us to say when we are no longer there? That we were more driven to succeed than anyone around us? Or that we stopped to ask if a sick child had gotten better, and stayed a moment there to trade a word of friendship?

"We have work to do. There are the homeless, lost and roaming. There are the children who have nothing—no love and no normalcy—there are those who cannot free themselves of enslavement to whatever addiction—drugs, welfare, the demoralization that rules the slums. There is crime to be conquered, the rough crime of the streets. There are the young women to be helped who are about to become mothers of children they can't care for and might not love. They need our care, our guidance."

George Bush, Inaugural Address, 1989

All across America we have heard about people who well deserve a pat on the back because of the kinds of volunteer initiatives they staff—and care about. President Bush is credited by many teens for having started the making-a-difference trend with his Points of Light program, a program that sees that ordinary Americans, including teens, are being honored for their community service efforts.

23 Do community service full-time before college.

"I work for City Year, which is nicknamed the 'Urban Peace Corps.' It is a year-long, full-time volunteer program based in Boston. I chose to spend almost a year doing this before going to college. We break up into six teams. After a short orientation, we go out on projects for the next nine months.

"Each group has a main project, which is called the 'flagship.' My group's flagship is educating others about violence prevention. After extensive research, with the help of the police department and a local hospital, we're going to go into an auditorium setting in junior high schools and do a presentation. This type of volunteering has given me so many life skills; it's a big commitment, but I've never regretted it. In no way is it missing a year." *Gloria Wong, Brookline High School, Brookline, Massachusetts (1990 graduate)*

24 Work at a crisis pregnancy center.

"I volunteer at a crisis center for pregnant teenagers. The center gives free pregnancy tests and shows films about abortion and about giving birth. If the teenagers want to put their babies up for adoption, the center arranges it. The center also maintains touch with the mothers throughout the entire pregnancy, and those who choose to keep their children can come back and borrow donated items until their babies outgrow them.

"My job is to arrange and sort all of the donations, which are items such as baby clothes, toys, and strollers. Even though I'm not actually counseling the clients, since only the certified counselors do that, I feel really good about what I do. I'm doing something that, no matter how trivial, really needs to be done." *Amy Wichern, twelfth grade, Kent Denver School, Englewood, Colorado*

25	**Interact with kids in a detention center.** "I am the head of a group of kids who go to a detention center to visit troubled teenagers. The kids

range in age from thirteen to twenty-one. They are there for committing such crimes as stealing, assault, and even murder. Because I live in the same environment as some of the people there are from, I am able to show them that something positive can be done in the community. When we're there, we give advice to the teenage males, play cards with them, watch TV with them, and basically get to know them. We create a bond that is often kept for good. Our presence is one of the only ways kids at the center have of talking to someone in the outside world." *Abel Rivera, twelfth grade, The Peddie School, Hightstown, New Jersey*

26	**Work at a science center.** "I volunteer at a Science Center. Last year, William Shatner, the actor from 'Star Trek,' came to the Center

to dedicate the new planetarium. While I was at the Center I realized it was a pretty cool place, so I decided to volunteer there. I'm responsible for a lot of things. I do demonstrations about physical science, such as showing basic practical applications of liquid nitrogen (it turns soft rubber into material as hard as a nail). The best thing about volunteering at the Center is working with people—both the people who come into the Science Center and the people with whom I work. I've learned a lot from such intelligent scientists.

"Sometimes my friends think I'm crazy to spend so much time volunteering at the Center—I couldn't pay some of them to come in even for an hour! But I want to be an astronaut someday, and I'm getting great experience and having a lot of fun." *Mark Solomon, eleventh grade, Valley High School, West Des Moines, Iowa*

27	**Volunteer as a firefighter.** "I am a volunteer firefighter. When I arrive at the firehouse for a fire or rescue, I put my gear on and

ride a fire truck to the scene. Once on the scene, I perform what-ever tasks are necessary. I am assigned to the rescue-and-salvage truck. My duties are operation of the generator, lights, and rescue equipment. There are many positive aspects of being a firefighter. It's easy to build friendships because of the importance of trust in the organization. This sort of community service is an opportunity to experience how the adult world operates." *Charles Limmer, twelfth grade, Newark Academy, Livingston, New Jersey*

More ideas:

28 **Start a community service club at school.**

29 **Have the members of your after-school club or athletic team pick a day on which to do something to benefit the community.**

30 **Give a school event (such as a concert or prom) a community service theme.**

31 **Have your class "adopt" a charity for which to raise money.**

32 **Put together a community-wide carnival.**

33 **Organize a local book swap.**

34 **Encourage your school to donate used books to schools with less funding.**

FACT

The term "volunteer" covers people engaged in a wide range of activities. It includes direct service providers, directors and officers of volunteer organizations, and certain state and local government officials.
(The White House, Office of the Press Secretary, December 1990)

FACT

Fifty-eight percent of teenagers volunteered in 1989. Teens averaged 3.9 hours of volunteer time each week, with a total of 1.6 billion hours of volunteer time by teens in 1989.
(*Volunteering and Giving Among American Teenagers 14 to 17 Years of Age*, Independent Sector, 1990)

FACT

Eighty-three percent of donations to charity are from individuals. Six and one-half percent are from bequests; 5.9 percent are from foundations; and 4.6 percent are from corporations.
(*Scholastic Update*, February 23, 1990)

How You Can Help

For more information about community service, contact:

American Youth Work Center
1751 N Street, NW
Suite 302
Washington, DC 20036
(202) 785-0764

B'nai B'rith International
1640 Rhode Island Avenue, NW
Washington, DC 20036
(202) 857-6600

Boy Scouts of America
1325 West Walnut Hill Lane
P.O. Box 152079
Irving, TX 75015-2079
(214) 580-2000

Campaign for Human Development
1312 Massachusetts
    Avenue, NW
Washington, DC 20005
(202) 659-6650

City Year
11 Stillings Street
Boston, MA 02210
(617) 451-0699

Girl Scouts of the U.S.A. National Headquarters
830 Third Avenue
New York, NY 10020
(212) 940-7500
1-800-223-0624

Junior Optimist Clubs
4494 Lindell Boulevard
St. Louis, MO 63108
(314) 371-6000

Key Club International
3636 Woodview Trace
Indianapolis, IN 46268
(317) 875-8755
1-800-879-4769

Keyette International
1421 Kalmia Road, NW
Washington, DC 20012
(202) 726-4619

Links
1200 Massachusetts
    Avenue, NW
Washington, DC 20005
(202) 842-8686

Organization of American States, Youth Office
1889 F Street
Washington, DC 20006
(202) 789-3000

The Salvation Army
799 Bloomfield Avenue
Verona, NJ 07044
(201) 239-0606

Visions International
RD 3, Box 106A
Newport, PA 17074
(717) 567-7313

Volunteers in Service to America
1100 Vermont Avenue,
    NW
Room 8100
Washington, DC 20525
1-800-424-8867

Volunteers of America
3813 North Causeway
    Boulevard
Metairie, LA 70002
(504) 837-2652

Volunteer—The National Center
1111 North 19th Street,
    Suite 500
Arlington, VA 22209
(703) 276-0542

Youth Service America
1319 F Street, NW, Suite
    900
Washington, DC 20004
(202) 783-8855

Youth Volunteer Corps
1080 Washington
Kansas City, MO
    64105-2216
(816) 474-5761

Teen to Teen
Counseling

"Students are, in general, more comfortable with other students than they are with adults. Teenagers want to talk to someone on the same level—someone who knows what's going on around them."
Jeff Eglintine, a twelfth grader at Woodstock High School,
Woodstock, Vermont

While some problems require the help of a professional, more and more schools and communities are turning to peer counseling as a means of handling minor problems. Many young people would rather talk about their problems and concerns with someone who is going through similar experiences. They turn to peer counselors to talk confidentially about everything from sex, drugs, AIDS, problems in school, and boyfriend/girlfriend relations to dealing with problems in our society, such as war and prejudice, understanding your feelings, peer pressure . . . basically anything that today's teens are concerned about. Most peer counselors have gone through a minimum of three months of training and have passed a written exam testing their interpersonal and communication skills. Teens helping each other may be one of the best ways for your generation to stick together and to work your way through many of the issues facing you.

150 Ways

Volunteer for a suicide prevention team.

35

"I am a member of my school's counseling and outreach team for suicide prevention. We don't call ourselves 'counselors,' since we're not certified, but we work really closely with the guidance counselors at school. Sometimes we'll seek people out who we think might be in need of help, because kids talk and everyone pretty much can see who is having problems. But, for the most part, they come to us. I've seen some really serious cases in which people actually have had their suicides planned out, and I always wonder whether I'm going to be effective in stopping them. But even though I get really nervous, it's the feeling that I'm helping someone that makes it all worthwhile." *Peg Van Gheem, eleventh grade, West De Pere High School, De Pere, Wisconsin*

Work as a crisis-intervention hotline counselor.

36

"I'm a volunteer on the Talk Line, which is a crisis-intervention hotline that people can call when they're upset or depressed and need someone to talk to. I work at the hotline about three hours a week. The most common types of calls I get are from people who are really depressed and say they don't know why they're living. I think it's not so much that they're intending to commmit suicide, more that they want to shock me, or shock themselves. We also get a lot of calls from people who are having problems in a relationship. I do find working on the hotline very difficult at times because I know I can't always make everything better." *Keith Donoghue, twelfth grade, Barrington High School, Barrington, Illinois*

Work as a peer counselor.

37

"I became a peer counselor at my school because I like to help kids with all sorts of problems. I think peer counseling helps a lot of people, because a lot of times students don't have someone to talk to at home and they don't want to talk to an adult in the school. As a counselor, I don't tell students what to do; rather, I give them options. A lot of the problems they have are basic high school problems like stress, boyfriend/girlfriend problems, parents, homework. Sometimes it's kind of hard to be listening to people who are my peers, and sometimes they seem a little bit uncomfortable. Even if what I say doesn't help them, at least I know they've gotten their problems off their chests." *Blanca Jackson, eleventh grade, Roaring Fork High School, Carbondale, Colorado*

38 **Counsel on a kids' hotline.**
"I'm a counselor on Phone Pal, which is a number that younger kids can call Monday through Friday from 3 to 6 p.m. Kids call if they're bored or lonely after school, or if their parents are still at work and the kids want someone to talk to. One time a child called in who seemed really violent. He said that he liked blood, and he said his sister fell off the Empire State Building. He kept calling me, and after a while he became a completely different person—he was nice, open, and honest. I really felt as though I had helped him a lot." *Jaynne Jacob, twelfth grade, Central High School, Grand Forks, North Dakota*

More ideas:

39 **Counsel new students at your school.**

40 **Work as a peer counselor at a sex education program for teens.**

41 **Counsel fellow students about substance abuse, eating disorders, or any other important issues.**

42 **Counsel pregnant teenagers.**

43 **If your school doesn't already have a peer counseling program, start one!**

FACT

In 1988, the U.S. suicide rate for 15-through 24-year-olds was 13.5 suicides per day, for a total of 4,929 suicides. (American Association of Suicidology, 1991)

FACT

In a survey of 535 pregnant or parenting adolescent women, 68 percent report having been molested or raped. (*Protecting Children*, American Association for Protecting Children, 1990)

FACT

Eighty percent of teenage pregnancies are unintended, and 80 percent of pregnant teenagers become high school dropouts. (Fact Sheet, Students Organizing Students, 1990)

How You Can Help

To learn more about counseling, contact:

Allied Youth and Family Counseling Center
310 North Windomere
Dallas, TX 75208
(214) 943-1044

American Youth Work Center
1522 Connecticut Avenue, NW
Washington, DC 20036
(202) 785-0764

The National Peer Helpers Association
1950 Mission Street
San Francisco, CA 94103
(415) 965-4011

National Runaway Switchboard
2210 North Halstead Street
Chicago, IL 60614
(312) 880-9860

Youth Service Line:
1-800-621-4000

Runaway Hotline
P.O. Box 12428
Austin, TX 78711
1-800-392-3352 in Texas
1-800-231-6946 elsewhere

Students Against Driving Drunk (SADD)
P.O. Box 800
Marlboro, MA 01752
(617) 481-3568

Women, Inc.
244 Townsend Street
Dorchester, MA 02121
(617) 442-6166

Women in Crisis
133 West 21st Street
New York, NY 10011
(212) 242-4880

Women in Transition
125 South Ninth Street
Suite 502
Philadelphia, PA 19107
(215) 922-7177

Youth Counseling League
138 East 19th Street
New York, NY 10003
(212) 473-4300

Youth Development
P.O. Box 178408
San Diego, CA
    92177-8408
(619) 292-5683
1-800-HIT-HOME
    (448-4663)

Youth Suicide National Center
1811 Trousdale Drive
Burlingame, CA 94010
(415) 692-6662

One of the most creative peer education organizations is PRIDE (Parents' Resource Institute for Drug Education). Five-member student teams from schools around the country are trained at PRIDE's national headquarters in Atlanta, Georgia. Once trained, the students return to their respective schools to perform plays, dance routines, and rap numbers about the dangers of drug abuse. If you'd like to form a PRIDE team at your school, contact:

PRIDE
The Hurt Building
50 Hurt Plaza, Suite 210
Atlanta, GA 30303
(404) 577-4500

If your school doesn't already have a peer counseling program, consider starting one. The National Crime Prevention Council can help with information and advice. They've also published two books: *Reaching Out: School-Based Community Service Programs* and *Prevention Power: Teens in Community Drug Prevention*. Both are available free of charge from:

The National Crime Prevention Council
1700 K Street, NW, 2nd
    Floor
Washington, DC 20006
(202) 466-6272

Gimme Art
Cultural Activities and the Arts

"Culture and the arts are things that everyone should be exposed to. To me, culture means heritage and the people around you."
Tami Dixon, an eleventh grader at Cleveland School of the Arts, Cleveland, Ohio

"During 1989, education was in the spotlight. Educators, business leaders, and elected officials all agreed that we are not doing a good enough job of educating our children. American schools are in trouble. Outmoded curricula, poverty, and drugs are all cited by experts as contributing factors which undermine our schools. . . . There was also a growing consensus among educators and Arts organizations about the importance of establishing the Arts as basic subjects in schools. . . . We at Young Audiences believe that the Arts can play a vital role in educational reform. By teaching our children about the Arts, we put them in touch with themselves, with the needs and aspirations of our society, and with all the achievements in the fine and performing arts that are part of our cultural patrimony. The Arts are crucial to a child's development because they offer positive alternatives and foster individual expression. Involvement in the Arts can help unlock creativity and inventive abilities; and we know that these attributes are just as important for a budding scientist or mathematician as they are for a future artist."

Young Audiences, Inc., 1990 Annual Report

The arts—performing and visual arts—have long been popular extracurricular activities and now, maybe more than ever, they have to be supported since when people do art, they unlock their most creative and most feeling selves. "When I sit down and work on my creative writing," said one student we met in Milton, Massachusetts, "I step outside my affluent setting and think about the frustrations that other people who are less fortunate experience daily."

44 Make art for a hospital.

"I joined an arts coalition that was created by an art teacher at my school. We wanted to make a large alphabet for a wall of the pediatric unit at an AIDS Hospital in Harlem. Everyone in the club decided which letter of the alphabet they would do, using canvas, paper, watercolors, whatever. Each week, people brought in what they had done, and we critiqued each other's work. Then the group went to the hospital and actually hung the alphabet from the walls, which was one of the best parts because we were able to see how excited the patients were and how much they appreciated what we had done." *Lowell Pettit, twelfth grade, Collegiate School, New York, New York*

45 Volunteer at a gallery.

"Due to my interest in art, I spend my summers working in a children's art gallery in which children are allowed to touch and build during certain hours. I take the kids through the gallery and talk about everything we see. To me, watching the kids learn, watching their expressions when they're experiencing new things, is the best thing in the world. My friends are really supportive of my volunteer work, although some people may wonder why I'm not doing a paying job. But any spending money I would make at a paying summer job would go to buy myself frivolous things that I don't really need." *Kahrna Stimley, eleventh grade, St. Joseph's Catholic High School, Jackson, Mississippi*

46 Help out at an arts and crafts fair.

"I work on an arts and crafts fair with the blind and visually impaired. I enjoy arts and crafts, so I usually help them with macrame and other crafts, such as pottery. People sometimes ask me, 'Did a blind person really make this?' and it's funny because after working with the visually impaired it's so clear to me that you don't need to be able to see to make a beautiful piece of artwork! It doesn't matter how you look or dress, or how old you are, you're helping the group, and they're so thankful for it. Volunteering at the fair has really broadened my horizons, and I'm able to listen much better." *Amy Bowles, tenth grade, Palo Verde High School, Tucson, Arizona*

47 Share your culture with others through an art form.

"I started learning Chinese dance when I was very young. Since then, I've been performing the dances at a number of fairs and festivals that encompass international cultures and at a children's museum in my area. In doing this, I feel sort of like a minister of culture. I think that volunteering in this way is so important, especially in the United States, where there are so many cultures mixed together and people need to learn more about others. It's a good feeling to introduce your own culture to others." *Cindy Tang, eleventh grade, The Webb School, Bell Buckle, Tennessee*

48 Start a film club to benefit a good cause.

"I serve my community through a film society that I started at my school. Films are shown once a week after school. Anyone who attends is asked to make a contribution to a local charity. In a way, it takes away unnecessary frivolity from entertainment. If students are aware of a worthy cause, they will not hesitate to support it." *Jon Green, twelfth grade, Dwight-Englewood School, Englewood, New Jersey*

More ideas:

49 **Work as a stagehand, costume assistant, or box-office ticket seller at your local theater, ballet, or opera.**

50 **Start a cultural awareness club at school.**

51 Take underprivileged children to a museum or concert.

52 Be a freelance theater critic for a charitable organization's newsletter or newspaper.

> **FACT**
>
> Many local nonprofit theater productions have gone on to Broadway and Hollywood fame, incuding *Driving Miss Daisy, Children of a Lesser God, A Chorus Line, M Butterfly, Annie,* and *The Great White Hope.* (National Endowment for the Arts, 1991)

> **FACT**
>
> Between 1966 and 1976, state support for the arts rose from $2.6 million to more than $100 million. Today, the figure stands at $284 million annually. (National Assembly of State Arts Agencies, 1991)

> **FACT**
>
> There are currently more than 3,000 local arts agencies. In 1960, there were approximately 60. (National Assembly of Local Arts Agencies, 1991)

How You Can Help

For more information about volunteer activities related to the arts, contact:

American Association of Museums	***American Council for the Arts***	***Association of American Cultures***
1225 Eye Street, NW	1285 Avenue of the	410 8th Street, NW
Suite 200	Americas, 3rd Floor	Suite 605
Washington, DC 20005	New York, NY 10019	Washington, DC 20004
(202) 289-1818	(212) 245-4510	(202) 393-8222

The Center for Arts Information
625 Broadway
New York, NY 10012
(212) 977-2544

National Dance Association
1900 Association Drive
Reston, VA 22091
(703) 476-3436

The National Endowment for the Arts
Public Information Office
1100 Pennsylvania Avenue, NW
Washington, DC 20506
(202) 682-5570

National Music Council
P.O. Box 5551
Englewood, NJ 07631
(201) 871-9088

Very Special Arts
1331 F Street, NW
Suite 800
Washington, DC 20004
(202) 628-2800
1-800-933-8721

Humans' Best Friends
Facilities and Services for Animals

"Animals have feelings, just like people have feelings. Some practices inflicted on animals, such as animal testing, are totally inhumane. The animals are suffering. There's got to be another way of testing products."
Andy Roberts, a twelfth grader at David Douglas High School, Portland, Oregon

"In a still unsolved and unexplained incident, a female black bear hibernating with her four cubs in Marengo, Wisconsin, was shot to death last winter. One of her three-month-old cubs was also killed. Paul Martin, Wisconsin Department of Natural Resources warden, said the 170-pound mother bear was shot at least seven times in the head with a .22 caliber firearm; the four-pound cub was shot once in the chest.

"Dr. Ray Anderson, professor of wildlife at the College of Natural Resources in Stevens Point, has been studying black bears in northern Wisconsin since 1980. He said, 'This is a malicious outright killing that is beyond my comprehension. The bears were defenseless, hibernating in their den and were not threatening anyone.' The three surviving cubs were found shivering and caked with mud in a sawdust pile about 100 yards from the den. They were taken to the nearest veterinary clinic, where they were nursed back to health."

Jeff Peters, as quoted in ASPCA Report, Summer/Fall 1990

Such "unsolved and unexplained" incidents involving cruel and deadly treatment of animals are by no means rare. They happen every day. But concerned citizens, many of them volunteers, have successfully brought the animal rights issue into the public eye, and they are making a difference.

When we first met Tiffany Defrance, a tenth grader from Nashville, Tennessee, she told us about her commitment to animals—this is why she makes time to volunteer at the local Humane Society. She also told us that many of her friends are moved by stories of unwanted pets who end up starving or being killed through sheer human negligence. What can teenagers do to change the way people regard animals, she asked; and then when we heard about her contributions, we couldn't help but think that if every interested teen followed her lead and mailed letters against puppy farms, advocated sterilization for household pets, and volunteered at an animal shelter, well . . . .

53 Work at a veterinary clinic.

"Sometimes I'm kept up at night thinking about the terrible treatment of animals. I've always loved animals and want to be a veterinarian, so I volunteer at a veterinary clinic on weekends. In the morning I clean and feed the animals; later in the day I watch surgery and sometimes, if I'm lucky, I am able to hand over instruments.

"The gratification I get is when I see a change and see that an animal is being treated better. One time a dog came out of surgery in terrible shape, shaking and bleeding, and the people in the clinic just put it in a cement box. I put a towel around it and took care of it, and I could tell I made it more comfortable. I've been active in getting other students involved in the animal rights cause. I've talked to a lot of classes about cruelty to animals and have informed students about things such as cosmetics testing on animals."
Emily Levine, twelfth grade, Augusta Preparatory Day School, Martinez, Georgia

54 Volunteer at an aquarium.

"I started my volunteer work at Mystic Marinelife Aquarium in Mystic, Connecticut, at the age of twelve.

I applied to the volunteer job opportunity program and was one of the lucky ones to be selected. Through the years, my general duties have ranged from cleaning the cages and feeding the seals, sea lions, sharks, penguins, and other small creatures to running an open classroom and handling crowd control during summer and school vacations. My responsibilities increased as I grew older, and I felt that I was an important part of the aquarium staff. Dealing with the public is not always a picnic, but it has its memorable moments." *Victoria Fisher, twelfth grade, Moses Brown School, Providence, Rhode Island*

55 Lobby for the rights of an abused species.

"Last spring I was watching a TV program, on one of the science channels, that depicted the slaughter of dolphins by tuna fleets. I felt very strongly about it and went to my biology teacher to discuss it with him. Together we worked out a plan as to how best to vocalize my feelings, making them more personal and more effective.

"Through friends in Pittsburgh, we came up with the home addresses of three of the top executives at the H. J. Heinz Company, which owns Starkist tuna. I went into my biology teacher's classes and distributed postcards to the students while informing them fully about the dolphin problem. The postcards, which were written with strong and personal emotions, were mailed, three per day, to the executives' homes.

"A short time thereafter, the Heinz Company announced its new policy not to catch any tuna at the expense of dolphins. The chairman of the company actually read some of the postcards at a press conference." *Joel Rubin, tenth grade, Cape Elizabeth High School, Cape Elizabeth, Maine*

56 Work at the zoo.

"I volunteer at the zoo. I like the animals because they're so loving. It's different from working with people: The animals take out their aggressions differently than do people. But working with animals does require some patience, maybe more so than working with people, because of the difficulty in communicating with animals at times. I've realized how much animals need to be saved. I've wondered whether or not there will be animals around for my children to visit at the zoo." *Christina Weigle, ninth grade, Bailey Magnet School, Jackson, Mississippi*

57 Volunteer at an animal shelter.

"I work at an animal shelter, where I'm teamed up with a disabled person who comes to play with the animals. For about the first half hour I show him or her how to groom and take care of one of the pets. For the rest of the time, we play games with the animals. It's really neat because the handicapped people are really into the animals. I feel like I'm finally doing something and helping both the animals and the individuals." *Rosie Ramos, twelfth grade, Portsmouth High School, Portsmouth, Rhode Island*

More ideas:

58 Write letters of protest to cosmetics companies that engage in animal testing for their products.

59 Start an animal rights awareness club at school.

60 Boycott products that you feel use animals unfairly.

61 Clean up water waste that is a threat to marine wildlife.

62 Throw birdseed instead of rice at weddings.

63 Join a national animal rights organization and contribute to its lobbying efforts.

FACT

Animals bred in zoos may be sold to laboratories for experiments, or to circuses, where their fate may be worse than in zoos. (*The Animal Rights Handbook: Everyday Ways to Save Animal Lives*, 1990)

FACT

Of all the garbage picked up during beach cleanups coordinated by the center for Marine Conservation, 62 percent is made of plastic, including bags, bottles, fishing lines, and six-pack holders. (*The Animal Rights Handbook: Everyday Ways to Save Animal Lives*, 1990)

FACT

Since the turn of the century, animal research has helped increase our lifespan by nearly twenty-eight years. (*Seventeen*, May 1990)

How You Can Help

For more information on what you can do to help animals, contact:

American Humane Association
Animal Protection
    Division
P.O. Box 1266
Denver, CO 80201
(303) 695-0811

ASPCA (American Society for the Prevention of Cruelty to Animals)
441 East 92nd Street
New York, NY 10128
(212) 876-7700

Animal Welfare Institute
Box 3650
Washington, DC 20007
(202) 337-2332

Beauty Without Cruelty U.S.A.
175 West 12th Street
New York, NY 10011
(212) 989-8073

Care About the Strays
P.O. Box 474
New Albany, OH 43054
(614) 855-2494

Friends of Animals
1 Pine Street
Neptune, NJ 07753
(201) 922-2600

Humane Society of the United States
2100 L Street, NW
Washington, DC 20037
(202) 452-1100

The National Wildlife Federation
1412 16th Street, NW
Washington, DC 20036
(202) 797-6800

People for the Ethical Treatment of Animals (PETA)
P.O. Box 42516
Washington, DC 20015
(202) 770-7444
Available from PETA is a free wallet-size list of companies that do and do not test their (cosmetics) products on animals.

The Wilderness Society
1400 Eye Street, NW,
  10th Floor
Washington, DC 20005
(202) 842-3400

World Wildlife Fund
1250 24th Street, NW
Suite 400
Washington, DC 20037
(202) 293-4800

For a catalog of non-animal-tested and environmentally safe products, write to:

Vegan Street
P.O. Box 5525
Rockville, MD 20855
(301) 840-1561

Recommended Reading

The Animal Rights Handbook, Living Planet Press, 1990

Wheelchair Heroes
Facilities and Services for the Differently Abled

"Just because someone has a handicap does not mean he or she should be treated any differently. They are people, too."
Amy Krocker, a twelfth grader at Brentwood Junior-Senior High
School, Pittsburgh, Pennsylvania

What do most of us feel when we see a person struggling to walk down the street because of a physical disability? Or a severely retarded baby who seemingly will never live life as we do? We feel sorry for them. But sympathy can make us feel embarrassed or uncomfortable. Sometimes it makes us avoid contact with people who are differently abled. We're not sure what to say or how to act, so we keep our distance. But this distance we maintain can prove a greater barrier to the differently abled than any handicap they might have.

People who know and work with the differently abled stress that those of us who have physical or mental disabilities and those of us who don't can, in fact, learn a great deal from each other. So ask yourself. When was the last time you had a conversation with a retarded person or a paraplegic? Maybe it's time to turn our sympathy into something more constructive.

Befriend a mentally retarded person.

| 64 |

"I was working at a restaurant and a family came in with their daughter, Laura, who has Down's Syndrome. I let them know that I was a senior in high school and had a pretty flexible schedule if they ever needed any help. They got in touch with me, and now Laura and I are together every day. She meets me at school when I have a free period. My main priority is to help Laura work with other people. I try to help her along with basic life skills.

"Laura is really well liked by all of my friends. Laura, I, and my boyfriend are going to the prom together. If I'm ever sick or out of school, my friends all watch out for Laura and make sure she gets lunch and has someone to be with. To me, Laura is more normal than 50 percent of the kids in my school. She's not handicapped—she has a mind of her own." *Charis Brooks, twelfth grade, Friday Harbor High School, Friday Harbor, Washington*

Help the physically challenged with a hobby.

| 65 |

"I volunteer in an art class for adults with cerebral palsy. I help to set up the equipment and assist the students with anything they might need. It's really incredible to see the things that they can do, such as painting with their feet and their mouths. It has been awkward at times, especially when I first started working there. Once when I was handing one man a pen he was having such trouble grasping it, and I wasn't quite sure how to react. But situations like that don't embarrass me anymore because I know that they don't embarrass the people with cerebral palsy." *Celina Schocken, twelfth grade, Lakeside School, Seattle, Washington*

Work as a counselor at a camp for the physically or mentally challenged.

| 66 |

"Last summer I worked at a camp for mildly to moderately physically and mentally handicapped children and adults. Every day, I spent time with a group of sixteen- to seventeen-year-old boys. There was one camper named Jim, who was an adult—about twenty-five years old. He reminded me of one of my friends at home, except he had a disease which stunted the growth of his brain, so he learned more slowly and forgot things easily. At first I just assumed that because of our differences we probably wouldn't be able to be friends. But we stayed up late every night after everyone went to sleep, just talking and laughing—about everyday, normal things. I'll never forget the lesson I learned from that." *Julia Tallant, twelfth grade, Crestwood High School, Atlanta, Georgia*

67 Raise a dog that will care for a physically challenged individual.
"My family cares for a dog names Zeek who will someday be a companion to a handicapped person. I also volunteer at the Canine Companions center, where I help vaccinate the dogs that are being trained to be guide dogs, tattoo them in case they get lost, and run them around. I come into contact with many handicapped people who really rely on their dogs. They thank us for taking care of the dogs that help them so much." *Sara Nesbit, seventh grade, Twin Hills School, Sebastopol, California*

68 Help a handicapped person with therapy.
"I am involved in guiding a man with an extremely rare muscular and nervous system disease through strength and motor coordination exercises. When we're together, I mostly give him directions on how to do his exercises and make sure he does them correctly. For some exercises, I provide minimal resistance to his motion. When the weather permits, I help him to take short walks down the street. Every time I see him we have a ritual that is particularly gratifying for me. Before I leave, we both give each other encouragement. He gives me advice and support for school and life in general. I help him to keep a positive attitude." *Heather Will, twelfth grade, Bay High School, Bay Village, Ohio*

69 Help a handicapped person shop.
"I volunteered for 'Handicapped Shopping' at a nearby department store. Throughout the day, members of my Key Club helped those in wheelchairs, the elderly, and the mentally handicapped with their Christmas shopping. For many of the shoppers, this was one of the few times teenagers had so cheerily and readily volunteered to help them. The determination on the shoppers' faces was enough to make us take a look at our

lives and see how much we really have." *Duncan Bachen, twelfth grade, Egg Harbor Township High School, Egg Harbor Township, New Jersey*

More ideas:

70 **Read to individuals who are visually or hearing impaired.**

71 **Lobby for handicapped-accessible features in public areas in your community.**

72 **Encourage your school to make its facilities available for handicapped students.**

73 **Run household errands for a person who uses a wheelchair.**

FACT

Over the last twenty-five years, more than 40,000 workers who are mentally retarded have been matched with employers through the National Employment and Training Program. (Association for Retarded Citizens of the United States, 1991)

FACT

It is estimated that 250,000 children are born in the United States each year with major birth defects. (Association of Birth Defect Children, Inc., 1990)

FACT

There are approximately 24 million deaf or hearing-impaired people in the United States. (Deafness Research Foundation, 1991)

How You Can Help

For more information on what you can do for the differently abled, contact:

American Foundation for the Blind
15 West 16th Street
New York, NY 10011
(212) 620-2000

American Mental Health Fund
2735 Hartland Road, Suite 302
Falls Church, VA 22043
(703) 573-2200
1-800-433-5959

Association of Birth Defect Children, Inc.
5400 Diplomat Circle, Suite 270
Orlando, FL 32810
(407) 629-1466

Association for Retarded Citizens of the United States
500 East Border Street, 3rd Floor
P.O. Box 1047
Arlington, TX 76004
(817) 261-6003

Canine Companions
1215 Sebastopol Road
Santa Rosa, CA 95407
(707) 528-9830

Deafness Research Foundation
9 East 38th Street, 7th floor
New York, NY 10016
(212) 684-6556
1-800-535-3323

Easter Seals Society for Disabled Children and Adults
2800 13th Street., NW
Washington, DC 20009
(202) 232-2342

Mainstream, Inc.
1030 15th Street, NW, Suite 1010
Washington, DC 20005
(202) 898-1400

National Alliance for the Mentally Ill
2101 Wilson Boulevard, Suite 302
Arlington, VA 22201
(703) 524-7600

National Down Syndrome Society, Inc.
666 Broadway, Suite 810
New York, NY 10012
(212) 460-9330
1-800-221-4602

National Information Center for Handicapped Children and Youth
Box 1492
Washington, DC 20013
(703) 893-6061
1-800-999-5599

Rehabilitation International
25 East 21st Street, 4th Floor
New York, NY 10010
(212) 420-1500

"He Ain't Heavy . . ."
Facilities and Services for the Economically Disadvantaged

"I worry about the fact that some people can have huge amounts of money and go from day to day worrying about their stocks and bonds, while there are homeless people and children dying in this world. This nation needs to start paying attention to the poor."
Catherine Nalmmens, an eleventh grader at Sacred Heart Preparatory School, Atherton, California

"Imagine a long, dusty road winding its way out into rural America to the yard of a broken-down shack in what is known as the Third World of the United States—the Mississippi delta. This area of the country has been in the news repeatedly over the years and agencies and committees have studied ways to meet the challenge of persistent poverty in the area. But do these studies extend a helping hand to a family as they look out of their doorway, watching the mailman drive up to their mailbox?

"No, they do not. But friendship and help from other Americans who care will come directly to them because of an organization located in Plainville, Connecticut. The mailman brings a letter to this family telling them that they have been matched with a sister-family from another part of the country. These people will be sending letters, their friendship, and boxes of good used clothing, food, small household items, books, toys, information, encouragement, and whatever else they can to help alleviate the need and to free up the family's income to pay bills and medical needs.

"A mother wrote in her first letter to The Box Project, . . . 'I am sorry for writing on the back of this paper. When you have six children it is so hard to keep thing around. We do our best to teach our children the good thing in life. Sometime I go all day without eating so my children can eat. I pray each day if there a will there a way. If it wasn't for God I don't think I could go on each day worrying. The few food stamp I get I try to stretch them as far as I can but my children is growing. I cook beans all the time trying to stretch. We jump for joy when I got The Box Project help. Now I can smile.'"

Nancy Normen, Executive Director, The Box Project

What these examples illustrate is that people are people, everywhere. If you want to make a difference for those whose circumstances are less fortunate than your own, we suggest you start off by recognizing that people are people, rich, middle class, and poor. Further, what those of us who are more fortunate can take for granted may be the bright hope for those who have had tougher luck. We were especially impressed by the respect that the volunteers we met the night we participated in a midnight run with Trevor's Campaign for the Homeless showed their clients.

74 Provide needy families with firewood.

"Every year when the first cold spell hits, I volunteer with Wood-for-Warmth. A group of students gather at a site where there is a lot of wood (a development site or a structure that was knocked down in Hurricane Hugo). We then chop the wood and provide it to families who can't afford to buy firewood. The families come with their trucks and are really grateful for what we do. And I'm glad that I'm no longer in my little, selfish shell." *Dabney Roversi, tenth grade, Ashley Hall, Charleston, South Carolina*

75 Have party guests bring supplies for the underprivileged in lieu of a gift.

"Everyone who is coming to my bar mitzvah has been asked to bring something to benefit The Storefront, which is an organization in my community that helps homeless children. My mom, dad, and I are asking each guest to bring not only canned food, but also socks, bread, milk—things that the homeless need. Most people think that all teenagers just want material things, but I'm not all that interested in 'stuff.'" *David Schatz, seventh grade, Lewis Junior High School, San Diego, California*

76 Volunteer at a soup kitchen.
"Every Saturday morning, a group of students and I work in a soup kitchen. I always meet new faces and see old, familiar faces. I also learn a lot from the homeless people's perspectives on life, politics, and philosophy. I respect them for their insights and big hearts. Their friendships are invaluable to me because they are special people in their own ways, even though they do not have many material possessions in this lifetime. You really have to give a volunteer job like this several tries before you give up, because the first day can be really difficult." *Kasasira Mwine, twelfth grade, Episcopal High School, Alexandria, Virginia*

77 Collect mittens for the homeless.
"Three years ago I went to the Salvation Army Hospitality House and served dinner there. I saw a strong need and wanted to do something about it. I came up with the idea of collecting socks, mittens, and hats for the people coming into the soup kitchen. The collecting is sometimes frustrating, but Christmas Day makes it all worthwhile. I wrap every item up and take them all to the soup kitchen, and when the people come up for Christmas dinner, I give them to everyone. This year I met my goal of 1,000." *Kerri Trusty, eighth grade, East Middle School, Great Falls, Montana*

More ideas:

78 **Deliver holiday meals to families with low household incomes.**

79 **Encourage your school to donate leftover cafeteria food to a local shelter.**

80 **Volunteer to pick up leftover restaurant food and deliver it to the homeless on the streets.**

81 **Run a canned-food drive.**

FACT

Some organizations have put the number of homeless people living in America at as high as 3 million. Others say the number is between 300,000 and 1 million. (Coalition for the Homeless, 1990)

FACT

There are more than 80 million homeless children living on the streets of the world's cities today. (Defense for Children International/USA, 1990)

FACT

Every fifty-three minutes, an American child dies because of poverty. That's 9,855 a year. (Children's Defense Fund, 1990)

How You Can Help

For more information on what you can do to help the economically disadvantaged, contact:

American Red Cross
National Capitol Chapter
225 E Street, NW
Washington, DC 20006
(202) 728-6479

The Box Project, Inc.
Dept. I
P.O. Box 435
Plainville, CT 06062
(203) 747-8182

Food for the Hungry
P.O. Box E
Scottsdale, AZ 85260
1-800-2 HUNGER
  (248-6437)

Habitat for Humanity
Habitat & Church Streets
Americus, GA 31709
(912) 924-6935

National Coalition for the Homeless
1621 Connecticut
  Avenue, NW
Washington, DC 20009
(202) 265-2371
or
105 East 22nd Street
New York, NY 10010
(212) 460-8110

or
311 South Spring Street
Los Angeles, CA 90013
(213) 488-9136

National Student Campaign Against Hunger
29 Temple Place
Boston, MA 02111
(617) 292-4823

The Salvation Army
799 Bloomfield Avenue
Verona, NJ 07044
(201) 239-0606

Second Harvest
343 South Dearborn
Chicago, IL 60604
(312) 341-1303

Trevor's Campaign for the Homeless
137–139 East Spring
 Avenue, NW, Suite
 400
Ardmore, PA 19003
(215) 642-6452

Generation to Generation
Facilities and Services for the Elderly

**"Some kids may think the elderly are really
different—but I think they still have the same hopes
and dreams as kids. They are really fun, and always
carry smiles on their faces."**
Toby Gillen, a twelfth grader at Cascia Hall Preparatory School,
Tulsa, Oklahoma

". . . Her name was Ada. She was eighty-six years old, and lived on
Martin Luther King Boulevard in Roxbury, Massachusetts. She was
all alone on Thanksgiving Day when a volunteer from Little Brothers—Friends of the Elderly in Boston knocked on her door, holding
a shopping bag, turkey dinner, and a bouquet of flowers. She
greeted him warmly and made him feel welcome. She was a sweet
woman, and clearly thankful for his visit."

Excerpted from Little Brothers—Friends of the Elderly, 1989
Annual Report

The elderly lady and the young volunteer became good
friends, and when she died two years later, he knew that he had
made an enormous difference in her life. She had made an enormous difference in his.

Throughout the country, thousands of elderly people spend
their lives alone, with not even a phone call to brighten their days.
Some are easy targets for greedy landlords. Others are neglected by
their own children or other family members. Many, either too
withdrawn or too ill to go through the necessary red tape, do not

receive needed government benefits and aid. They virtually slip through the cracks. Even those in decent nursing homes yearn for the sight of a fresh, young face and conversation with a young person experiencing new and different things. Disheartened as some may seem, the elderly can offer a great deal of wisdom and knowledge. Young people working with the elderly not only give—they take as well.

One thing we were pleasantly surprised to hear, again and again, is the number of teenagers who consider their grandparents and other older relatives among their closest advisers. There is so much that they report they learn from these seniors—and students who volunteer with the elderly reported similar satisfactions especially "once they bond" with the people they're helping. A student in Miami told us, "I think I actually get more from befriending the two elderly people I visit weekly than they get from me. They have so much wisdom—and warmth."

82 Love an elderly person.
"I have two friends who are senior citizens. They love me so much, and I love them back. One of them said to me recently, 'Nobody has loved me like this before.' Some people don't want to be friends with old people because they're afraid the old people are going to die, but you should know that even if they do die, you made a difference in their lives." *Cynthia Moran, eleventh grade, Berwick Academy, South Berwick, Maine*

83 Reach out to an elder in need.
"Through a reach-out program at school I became acquainted with an elderly, slightly impaired gentleman. One might look upon a 'job' with the elderly as work, but for me it is a welcome opportunity to share in the lives of the aged. Working with him is such an enriching and valuable part of my life. You can only benefit from the wit, wisdom, and love of life that the elderly in our society can give." *Nate Coffin, twelfth grade, Mount St. Joseph Academy, Rutland, Vermont*

84 Share your pet with the elderly.
"I bring dogs and cats to a nursing home twice a week. There are a number of blind and deaf people at the home, and blind people seem to benefit the most from

holding and petting the animals. Just the feel of the pet really is important to them. I love going to the nursing home. I even go there when I'm on vacation from school and on weekends. Once we were on the mentally handicapped floor, and there was one man who, the nurses told us, hadn't responded to anything in five years. He didn't smile, talk . . . nothing. The nurse said, 'Don't expect a response.' We touched the dog to his face, and he opened his eyes up a little bit and smiled. The staff couldn't believe it. That kind of thing makes everyone happy. But there are other days when someone just sees the dog and starts to cry. That can be really hard to deal with at the beginning." *Michelle Orzoff, twelfth grade, Roycemore School, Evanston, Illinois*

More ideas:

85 **Send letters and cards to someone in a nursing home.**

86 **Read to or run errands for a senior citizen living alone.**

87 **Interview an elderly person about his or her life.**

88 **Clean up an older person's home or yard.**

FACT

Approximately 25 percent of America's elderly persons live in homes that have serious problems, including leaking roofs, inadequate plumbing and electrical wiring, and unvented room heaters. (*The Good Heart Book: A Guide to Volunteering*, David E. Driver, Chicago: The Noble Press, Inc., 1989)

FACT

According to the American Association of Suicidology, 20 percent of all suicides in America are committed by elderly persons. (*Volunteer U.S.A.*, Andrew Carroll, New York: Fawcett Columbine, 1991)

FACT

On average, 12 percent of the population is sixty-five years of age and above. In rural America, that average is 25 percent. (The National Council on the Aging, Inc., Annual Report, 1990)

How You Can Help

☎ ✍

For more information on how you can become involved with the elderly, contact:

American Association of Retired Persons
1909 K Street, NW
Washington, DC 20049
(202) 662-4895

Generations United
c/o The Child Welfare League
440 First Street, NW, Suite 310
Washington, DC 20001
(202) 638-2952

Little Brothers—Friends of the Elderly
530 Columbus Avenue
Boston, MA 02118
(617) 536-2404

National Council of Senior Citizens
925 15th Street, NW
Washington, DC 20005
(202) 347-8800

National Council on the Aging
600 Maryland Avenue, S.W.
West Wing 100
Washington, DC 20024
(202) 479-1200

We Are the World
International Service or Relief Organizations

**"Hopefully, the world will join its people together
in order to save itself."**
Sarah Abbott, a tenth grader at Ben Franklin High School,
New Orleans, Louisiana

We've all heard people say that our world is shrinking. Advanced technology has connected us to peoples in the farthest corners of the world, and as the years go by we seem more and more interdependent: A plunge on the New York Stock Exchange causes panic in Tokyo; the destruction of rain forests in Brazil threatens the ecosystem of the entire planet. It has become clear that in order to survive we must work together as a global community.

The problems that face us in this country—massive budget deficits, homelessness, AIDS, drug abuse, to name but a few—can seem overwhelming. Yet, when we look at the troubles of other nations, it becomes apparent that Americans are, in fact, exceptionally fortunate. Each day, 40,000 children in Third World countries die of starvation or related illnesses. Thousands of people are imprisoned, tortured, and killed every year by despotic governments interested more in power than in the people they rule. And children in impoverished countries throughout the world grow up without even the faintest glimmer of hope that their situations might someday improve.

American youth will not be able to solve the world's problems singlehandedly. But you can make a difference in the lives of those you touch, and you can work together with others to forge global solutions to our most pressing problems. There are countless international service organizations you can join and support, and there will never be a limit on opportunities to extend your hand to someone in need in another country. All that's required is that you care enough to make that commitment.

89 Volunteer at a Third World orphanage.

"My family has spent several weeks over the past few years working in different Third World countries. Last summer we spent two weeks in an Acapulco, Mexico, orphanage. The orphanage is in terrible shape because, for some bureaucratic reason, the government doesn't give them any assistance. The orphanage doesn't have any windows—just holes in the bricks. One time a scorpion was on my leg and I didn't notice it until one of the small children began jumping around and acting out this charade. There was a real language barrier because my Spanish wasn't too good. The child got a leaf and calmly took the scorpion off my leg. There was such a bond then." *Seth Holmes, tenth grade, Lewis and Clark High School, Spokane, Washington*

90 Start a human rights club chapter at your school.

"I decided to start an Amnesty International chapter at my school when I found out about all of the abuses going on in the world. It's really sickening. We circulate petitions concerning prisoners of conscience—people who are being detained on the basis of their beliefs. Amnesty also sends us 'Urgent Actions,' which are appeals for immediate help for a particular prisoner. We send petitions and letters to heads of government on behalf of the prisoners. Amnesty is really effective. When heads of state get hundreds and hundreds of letters, they really do make changes." *Sarah Bardeen, twelfth grade, Grosse Pointe South High School, Grosse Pointe, Michigan*

91 Work with an underprivileged overseas community.

"I joined AMIGOS de las Americas, which is going to be sending me to Mexico or South America over the summer.

During the school year, we meet once a week and see films and hear people speak on topics like poverty and hunger or the importance of the rain forests. We go through seminars on how to relate to the people in less developed countries. Then, on the weekends, we do local community service, such as yard work for elderly people or helping refugees from other countries. We kind of get into the community service mode by doing it." *Courtney Munch, tenth grade, Kinkaid School, Houston, Texas*

92 Join a peace camp.

"I spent four weeks at a Worldpeace camp in the Soviet Ukraine. There were delegations there from all over the world. The best thing about the experience was what I learned about other people. In general, the Soviet kids aren't so into being cool; there isn't that much peer pressure. In a sense, they're less mature than American teenagers, but I think the way they are is much better. They all seem to be friends no matter what clothes they're wearing. I realized when I was there how closed-minded Americans can be." *Jill Rubin, tenth grade, Horace Greeley High School, Chappaqua, New York*

93 Do support work for an international relief group.

"I volunteer with Heifer Project International, an organization that helps people all over the world become self-sufficient. HPI does this by teaching them how to use their surroundings to the best advantage, by giving them animals to raise and sell or use for food, and by having each person pass on their new knowledge. The organization has two farms in the U.S., in Massachusetts, which is where they collect donated animals or animals they have bought. I lived on one of the farms for five weeks over the summer. I fed animals, cleaned the barn, cut down trees, built fences, took care of sick animals, cut grass, chopped and stacked wood, gave presentations, and helped with fund raising. When you work at HPI, you actually meet people from villages HPI has helped out. They tell you personally what a difference HPI made in their lives." *Beth Fraser, twelfth grade, Calhoun High School, Merrick, New York*

94 Adopt a foster child.

"Last year I went to Honduras for ten days to meet a foster child that my Spanish Club had adopted. I was able to go because I won an essay contest sponsored by Foster Plan International. It was really kind of depressing to see what goes on there and everything that the Hondurans have to go through. The money that we send goes to the village, but much of it goes to our foster child's family as well. They were really proud of everything and were offended if I didn't want to go and see anything. My foster child was so happy to meet one of the people who are helping to support her." *Trista Dunagan, eleventh grade, Cactus Shadows High School, Cave Creek, Arizona*

More ideas:

95 **Send care packages to a family overseas.**

96 **Raise money for internationl hunger or disaster relief.**

97 **Write to a pen pal in a foreign land.**

98 **Have your class "adopt" a class in a Third World country.**

99 **Host an international exchange student.**

FACT

Thousands of people are in prison because of their beliefs. Many are held without charge or trial, and torture and imposition of the death penalty are widespread. Men, women, and children in many countries have "disappeared" after being taken into official custody. (*The Human Rights Library*, Amnesty International, 1990)

FACT

There are more than 10 million child refugees around the world, many of whom have fled death. (Defense for Children International—USA, 1990)

FACT

Thirteen million children around the world live in poverty. (*The Children's Campaign*, Child Welfare League of America, 1990)

How You Can Help

For more information on international service programs, contact:

The Africa Fund
198 Broadway, Room 402
New York, NY 10038
(212) 962-1210

Africare, Inc.
440 R Street, NW
Washington, DC 20001
(202) 462-3614

American Field Service
313 East 43rd Street
New York, NY 10017
(212) 949-4242
1-800-AFS-INFO
(237-4636)

Amnesty International
322 Eighth Avenue, 10th
Floor
New York, NY 10001
(212) 807-8400

CARE
660 First Avenue
New York, NY 10016
(212) 686-3110

Christian Children's Fund
203 East Cary Street
Richmond, VA 23261
(804) 644-4654
1-800-776-6767

Council on International Educational Exchange
356 West 34th Street
New York, NY 10001
(212) 695-0291

The Foster Parents Plan
155 Plan Way
Warwick, RI 02886
(401) 738-5600
1-800-556-7918

Ground Zero Pairing Project
P.O. Box 10329
Portland, OR 97219
(503) 245-3519

Human Rights Watch
485 Fifth Avenue, 3rd
Floor
New York, NY 10017
(212) 972-8400

Operation Crossroads Africa, Inc.
150 Fifth Avenue
New York, NY 10011
(212) 242-8550
1-800-422-3742

Oxfam America
115 Broadway
Boston, MA 02116
(617) 482-1211
1-800-448-1355

Save the Children
The National Volunteer
Program
54 Wilton Road
P.O. Box 950
Westport, CT 06881
(203) 226-7271

Service Civil International
c/o Innisfree Village
Route 2, Box 506
Crozet, VA 22932
(804) 823-1826

United Nations Volunteers
1889 F Street, NW
Washington, DC 20006
(202) 955-5613

Volunteers for Peace International Work Camps
43 Tiffany Road
Belmont, VT 05730
(802) 259-2759

WorldPeace Camp
c/o Samantha Smith
Center
9 Union Street
Hallowell, ME 04347
(207) 626-3415

Youth of All Nations
16 St. Luke's Place
New York, NY 10014
(212) 924-1358

First Aid
Medical Facilities and Services

"Medical facilities are a necessity in the world—places of healing and caring compassionately."
Sara Renaud, a twelfth grader at Bellaire High School,
Bellaire, Michigan

An illness can attack not only a person's body, but also his or her sense of self-sufficiency and worth. When hospitalized or bedridden, people of every age need comfort and support. Some get these from family members; others must rely on the efforts of medical staffs and volunteers. If you've ever spent any time in a medical facility, you're no doubt well aware that the little things—a change of bed sheets or a fresh glass of water—can make all the difference in a patient's recovery. Whether you choose to get involved by delivering flowers and food or by providing a helping hand and a sympathetic ear, your concern and care will make a difference to the patients whose lives you touch.

100 Work in an operating room.
"I work in a veterans' hospital. One time I saw a pacemaker being put into someone. I was in the operating room and had on the whole scrub suit and everything. I almost passed out. I don't think I would want to do something like that again. I also helped to put a cast on an amputee patient. It was

kind of hard to block out the fact that the patient didn't have a whole leg under the cast, but it was a good learning experience. The veterans like telling a lot of interesting stories, and I've gotten to meet some neat people." *Brenda Agenbroad, twelfth grade, Wayne High School, Wayne, Nebraska*

101 Organize a blood drive.

"I first got involved with the Red Cross because when I was young I had a friend who died of leukemia. When she was going through treatment, her mother came to the school to talk to us about giving blood for her benefit. I decided then and there to become involved with the blood drives both at my school and in my city. Regardless of the fact that I don't know who my blood is going to, or even whether or not it can be used, I feel that I'm doing something very important." *Robby Blalock, twelfth grade, Abbeville High School, Abbeville, Alabama*

102 Work at a rehabilitation center.

"Five days a week, four hours a day every summer, I volunteer at the Rehabilitation Hospital of the Pacific. In a speech-therapy class the therapists and I help rebuild the patients' speaking ability. We ask them questions that would seem simple to us, but are a challenge for the patients to answer. After the day is done, I have a vast sense of pride and can gladly say I helped someone, even if it was something little. Sometimes you can get frustrated and go a little insane, but you must never show that kind of feeling around the patients." *Sherri Seto, eighth grade, Mid-Pacific Institute, Honolulu, Hawaii*

103 Educate others about prospective medical careers.

"I am president of one of the posts of Medical Explorers, an association which helps teenagers see different aspects of careers in the medical field. As president I arrange for speakers, tours, and field trips for our groups, and I run our meetings, which are once a month. Medical Explorers helps teenagers decide whether or not they want a career in the medical field. Many kids don't know that you can work in a hospital and be a business administrator, a dietician, or any number of things. And after being fully informed, some may even decide that they don't want to go into medicine. But it's a great way to learn as much as you can about it." *April Yuchnitz, twelfth grade, Furman High School, Sumter, South Carolina*

104 Volunteer at a children's hospital.

"On Saturday mornings I work at the Blythedale Children's Hospital. I get there at about 9:15 a.m., grab a cup of coffee, and head upstairs. Upon leaving the elevator, I'm in another world. The children don't run around—most are in wheelchairs, on stretchers, or in strollers. But only their physical appearance is different from other kids. As smiling faces greet me, I know that volunteering is the most useful thing I could be doing on any Saturday morning. Regardless of the problems they have faced, these children have survived and thrived. The most positive aspect of volunteering is what you realize when you drive home—that, although it was only a couple of hours, you made a difference." *Vandana Purohit, twelfth grade, Edgemont High School, Scarsdale, New York*

105 Work at a center for the mentally disabled.

"Every Monday, I go to the Allegheny Health Center and work with people with such disablements as autism and schizophrenia. I've seen people having seizures and naked people walking around looking lost. I've also dealt with being poked at and fondled. But these are all little things that don't really affect the way I feel about my volunteer work. These people want and need attention from us, and, through talking and playing with them, I feel as though I'm doing something really good for them. It's been a great experience for me, and something I wouldn't pass up." *Stacey Walton, twelfth grade, Appleton High School East, Appleton, Wisconsin*

106 Volunteer as an emergency medical technician.

"I work as an emergency medical technician. After my training, the first task I was given was to get the vitals—blood pressure, pulse, and rate of respiration—of three patients. It was unlike anything I had ever done before. In the classroom, everyone's vitals had always been virtually normal, but these patients' vitals were not. My next job was to restrain a patient's arm so that the nurse could insert an intravenous tube. Then I helped a doctor put stitches in a man's head. Perhaps the hardest thing was seeing a man die and then putting him into a body bag. I think you can volunteer in this environment only if you are both mentally and physically trained to face the realities of life. But it's an unforgettable experience." *Steven Shames, eleventh grade, Wilton High School, Wilton, Connecticut*

More ideas:

107 **Volunteer at a home for the families of terminally ill children.**

108 **Work at a doctor's office.**

109 **Be a lab assistant at a medical research facility.**

110 **Help a person with AIDS (or another illness) with meals and daily errands.**

111 **Volunteer at a pregnancy clinic.**

112 **Work in a clinic for low-income patients.**

113 **Take classes in CPR (cardiopulmonary resuscitation) or first aid.**

FACT

Sixty-five percent of all of the hospitals in the United States have volunteer-services departments. (*Hospital Statistics,* American Hospital Association, 1989–90)

FACT

A short time ago, the median life expectancy for a person with AIDS was just 30 weeks. However, many AIDS patients now live for over three years. (National AIDS Information Clearinghouse, 1990)

FACT

There will be an estimated 27,800 new cases of leukemia this year, half of them acute and the other half chronic. (Leukemia Society of America, Inc., 1990)

How You Can Help

For more information about what you can do in the medical field, contact:

AIDS National Interface Network
300 Eye Street, NE
Suite 400
Washington, DC 20002
(202) 546-0807

American Cancer Society
3340 Peachtree Road, NE
Atlanta, GA 30026
(404) 320-3333
1-800-ACS-2345
(227-2345)

American Heart Association
7320 Greenville Avenue
Dallas, TX 75231
(214) 373-6300

American Lung Association
1740 Broadway
New York, NY 10019
(212) 315-8700

American Red Cross
18th and D Streets, NW
Washington, DC 20006
(202) 639-3589

Arthritis Foundation
1314 Spring Street, NW
Atlanta, GA 30309
(404) 872-7100

Cancer Care, Inc. & The National Cancer Care Foundation, Inc.
1180 Avenue of the
    Americas
New York, NY 10036
(212) 221-3300

March of Dimes
1275 Mamaroneck
    Avenue
White Plains, NY 10605
(914) 428-7100

Muscular Dystrophy Association
810 Seventh Avenue
New York, NY 10019
(212) 586-0808

National AIDS Network
1012 14th Street, NW
Washington, DC 20005
(202) 347-0390

National Easter Seal Society
70 East Lake Street
Chicago, IL 60601
(312) 726-6200

National Emergency Medicine Association
306 West Joppa Road
Baltimore, MD 21204
(301) 494-0300
1-800-332-6362

National Federation of the Blind
1800 Johnson Street
Baltimore, MD 21230
(301) 659-9314

National Kidney Foundation
30 East 33rd Street
New York, NY 10016
(212) 889-2210
1-800-622-9010

National Mental Health Association
1021 Prince Street
Alexandria, VA 22314
(703) 684-7722

National Multiple Sclerosis Society
205 East 42nd Street
New York, NY 10017
(212) 986-3240

United Cerebral Palsy Association
710 Penn Plaza, Suite 804
New York, NY 10001
(212) 268-6655

Hotlines

Teens Teaching AIDS Prevention: 1-800-234-TEEN (8336)

AIDS National Hotline: 1-800-342-2437

If I Had a Hammer . . .
Neighborhood Improvement and Housing Rehabilitation

"You don't need to have construction skills—the only thing a person needs to help to renovate buildings and houses for homeless people is the eagerness to work."
Matthew Leaf, a twelfth grader at Friends Academy,
Locust Valley, New York

"As with most [Habitat for Humanity] projects, plans for the work in Chicago were made with a lot of faith and a little money. But both money and building supplies were ready when the crews, along with Jimmy and Rosalynn Carter, began work . . . the homeowners-to-be were on the site, too. Arbie Nelson was one of them. She was living in a nearby condemned apartment with her family of nine. Electricity and water had been shut off. The week we were there a nest of roots fell from the ceiling onto one of the beds of her children. Buckets were used to bring water from a neighbor's house, and the kitchen was a grill in the backyard. For this deplorable dump, Arbie paid $400 a month.

"As the workers pounded the studs for the walls into place . . . and as scores of people scurried around, taking measurements and yelling instructions, Arbie was overcome with emotion. She started at one side of the concrete slab and walked the length of it with arms upraised, tears flowing from her eyes, crying out again and again, 'It's a miracle! It's a miracle! Praise God. We're gonna have a house. It's a miracle.'"

Excerpted from The Excitement Is Building *by Millard and Linda Fuller (WORD Publishing, Texas, 1990)*

In fact, some of the best teenage social scenes we've heard about are Habitat sites where people of both sexes are making affordable housing a reality for families who might never be able to live independently. We were talking with Sarah Beatty, a student from Princeton, New Jersey, and she told us, "Maybe you'd be surprised but one of the best places to see the really cute guys from around here is down at the Habitat house in Trenton. . . ." And, a college student we know, Hillary Goldman, who attends the University of Vermont, spent spring break 1991 at the Habitat site in New York City. "It was a very fun, very satisfying week. I made great friends and felt wonderful about creating homes for people who truly need them."

114 Rehabilitate a city block.
"I volunteered for a local organization that buys an entire city block that has become run-down or crack-ridden. For each block that it purchases, about three years are spent beautifying it. By the time I became involved, this particular block was in the finishing stages, so we picked up a lot of trash that had been thrown around during the renovation process. We also mowed weeds and worked on the roof of a house. Many of the people on the block were elderly people who had lived there for years and were slowly overridden by drug dealers. It gave me a great sense of gratification to be able to help them out. The only depressing thing was the state of squalor that these people lived in. The grass was growing up through the floor in some of the places, but we cleaned up their houses around them." *Brian Ullmann, twelfth grade, Shawnee Mission East High School, Shawnee Mission, Kansas*

115 Rehabilitate a church.
"Through a mission group in my church, I traveled to Virginia by bus with about twenty-five other young people to spend four days helping to put the finishing touches on a newly built church. I stayed with one of the families who would be future parishioners of the church. We cleaned up everything on the

inside, finished up the parking lot, and planted a lot of trees. It was really strenuous work because it was so hot. People may think that twenty-five or so kids wouldn't be able to make any sort of difference, but I really think we did." *Jennifer Osborn, twelfth grade, McClellan High School, Little Rock, Arkansas*

116 Volunteer in a less affluent part of the country.

"Through an Appalachian service project, I spent a vacation in a mountainous region of North Carolina. When we first got down there I didn't know what to expect. But the house was in a complete state of disrepair. A typical day involved working for about three to four hours on the house, eating, and then working for about four to five more hours. We did everything from pouring a concrete foundation (the house had been propped up on cinderblocks) to painting the entire house. To do this kind of work you really have to be prepared to get dirty—and not be unsettled by poverty." *Elisha Sessions, eleventh grade, Bearden High School, Knoxville, Tennessee*

More ideas:

117 **Clean up a local beach, park, or playground.**

118 **Adopt a section of highway and keep it free of trash.**

119 **Plant a tree or garden in a public area.**

120 **Paint a park bench.**

FACT

Over the last decade, the federal housing budget has been slashed by nearly 80 percent. (Coalition for the Homeless, 1990)

FACT

There are over 500 projects affiliated with Habitat for Humanity in the United States, Canada, and Australia, and more than 100 sponsored projects in 28 developing countries. (*Fact Sheet,* Habitat for Humanity International, 1991)

FACT

More than 25 percent of homeless adults work full-time but are unable to find affordable housing. (Coalition for the Homeless, 1990)

How You Can Help

For more information on what you can do to renovate substandard housing or beautify a neighborhood, contact:

Church World Service
P.O. Box 968
Elkhart, IN 46515
(219) 264-3102
1-800-456-1310

Habitat for Humanity
International
121 Habitat Street
Americus, GA 31709
(912) 924-6935

Plenty U.S.A.
P.O. Box 2306
Davis, CA 95617
(916) 753-0731

Youth Volunteer Corps
1080 Washington
Kansas City, MO
64105-2216
(816) 474-5761

Desk Jockeys
Office Support and Fund-Raising

"Working in an office environment can be great—you work in the same place every day and build good relationships with those around you."
Joshua Houston, a twelfth grader at Avon Lake High School,
Avon Lake, Ohio

The nuts and bolts of any nonprofit organization are primarily office related—fund-raising, stuffing envelopes, making phone calls, data processing, and other light clerical duties. Office workers are crucial to the success of any program, and most organizations depend on volunteers to fill those roles. Consider volunteering to work in the office of an organization whose work you admire or to raise funds for the group. You'll not only learn more about the organization—and the cause with which it's involved—you'll also learn skills that will prove helpful when you begin a paying job. Why not get a head start on your career?

121	**Do office work for an AIDS foundation.**

"I saw a flier from the San Francisco AIDS Foundation asking for donations to the AIDS cause, and since I didn't have any money to donate, I decided that what I could give was my time. I went to one orientation to familiarize me with the setting, but since I wasn't going to be doing work that required any specific training, that was all I had to do to get ready. I wrote personal letters to people who had written in asking for information. I explained to them why their interest in the AIDS Foundation was so important. Through my work there, I now have a better understanding of people in general. I worked with people who were considerably older than I was; it helped me to deal with people out of my peer group and from different backgrounds." *Genevieve Ng, eleventh grade, George Washington High School, San Francisco, California*

122 Raise money for a national medical organization.

"Someone called my house one night and asked if I would be interested in volunteering for the Leukemia Society of America, and I have a friend who has leukemia, so it really struck me that this was something that I should do. I was asked to go around to each of my neighbors' houses and ask them for cash donations. I got to know some of my neighbors with whom I wasn't familiar beforehand. Most people were really receptive to me, although there were a few who weren't too friendly. I had a great feeling when I finished and turned the money over to the organization." *Jennifer Crenshaw, twelfth grade, Choctow High School, Choctow, Oklahoma*

123 Take part in an event for a good cause.

"One outstanding project I've participated in for the past couple of years is raising money for the Make-a-Wish Foundation. We had an all-night volleyball tournament. In order to participate in the volleyball games, you had to raise a certain amount of money. The tournament ended as the sun was rising. All 300 participants walked onto the front steps of the school and had a candlelight vigil. On the bottom of each card that was used to collect wax was the name and address of a terminally ill child. I wrote to my child, Candy, until she passed away four months ago. The money goes to make a terminally ill child's wish come true. I know Candy's last wish came true." *Jonell Lucca, twelfth grade, Hammonton High School, Hammonton, New Jersey*

More ideas:

124 **Put up posters and give out flyers for a charitable organization.**

125 **Organize a bazaar or raffle to raise money.**

126 Sponsor a student-run dinner and concert for parents and donate the money to a good cause.

FACT

The March of Dimes Birth Defects Foundation was founded by Franklin D. Roosevelt in 1938 to fight polio. The organization represents every community in America through a nationwide network of 138 chapters and hundreds of thousands of volunteers. (March of Dimes Birth Defects Foundation, *Fact Sheet*, 1991)

FACT

There are 2,300 United Ways operating throughout the country. Each one conducts its own fund-raising campaign. (United Way of America, 1991)

FACT

Over the past five years, total annual giving to educational institutions in the U.S. has risen 55 percent, with contributions from individuals up nearly 70 percent. (*Chronicle of Higher Education Almanac*, 1991)

How You Can Help

For more information about fund-raising for the organizations mentioned in this chapter, contact:

Leukemia Society of America, Inc.
733 Third Avenue, 14th
    Floor
New York, NY 10017
(212) 573-8484

The Make-a-Wish Foundation
2600 North Central
    Avenue
Phoenix, AZ 85004
1-800-722-9474

March of Dimes Birth Defects Foundation
1275 Mamaroneck
    Avenue
White Plains, NY 10605
(914) 428-7100

Toys for Tots (holiday season only)
Armed Forces Reserve
    Center, Building 351
Anacostia Naval Station
Washington, DC 20374
(202) 433-3612

United Way of America
701 North Fairfax Street
Alexandria, VA
    22314-2045
(703) 836-7100

Sports: The Common Denominator
Sports and Recreation

"The importance of sports as community service is that it is the beginning of the idea of teamwork and working together to achieve a goal. By coaching younger kids, I can pass the knowledge I have to younger people who are less experienced."
John Smitty, a twelfth grader at Central High School, Milwaukee, Wisconsin

The importance of sportsmanship and teamwork is something everyone learns as a child. Playing and working together as a team builds a sense of camaraderie that goes far beyond the pursuit of a common goal. Playing a sport also builds self-confidence and self-esteem. But some people might ask, "What do sports have to do with community service?" Quite a bit. Involvement in sports, whether one is coaching, teaching, or playing on the team, is an important form of socialization. Sports allow us to communicate with another person, another team, or even nature.

When you're playing a sport, try to see what you're doing as not simply a personal challenge but as an opportunity—an opportunity to build school or community spirit, to develop personal traits, and, perhaps most important, to pass on to someone else what you have learned. That's what being a good sport is all about.

127 Teach elementary school students to ski.

"I'm involved with Rug Rats, a program in my school in which we teach students at a nearby elementary school to ski. I became interested in the program because when I was in the fifth grade I was one of the students in the Rug Rat program. So, basically, I wanted to give back what I had gotten, because I remembered the program as being a lot of fun and really helpful in getting me out on the slopes twice a week.

"At first, we went through clinics, which showed us how to start off working with the kids. For example, they showed us the kinds of wedges that beginners must use to stop. We also learned some games so it would be easier for the kids. We go twice a week after school, and the students pay a reduced fee for the lift tickets. I think it's great just to help these kids have some fun and learn, because a lot of them don't get to go skiing that much. Even if it's only two days a week, they'll get something out of it." *Josh Paquette, ninth grade, Gould Academy, Bethel, Maine*

128 Coach a basketball team.

"When I was younger I used to play basketball at the community center run by the Salvation Army, and my sisters are on the team now. I'm good at basketball, and I enjoy doing things for a good cause, so now I'm a volunteer coach for about two to three hours in the evening each week. Our games are usually on weekends. The kids are in the third and fourth grades and it's a lot of fun. I've learned a lot of patience and teaching skills that I know will work to my advantage in the long run.

"I would say that if you're good at sports and you're willing to put in some extra time to make a difference in someone's life, volunteer coaching is a great idea. A lot of my friends think what I do is really neat, and several of my friends have begun to do similar things." *Kim Hewitt, eleventh grade, East High School, Des Moines, Iowa*

129 Teach swimming classes.

"As a volunteer worker at the Y.M.C.A., I run swimming parties for children. The kids arrive at the center and after we greet them we give them a game or two to play as they are waiting for the others to arrive. We encourage the kids to blow up some balloons and tape them to the wall or put them on paper feet with their name on it. After everyone arrives, we take the kids down to the locker room, sit them down, and give them the buddy system speech and draw numbers for their partners. They are allowed five minutes to change into their swimsuits. We take them out into the pool and set out a few toys if the pool is not too full. The kids and teachers play for a half an hour. Then we get into a group and play a game like dodgeball. After an hour, we go into the locker room and shower and change. The kids then go upstairs and have snacks until their parents come to get them. The teachers all get the privilege of cleaning up afterwards." *Tyrell Allardyce, twelfth grade, T. F. Riggs High School, Pierre, South Dakota*

130 Volunteer for a community-wide recreational association.

"I am the student president of the Rodeo Association, an extremely popular group on the Navaho reservation where I live. It is a nonprofit organization that revolves around rodeo, a prevalent pastime around here. The association is for kids up to the age of eighteen, but we interact with adults as well. I help with a lot of fund-raising and also act as an ambassador between members of the association and adults. I attend board meetings and then address the students about what went on there. My leadership skills have improved a great deal.

"The best thing about the association is that it is based on something that is very important in our community. Rodeos bring people together from all around our area, and it is a special gathering for us. It makes me feel as though I'm a part of something that everyone appreciates." *Germaine Daye, twelfth grade, Tohatchi High School, Tohatchi, New Mexico*

More ideas:

131 **Teach a game such as chess to an underprivileged youth.**

132 **Coach or referee a Little League team.**

133 **Accompany kids on weekend "fresh air" trips to the country.**

FACT

Ninety-five percent of high school principals who answered a national survey believe that participation in sports teaches students valuable lessons that cannot be learned in a regular class routine. (National Federation of State High School Associations, 1991)

FACT

The Special Olympics were begun by the Joseph P. Kennedy Jr. Foundation and maintain ties to the Kennedy family. Rosemary Kennedy, a sister of the late president, is mentally retarded. (Special Olympics International Headquarters, 1991)

FACT

Each summer, more than 8,000 amputees, paraplegic and blind veterans, and physically limited civilians spend time at Confidence Through Sports programs in Ossining, New York, free of charge. (The 52 Association for the Handicapped, Inc., 1990)

How You Can Help

For information about sports and recreation for the physically challenged, contact:

The 52 Association for the Handicapped, Inc.
350 Fifth Avenue, Suite 1829
New York, NY 10118
(212) 563-9797

National Handicapped Sports Education Office
1145 19th Street, NW
Suite 717
Washington, DC 20036
(301) 652-7505

Special Olympics International Headquarters
1350 New York Avenue, NW, Suite 500
Washington, DC 20005
(202) 628-3630

Playing It Straight
Prevention of Substance Abuse

"One of my largest concerns and what worries me most is dealing with the pressures of drugs and alcohol. My self-esteem is high, but dealing with this worries me because I don't want to lose friends."
Joey Williams, a twelfth grader at William Chrisman High School, Independence, Missouri

"It is encouraging to hear about students like yourselves who are determined to lead drug-free lives. I understand the pressures facing kids today, especially from peers seeking to influence you to try drugs. Whenever you're confronted with drugs, have the courage to resist. And, because you're young, the same goes for alcohol too.

"In the war against illegal drug use, the heroes are not those who use drugs and quit; they are those who never use them in the first place. I am counting on you to be heroes in the war on drugs, standing firm in your commitment never to use drugs.

"By taking a public stand against illegal drugs, you are setting an excellent standard for others to follow. With support from concerned students like you, I am confident that we can win this war."

William J. Bennett, former Director, Office of National Drug Control Policy, as stated in an open letter to members of Students Against Driving Drunk

It's not enough to just say no yourself, corny as that may sound. It's important to also encourage your friends to say no to drinking and drugs and to say no to taking car rides with people who have had a drink or who have been using drugs. The safe rides programs we've heard about certainly make a difference, especially because it's a matter of teens helping other teens stay safe. Kaz Watanabe, a junior from Darien, Connecticut, explains, "Everybody knows that teenagers like to party. What we do is make sure that there are people who stay sober to ensure that everyone can have a safe ride home."

134 Talk to younger kids about avoiding drugs.

"I've seen some kids with drug problems in my high school, so a friend of mine and I thought that if we could reach kids at a younger age, it might do something to change the way they thought about drugs. We went to our principal and were set up with a sixth-grade teacher. Every week for a few hours, we'd go over to the elementary school with worksheets and exercises we had planned pertaining to alcohol, self-confidence, and self-esteem. The kids learned to expect us every week, and we got great feedback from them." *Paul Murrell, eleventh grade, Washburn High School, Minneapolis, Minnesota*

135 Start an Alcoholics Anonymous chapter at school.

"Since there are a lot of kids with drug and alcohol problems at my school, I called the Alcoholics Anonymous Association and talked with them about how to start a chapter. They sent me a packet about it—it was actually pretty easy. A lot of my fellow students find it hard to kick the habit, and it makes me feel really good to know that I'm helping others." *Jason Russell, twelfth grade, Mountain Home High School, Mountain Home, Idaho*

136 Encourage kids not to drink and drive.

"National Red Ribbon Week is a week during which people tie a red ribbon onto their cars or pin one onto themselves in order to symbolize their commitment not to drink and drive. Our cheerleaders performed the Red Ribbon Rap at a pep rally! As it turned out, our participation helped a lot—a lot of people were really involved with the event and didn't drink. Our rap went like this:

> Come on, folks
> We've gotta rap
> About this drinking and driving crap
> I've got a word for you that's true
> All this boozin' and cruisin' is through.
> I'm telling you straight
> And that's no jive
> It just ain't right to drink and drive.
> Boy in your beat
> Better buckle your seat
> If you want to stay alive
> Don't drink and drive."

Jennifer Encinas, eleventh grade, Devils Lake Central High School, Devils Lake, North Dakota

137 Join an anti–drinking and driving club.

"My boyfriend was involved in a drunk-driving accident in which someone died, which might be why I feel so strongly about drunk driving. I'm involved with SADD [Students Against Driving Drunk]. The organization tries to develop a sense of responsibility in teens and especially tries to make them realize how their actions can affect themselves and others. We recently had a speaker whose son had been killed in a drunk-driving accident. When I'm at a party, I'm the 'key master,' the person who holds everyone's car keys and gives them back only to drivers who are sober. If I can stop one person from drinking and driving, I'll be happy." *Cary Seston, twelfth grade, Lake Forest Academy, Lake Forest, Illinois*

138 Join a Saferides program.

"I'm involved with a program that offers a safe form of transportation to students who are too drunk to drive home. For four hours every Saturday night, three or four students and one adult monitor a phone line that kids who have been drinking can call. Although we're not attempting to end world hunger or help the homeless, we may save a life, or at least eliminate the risk of any accident." *Ramez Habib, twelfth grade, Herricks High School, New Hyde Park, New York*

More ideas:

139 **Volunteer at a substance-abuse rehabilitation clinic.**

140 **Organize an effort to "take back" a park or other public area that has been taken over by drug dealers.**

141 **Set up an awareness campaign about the dangers of dealing drugs.**

FACT

In 1990, the actual number of alcohol-related traffic fatalities in the United States was 22,083. (Mothers Against Drunk Driving, 1991)

FACT

Drinking and driving continues to be the leading cause of death for teenagers. More than 40 percent of all deaths for people aged 15 to 20 result from motor vehicle crashes, and about half of these motor vehicle fatalities involve alcohol. (National Highway Traffic Safety Administration, 1991)

FACT

By age 16, one teen in three is approached to buy or use drugs. (*Drug Use Among Youth*, The American Council for Drug Education, 1990)

How You Can Help

For more information about the prevention of drug and alcohol abuse, contact:

Al-Anon Family Group Headquarters
P.O. Box 862, Midtown
    Station
New York, NY 10018
(212) 302-7240

Alcoholics Anonymous World Services
Box 459, Grand Central
    Station
New York, NY 10163
(212) 686-1100

Alcohol Education for Youth and Communication
362 State Street
Albany, NY 12210
(518) 436-9319

The American Council for Drug Education
204 Monroe Street, Suite
    110
Rockville, MD 20850
(301) 294-0600
    or

136 East 64th Street
New York, NY 10021
(212) 758-8060

Cocaine Hotline
1-800-COCAINE
    (262-2463)

Just Say No Clubs
Just Say No Foundation
1777 North California
    Boulevard
Walnut Creek, CA 94596
(415) 939-6666
1-800-258-2766

Mothers Against Drunk Driving (MADD)
P.O. Box 541688
Dallas, Texas 75354-1688
(214) 744-6233
1-800-GET-MADD
    (438-6233)

Narcotics Anonymous
P.O. Box 9999
Van Nuys, CA 91409
(818) 780-3951

National Association on Drug Abuse Problems
355 Lexington Avenue
New York, NY 10017
(212) 986-1170

National Council on Alcoholism
12 West 21st Street
New York, NY 10010
(212) 206-6770

Students Against Driving Drunk (SADD)
P.O. Box 800
Marlboro, MA 01752
(508) 481-3568

Teen-Age Assembly of America/Youth Against Drugs Project
905 Umi Street
Honolulu, HI 96819
(808) 841-1146

Recommended Reading

Fight Drug Abuse with Facts, a free catalog, available from The American Council for Drug Education (see address above)

Trading Places in the Classroom
Teaching and Tutoring

"I think the most difficult thing teachers must do is convey to students that the teachers aren't merely there as educators, but as friends."
Neil Autrey, a twelfth grader at Columbia High School,
Columbia, South Carolina

Education is the key to our future. Yet it could also be a factor in America's decline. One out of every five American adults is functionally illiterate, unable to read the most basic material—road signs, job applications, medicine bottles, a restaurant menu, or a child's report card, according to the Literacy Volunteers of America (*Facts on Illiteracy in America*, 1989). And our population's overall academic awareness palls in comparison with that of our biggest economic competitor, the Japanese. Many of our young people do not receive the individual attention that they need and deserve in the classroom. Teachers, especially in large public schools, are overwhelmed and overworked. And with the prevalence of single-parent households and dual-income families, few children receive the help they need at home.

Will the United States reach its goal of having the most-educated work force in the world by the year 2000? It seems unlikely, particularly in light of the constraints that the federal budget deficit has put on education spending. George Bush has indicated his desire to be known as the "education president," yet his budget for education is less than his predecessor's.

It's clear that education needs to be treated as a top national priority. And it's also clear that the government will not be able to revamp our educational system on its own. So what can teenagers do to help? Aside from working to make improved education a legislative priority, you can work to raise our nation's educational level on a person-to-person basis. Tutoring a child after school or helping an illiterate adult learn to read might not seem like much. But to the person you help, it can mean the difference between a lifetime of limitations and a lifetime of achievement.

142 Tutor a child who needs special attention.

"My mother thinks that I should be a teacher, and she tells all of her friends that I'll tutor their kids! So one woman came to me and asked me to help out her daughter, who was in danger of having to redo the third grade. I never was really sure if I was helping her, until she got her report card and her mom was so happy. My advice to people who are considering tutoring someone is to become his or her friend from the very start. Don't even tutor the person during the first session—just talk. If you're not that person's friend, he or she won't get anything out of it." *Stephanie Crane, twelfth grade, Golden West High School, Visalia, California*

143 Tutor an adult who is going back to school.

"A next-door neighbor of mine asked me for help in algebra and chemistry because he was going back to school. I was really pretty flattered and was interested in helping him because I like the idea of teaching and explaining things to people. I used the exact methods that my teachers used with me, and I also devised a few methods of my own. Every time he needs my help he'll give me a call. I think it's a real challenge to try to get something through to someone." *John Alexander Lobur, twelfth grade, Ann Arbor Greenhills School, Ann Arbor, Michigan*

144 Teach religious instruction.

"Every other Sunday, I teach Sunday school. When all of my kids arrive, we start off with a prayer and a song. Then we read a story and work in workbooks. After we've finished, we sing songs until it is time to go. I really want to make a difference in one of my kids' lives." *Amy Holsing, ninth grade, Roncalli High School, Aberdeen, South Dakota*

145 Volunteer at a kindergarten.

"I was a volunteer at an all-day kindergarten for a semester and tutored about ten children. I helped these children with sounds, letters, and numbers. I also helped them with shapes, colors, and sight words. By the end of the semester, most of the children knew their numbers up to twenty or beyond, all their sight words, their colors, shapes, and letters. The experience was very rewarding for me in many ways. I feel that the children very much improved through the work that I did with them." *Kris Brown, twelfth grade, Hartford Union High School, Hartford, Wisconsin*

146 Teach English as a Second Language.

"I teach English as a Second Language. I have always been interested in the ESL program because of my involvement with teaching some of my relatives to speak English. One really positive aspect of teaching ESL is the insight I get into the students' native countries and into the kinds of lives they led and still lead. One of my favorite students, Long, was born during the Vietnam War. He is Amerasian—half American, half Asian. He told me, in very broken English, about his home, or lack of one. He told me that he lived on the street with his friend. He has no family. He does not even know when his birthday is. I know I can't change his past, but perhaps with my help he has a better chance in the future." *Jennifer Kim, twelfth grade, Roslyn High School, Roslyn, New York*

More ideas:

147 **Teach an illiterate adult to read.**

148 **Set up an after-school peer tutoring clinic at your school.**

149 **Teach at a reading clinic for underprivileged youth.**

150 **Tutor individuals preparing for the high school equivalency exam.**

FACT

According to the U.S. Department of Education, 1 in 5 American adults is functionally illiterate—20 percent of the total adult population in this country. In addition, another 34 percent of American adults are only marginally literate. (Literacy Volunteers of America, Inc., 1991)

FACT

Fewer than 5 percent of the 17-year-olds in our schools read well enough to comprehend average college or business writing. (Reading is Fundamental, 1990)

FACT

Every day in America, 1,375 teenagers drop out of school. (*Partners in Education*, National Association of Partners in Education, November 1990)

How You Can Help

For more information on what you can do to help educate others, contact:

Literacy Volunteers of America, Inc.
5795 Widewaters
  Parkway
Syracuse, NY 13214
(315) 445-8000

National Community Education Association
119 North Payne Street
Alexandria, VA 22314
(703) 683-6232

Reading Is Fundamental, Inc.
Smithsonian Institution
600 Maryland Avenue,
  SW, Suite 500
Washington, DC 20560
(202) 287-3220

Part II
Choosing the Volunteer Job That's Right for You

_____

**"I guess this is a message for my friends and teens all
over. I don't do community service for my college
transcript, I do it because I enjoy making a difference.
We are the fortunate ones, and it's easy to forget
that. Everyone has something inside them to give
back. Discover it, use it, and be proud that you've
made someone's life a little bit brighter and easier."**
Sarah Beatty, a twelfth grader at Princeton Day School,
Princeton, New Jersey

In today's world, finding a volunteer opportunity will be a piece of
cake. Everywhere we turn, we see people in need and problems
crying out for solutions. You probably wish you could do something for the child born with AIDS, the homeless family that lives
under the bridge, the animals on the verge of extinction—all at the
same time. Clearly, that's not possible.

What you must do instead is make a difficult choice. You
must decide how, when, and where you are going to focus your
energies, and in so doing you must consider your own needs,
interests, and schedule. Don't feel selfish because you want a
volunteer job that's right for you. As spokespeople from several
nonprofit organizations have told us, too many people rush into a
volunteer commitment without taking the time to examine just
what the job will entail. After a few weeks, these volunteers simply

fail to show up, with the result that valuable time has been wasted on orientation and training.

So to avoid reneging on a volunteer commitment, take the time beforehand to examine exactly what you want. Ask yourself the following questions.

What are my strengths?

Don't let modesty stand in your way—no one's going to publish your answers in the local paper. And keep in mind that just because you might not be an honor student or varsity athlete doesn't mean you don't have plenty going for you. Just jot down any words you would use to describe yourself in a positive way, any quality that could be used to someone's benefit. By determining your strengths, you'll be better able to decide the type of activity at which you'll excel.

What are my hobbies and interests?

Doing good doesn't have to be painful. Why not combine volunteering with an activity you enjoy? By making the experience more pleasant for yourself, you'll be more likely to stick with it for an extended period. And don't feel that you're limited to "traditional" volunteer activities. No rule says that you can't create one of your own. For example, if you'd like to work at a soup kitchen but you were hoping to make use of your musical skills, why not volunteer to perform during or after meals? Soothing music would be just as appreciated there as at any restaurant.

Are there any tangible benefits I'd like to gain from my volunteer experience?

Think of your volunteer job as a modern-day apprenticeship. Is there some skill you want to learn or improve? What about typing or computer skills? Or maybe you'd like some practice in public speaking or canvassing. As long as you're working for a cause, you might as well take advantage of the opportunity to broaden your abilities, particularly if a college or job application is looming.

Do I want to work one-on-one with someone or would I prefer to work in a group or on my own?

Some volunteers get great satisfaction out of developing a relationship with one person. They turn to volunteer opportunities such as being a "big brother" or "big sister," a tutor, or an aide to a disabled or elderly person. Other volunteers prefer a less personal, but no less important, approach to volunteerism. They take part in fund-raising drives, work as tour guides, or play instruments in a community orchestra. Volunteers who prefer to work independently may not even want to join an organization. They may choose to make a difference from within their own homes—by writing letters to policymakers, sending care packages to needy families overseas, or contributing in any other way they can. By deciding which type of experience you'd like to have, you'll be able to narrow your focus considerably.

Now take a look at the issues for which you'd consider volunteering. Perhaps you have a personal reason for choosing your cause—a classmate was killed in a drunk driving accident, you witnessed child abuse, or have a mentally retarded friend or relative. If it's not quite so easy for you to choose a cause, see how you'd answer these questions:

- If you had $100,000 that you had to give to a cause, what cause would it be?
- When you look at the problems of the world, what bothers you most?

Now read about what several of this book's teen coauthors have done and why.

Background: Maya Beasley, a tenth grader at Bethesda–Chevy Chase High School in Bethesda, Maryland, was struck by the many problems in Washington, DC. At the same time, she was struck by how little her classmates seemed to know or care about the issues involved.

The Volunteer Solution: Along with her best friend, Maya began a 30-person organization called YES (Youth Engaged in Service) at Bethesda–Chevy Chase High School. The organization has collected nearly a thousand blankets and coats for the homeless, has sponsored a foster child in Bangladesh, and has held numerous parties and field trips for underprivileged teens in Washington.

Background: Sylvia Heredia, a twelfth grader at Bronx High School of Science in New York, is very patient, loves children, and is academically oriented. As a New York City teenager, Sylvia knows people who she feels haven't been given a fair shot at an education and have consequently dropped out of school. She had some spare time on her hands and decided she wanted to contribute her time to furthering education.

The Volunteer Solution: Sylvia saw a television commercial for an organization called Project Literacy and knew right away that that was the job for her. She now tutors fourth graders and has the satisfaction of knowing that she's playing a big part in their futures.

Background: Sean Snowball, an eleventh grader at East High School in Anchorage, Alaska, loves sports. He is a member of his school's basketball, baseball, and track teams and hopes to become a physical education teacher or coach someday. Sean wanted to get involved in a community service activity that ties in with his abilities in and enthusiasm for athletics.

The Volunteer Solution: Sean took part in the Native Youth Olympics, an athletic competition based on sporting events indigenous to the Eskimos. Sean says, "Some young people are negative about the Eskimo culture, and I wanted to do something that would help shed a positive light on our culture." Sean had a great time participating in the Olympics, and he was a finalist in the one-arm reach and the Alaskan high kick, games his forefathers had enjoyed many years before.

Background: John and Nicole Gaghan, twelfth and eleventh graders, respectively, at Cherry Hill High School East in Cherry Hill, New Jersey, live in a community in which the trees seem to be disappearing before their very eyes. Over the years, the woods in which they used to play have been turned into shopping malls and parking lots. As teenagers, they felt that they had little power to challenge the developers, but they wanted to make their opinions known.

The Volunteer Solution: John and Nicole now serve on a committee that raises environmental awareness in their community. They attend town meetings and lobby for fewer new developments. They've inspired other young people at school to stand behind the issue with them, and together they have become a force to be reckoned with in the Cherry Hill area.

Background: Dan Altman, an eleventh grader at Georgetown Day School in Washington, DC, was frustrated by the powerlessness he and other teenagers felt to effect change in the world. His school had a community service requirement of 10 hours per year, and many students performed their obligatory 10 hours without contributing or benefiting very much. Dan felt that a greater emphasis needed to be placed on volunteer work.

The Volunteer Solution: Dan wrote a proposal and used it to convince his school's administration to raise the community service requirement from 10 hours per year to 120 hours per year. Though some students gave him a hard time at first, three years later 60 percent of the students at Georgetown Day spent over three times the required time in volunteering.

Background: Hilary Grabe, a tenth grader at Clearlake High School in Houston, Texas, is a competitive swimmer. She is a member of both her school's swim teqm and a private club team, and practices before school, after school, and at night four or five days a week. Hilary excels in the 100-meter backstroke and the 100-meter freestyle events and aspires to make the nationals in the near future. Since most of her time is spent with her school swim team, Hilary wanted to participate in a community service activity that included the group.

The Volunteer Solution: Hilary and her entire swim team walked 12 miles for the March of Dimes WalkAmerica walkathon and raised a good deal of money for the organization. She says, "It was great walking with the team, because we always have a good time together, and we knew we were doing this for a great cause."

Background: Jongnic Bontemps, an eleventh grader at The Portledge School in Locust Valley, New York, lives in an area that some people might consider "rough." Jongnic is fortunate to have more than many of his neighbors have, and he wants to give something back to the community.

The Volunteer Solution: Jongnic led a student group in helping out at a soup kitchen in his area. He has established ties with some of the soup kitchen's clients, an added bonus to his volunteer work. He says, "I like the continuity of serving the same people and getting a chance to know them on a person-to-person basis."

Background: Jeannie Hoffman and Missy Wagner, both twelfth graders at Tower Hill School in Wilmington, Delaware, are global teenagers. They're well aware of the problems that exist in Third World countries, and they wanted to contribute toward that cause.

The Volunteer Solution: While many of their classmates basked on beaches, Jeannie and Missy spent their spring vacation volunteering at Tower Hill's sister school in rural Jamaica. Though their school contributes money raised by students like Jeannie and Missy toward the Jamaican school, the girls wanted to have a more personal volunteer experience overseas. At the school, they rebuilt the kitchen and engaged in some very arduous physical labor.

Background: Andy Schocken, an eleventh grader at Lakeside School in Seattle, Washington, feels very fortunate. His parents have been generous, and Andy has pretty much had everything he has needed his entire life. He wanted to share his good fortune with others.

The Volunteer Solution: When Andy was bar mitzvahed at age 13, he asked his guests to contribute money instead of gifts. He put that money into a special account, and each year makes a generous contribution to an organization that he wishes to help. Andy says, "It was the most gratifying thing I have ever done. All my friends were getting thousands of dollars, and I thought it was a waste."

Background: Jane Odiseos lives in Greenwich, Connecticut, a wealthy community that is worlds apart from the slums of nearby New York City. When Jane spent time in New York and saw inner-city poverty there, she wished she could do more. But because she lives in the suburbs, she saw her options as somewhat limited.

The Volunteer Solution: Jane joined Meals on Wheels, an organization that transports food from Greenwich into New York City every Saturday morning. While it's hard work, Jane finds it very gratifying and says, "I get to enjoy Greenwich every day of the week—so giving up one morning to get a taste of how other people live is no sacrifice at all."

Background: Chris Pennisi, an eleventh grader at Manhasset High School in Manhasset, New York, always needs to be doing something. He is a self-described "hyper" guy. He likes to communicate with people, is dedicated, and has a strong interest in taking a leadership position and "getting the job done."

The Volunteer Solution: Chris joined the Key Club to keep himself busy and serve the community at the same time, and in a short time he has risen to the rank of District Board Director, in which capacity he is in charge of sixteen Key Club chapters in his district. He says, "I like the feeling of being in charge and running an organization that does community service."

Background: Tiffany DeFrance, a ninth grader at Harpeth Hall School in Nashville, Tennessee, has always loved animals, but she had an experience while on spring vacation with her family that convinced her to dedicate her free time to the cause of animals. While in the Bahamas, Tiffany dove off a boat and swam for several minutes directly alongside a dolphin. She says, "I realized how beautiful and special the dolphins are. It was an experience I'll never forget." This experience led directly to Tiffany's decision to volunteer in some activity that would help animals.

The Volunteer Solution: Tiffany washes and walks animals at her local Humane Society at least once a week. It is one of her favorite activities. She recently applied to volunteer for Earthwatch, a research organization based in San Francisco. If accepted, she'll get involved in all aspects of the work the organization does for dolphins.

Background: John Boris, a twelfth grader at Brunswick School in Greenwich, Connecticut, wanted to do something about the many problems in our society and had a difficult time choosing one specific cause to which to dedicate his time.

The Volunteer Solution: John keeps himself busy with four ongoing service projects that he has nicknamed his "rituals." He began a recycling program at Brunswick School, he heads up all of the Red Cross activities there, is a Peer Leader for underclassmen at school, and is a Big Brother to a preschooler who recently lost his mother. He is also involved with clothing drives for the economically disadvantaged and with the Make-a-Wish Foundation.

Background: Sarah Beatty, a twelfth grader at Princeton Day School in Princeton, New Jersey, is popular and well respected at school. Her friends look up to her and ask her for advice. She wanted to make herself available to her peers who weren't necessarily just her best friends.

The Volunteer Solution: Sarah became a student counselor at Hi Tops, an educational program on sexuality for male and female adolescents. Sarah was trained in peer leadership and sex education and gives workshops to her peers on topics pertaining to sex and contraception. She says, "Sometimes people come up to me in the hallways and ask me questions about birth control. They really trust me and rely on me to be able to answer their questions. It's a good feeling."

Making a difference in the world is a reward in its own right. The satisfaction you'll gain from lending a helping hand will outweigh all other considerations. But don't forget that a volunteer experience very often provides other rewards as well. All the while you're giving of yourself, you're also learning new skills, defining and refining your current and future interests, and trying out possible life and work styles.

As you go through your high school years and devote time to community service, extracurricular activities, and volunteer jobs, be sure to keep a log of what you're accomplishing. This log will prove invaluable, whether you use it to record your experiences for college or job applications or whether you simply want to keep track of your progress as a volunteer.

For each thing you do outside the classroom, be sure to record as much as you can, as you're doing it. Here is a sample of what we're describing, created by one of our hundreds of high school contributors, Barbara Wojcik, of Brick, New Jersey, a twelfth grader at Brick Township High School.

Organization	Medical Center of Ocean County
Location	Point Pleasant, NJ
Address and Phone Number	2121 Edgewater Place Point Pleasant, NJ 08742 (908) 892-1100
Adviser/Group Leader	Tammy Texter, assistant director of volunteer services
Description of Activity	Junior volunteer
Accomplishments/Goals/Tasks	Anything and everything to make patients more comfortable
Abilities/Skills Gained	Familiarity with the medical field; developed strong personal relationships with patients and hospital staff members

Notes

Working as a junior volunteer at the Medical Center of Ocean County is the most fulfilling volunteer activity in which I participate. I really cannot describe a typical day, for each day is different and exciting in its own way. Some days I work on a surgical floor as a patient aide, getting water, juice, newspapers, etc., for the patients; helping them to write letters, eat, contact their families by phone; and just being there to listen, talk, or lend a shoulder to cry on. Other days are spent transporting patients to and from the radiology department and helping with any paperwork and filing there. Yet other days are spent at the front desk, speaking with the families of patients and regulating visitors. I also take new patients to their rooms and take discharged patients to their cars.

The most positive aspect of this volunteer activity is the immediate difference I can make in a person's life. A squeeze of my hand or an unspoken thank you that shows so clearly in a patient's eyes and face is worth more than gold.

Health Occupations Students of America (HOSA) was the most influential organization in encouraging my involvement as a junior hospital volunteer. It is a vocational student organization that encourages leadership and personal growth while educating about health care. Working as a volunteer is one of the many community services in which my local chapter of HOSA participates. The time I spend volunteering is repaid many times over.

Keeping track of your volunteer achievements can help you to determine which direction you'd like to go in—academically, in your career, and as a volunteer. Periodically take stock of your skills, knowledge, and strengths so that you have a clearer, more organized view of your present and future capabilities. Use action words to describe your achievements, and use good descriptors in defining your own capabilities. The following lists contain examples of strong and meaningful words to help you get started.

ACTION WORDS

accomplished	collaborated	evaluated
achieved	communicated	examined
addressed	conceived	executed
administered	conceptualized	expanded
advised	conducted	expedited
affected	coordinated	explained
analyzed	counseled	facilitated
anticipated	created	familiarized
appraised	decided	formulated
approached	decreased	generated
approved	defined	guided
arranged	delegated	handled
assembled	demonstrated	hired
assessed	designed	identified
assigned	determined	implemented
assisted	developed	improved
budgeted	devised	increased
built	doubled	initiated
calculated	drafted	inspected
clarified	edited	instructed
	established	integrated

interpreted
interviewed
introduced
invented
invested
investigated
launched
led
maintained
managed
marketed
mediated
merchandised
minimized
modified
monitored
motivated
negotiated
obtained
operated
organized
originated
participated
performed
planned
presented
processed
produced
proposed
provided
published
purchased
recommended
recruited
redesigned
reduced
reported
researched
resolved

revised
revitalized
saved
scheduled
served
shaped
simplified
sold
solved
stimulated
studied
supervised
supported
surveyed
synthesized
taught
tested
traded
trained
translated
tripled
utilized
wrote

COMMUNICA-TIONS SKILLS
defining
describing
drawing/illustrating
editing
explaining
interpreting
listening
negotiating
persuading
reading
reporting
speaking
writing

RESEARCH SKILLS
analyzing
clarifying
classifying
collecting
compiling
coordinating
evaluating
examining
hypothesizing
interpreting
investigating
surveying
synthesizing

MANAGEMENT SKILLS
coaching
counseling
deciding
delegating
developing
guiding
interviewing
leading
monitoring
motivating
organizing
planning
relating
strategizing
supervising
teaching

KNOWLEDGE
foreign language
graphic design

word processing (and so on . . . there are no limits to the types of knowledge one can attain)

STRENGTHS

ability to work
  under pressure
ambition

common sense
competitiveness
cooperation
creativity
dependability
determination
diplomacy
direction
enthusiasm
flexibility

high energy level
initiative
intelligence
judgment
leadership
objectivity
patience
perspective
resourcefulness
tolerance

Part III
State-by-State Directory of Associations

The following is a sampling of nonprofit organizations nationwide that accept teenage volunteers. There are thousands of such organizations in each state, and this list is not intended to be either comprehensive or necessarily representative. Associations listed within each chapter are not repeated in this list. Inclusion of an organization in this list does not imply the support of the authors or the publisher.

Alabama

Alabama Special Camp for Children and Adults
P.O. Box 21
Jackson Gap, AL 36831
(205) 825-9226

Contact: Jerry Bynum

A camp for mentally or physically disabled individuals. Volunteer counselors needed to help with fishing, swimming, the petting zoo, rifle range, and demonstration farm.

Alabama Special Olympics
560 South McDonough
Montgomery, AL 36130
(205) 242-3383

Contact: Eric Dresser

Provides sports training and athletic competition in a variety of Olympic-type sports for children and adults with mental retardation. Volunteers needed to chaperone events, keep score and time, act as

huggers, and bestow awards on participants.

American Cancer Society
3617 Debby Drive
Montgomery, AL 36111
(205) 288-3432

Contact: Frieda Banton-Posey

Dedicated to eliminating cancer as a major health problem through research, education, and service. Volunteers needed to help with clerical duties, events, health exams in clinics.

Bay Area Food Bank
551-C Western Drive
Mobile, AL 36607
(205) 471-1607
Contact: Darlene Lee

The Food Bank receives salvaged food (e.g., dented cans) from local sources, sorts through it, and distributes whatever is still good to the hungry. Volunteers needed to inspect donations, to repackage and shelve items, and to work in the office.

Capitol City Boys and Girls Clubs
P.O. Box 9104
2840 Boys Club Road
Montgomery, AL 36108
(205) 269-2191
Contact: Hattie Brown

Volunteers act as counselors in health and physical education, citizenship and leadership development, social recreation services, outdoor and environmental education, cultural enrichment services, substance-abuse education, and tutoring services.

Children's Hospital of Alabama
1600 7th Avenue, South
Birmingham, AL 35233
(205) 939-9621
Contact: Sherry Coleman

A medical, research, and teaching facility dedicated exclusively to pediatric care. Volunteers needed for patient services, to assist nurses

and run errands, and for various clerical duties.

Community Concern
222 Woodvale Drive
Prattville, AL 36067
(205) 365-4080
Contact: Martha Marsten

A coalition of churches in the community that helps with emergency situations for those in need. Volunteers help distribute food, clothing, and prescription medicine for the needy. Teenage volunteers are welcome.

The Cystic Fibrosis Foundation
P.O. Box 530442
Birmingham, AL 35253
1-800-523-2357
(205) 879-0527
Contact: Beth Killough-Chapman

Seeks to develop the "means to control and prevent cystic fibrosis and to improve the quality of life for people with the disease." Volunteers needed for fund-raising and office assistance.

Easter Seal Society Inc., Alabama
Corporate and Administrative Office
P.O. Box 20320
2125 E. South Boulevard
Montgomery, AL 36120-0320
(205) 288-8382
Contact: Johnny Webster

Identifies the needs of people with disabilities and provides them with appropriate rehabilitation. Volunteers help with basic office

needs such as opening mail, filing, counting money, and typing.

Father Walter Memorial Child Care Center
2815 Forbes Drive
Montgomery, AL 36110
(205) 262-6421
Contact: Elizabeth Washington

A pediatric nursing home for mentally and physically disabled children, most of whom use wheelchairs. The organization is run by the Resurrection Catholic Mission. Volunteers needed to work one-on-one with children, give parties, finger paint, play, attend parties. Minimum age 14.

Gift of Life Foundation
17222 Pine Street
Suite 507
Montgomery, AL 36194
(205) 281-9797
Contact: Martha Jinwright

Provides prenatal and obstetric care for low-income and indigent women. Volunteers needed to put together packets containing educational materials for maternity patients.

Landmarks Foundation, Old Alabama Town
310 North Hull Street
Montgomery, AL 36104
(205) 263-4355
Contact: Krys Conner

The Landmarks Foundation strives to preserve Montgomery's historic structures. Volunteers needed for artistic and administrative tasks, hospitality, to work in the gift shop, and help with educational projects, special projects, and admission ticket sales. The Foundation uses a lot of young volunteers, especially in the spring.

Salvation Army
P.O. Box 1025
Mobile, AL 36633
(205) 438-1625

Contact: Major Fuqua

Works with the

homeless, drug addicts, unwed mothers, prisoners, the poor, children, and senior citizens and supplies basic human necessities and counseling. Volunteers needed especially during holiday seasons for special events.

Veterans Administration Medical Center
215 Perry Hill Road

Montgomery, AL 36109-3798
(205) 272-4670, Ext. 4149

Contact: Pamela Parker

Provides medical services for U.S. veterans. Volunteers perform clerical duties, assist with the book cart, work with arts and crafts, escort patients to appointments, run errands for patients, and help them with ambulatory care.

Alaska

Alaska Environmental Lobby
P.O. Box 22151
Juneau, AK 99802
(907) 463-3366

Contact: Marna Schwartz

This organization works with 20 other environmental groups in lobbying to improve Alaska's environmental laws. The agency is run almost entirely by volunteers. The organized volunteer program during legislative periods (January through May) has no minimum age requirement, though volunteers must work on a full-time basis for a month. In addition, volunteers are needed on an "on call" basis in the office to assist with clerical tasks.

Alaska Health Fair, Inc.
P.O. Box 202587
Anchorage, AK 99520
(907) 278-0234

Contact: Judith Muller

The Health Fair organizes events promoting health. Volunteers work on special events committees, gathering statistics and information, helping at the events, assisting the medical volunteers. Students also organize their own events, called Student Health Learning Centers. Also has branches in Juneau and Fairbanks.

Breadline
P.O. Box 73715
Fairbanks, AK 99707
(907) 456-8317

Contact: Sharon Hunter

This food kitchen is run almost entirely by volunteers, who do anything from answering phones to peeling potatoes to mopping floors.

Denali Center
1949 Gillam Way
Fairbanks, AK 99701
(907) 452-1921

Contact: Carol Switzer

The Denali Center provides long-term care for patients of all ages. Young adult volunteers read to patients, take them on walks, and provide companionship and entertainment.

Fairbanks Community Food Bank
517 Gaffney Road
Fairbanks, AK 99701
(907) 452-7761

Contact: Samantha Castle or Rhoda Clarkson

The Food Bank salvages food and distributes it to food kitchens in the area, in addition to packaging boxes of food and getting it to those who need it. Volunteers do anything from cleaning in the warehouse to sorting, separating, and repacking food.

Fairbanks Memorial Hospital Auxiliary
1650 Cowles Street
Fairbanks, AK 99701
(907) 451-3597

150 Ways

Contact: Chris Pastro

Volunteers aged 13 to 18 work in a variety of capacities, such as in pediatrics or on the medical floor, or in the human resources offices.

Fairbanks Pioneers' Home

2221 Eagan Avenue
Fairbanks, AK 99701
(907) 456-4372

Contact: Bonnie Toleman

State-operated retirement and nursing home. Youth volunteers work with the residents in many different ways, such as reading to them, going for a walk with them, or participating in their activities.

Fairbanks Resource Agency

805 Airport Way
Fairbanks, AK 99701
(907) 456-8901

Contact: Mary Matthews

This agency provides services for individuals with developmental disabilities. Volunteers work one-on-one with disabled individuals.

Festival Fairbanks

514 Second Avenue
Suite 102
Box 74086
Fairbanks, AK 99707
(907) 456-1984

Contact: Michelle Roberts

Festival Fairbanks is responsible for the upkeep of the Golden Heart Plaza in downtown Fairbanks. Volunteers are involved with gardening in and general maintenance of the park.

Fort Wainwright Child Development Services

Box 35046
Fort Wainwright, AK 99703
(907) 356-1550

Contact: Norie McCall

Promotes the development of motor and other skills in children through activities. Volunteers set tables and help teachers and supervisors by playing with children as part of the program.

The Georgeson Botanical Garden

Agricultural and Forestry Experiment
309 O'Neill Resources Building, University
Fairbanks, AK 99775
(907) 474-6921

Contact: Patricia Wagner, Pat Holloway (474-7433)

The Garden cultivates a variety of plants for display. Volunteers participate in construction, gardening, maintenance, graphics, and computer tasks.

Immaculate Conception Church Soup Kitchen

115 North Cushman Street
Fairbanks, AK 99701
(907) 452-3533

Contact: Jim Partridge

The Kitchen serves meals to anyone who comes in on Saturdays and Sundays. Volunteers prepare and serve food and clean up the dining area afterward. Volunteers must be at least 16 unless they are with a parent or guardian.

Main Street Fairbanks

547 Third Avenue
Fairbanks, AK 99701
(907) 452-8689

Contact: Billie Ellis or Karen Lavery

Main Street Fairbanks is involved in the economic development and growth of the Fairbanks area. Because funding is minimal, volunteers are especially appreciated to help with such tasks as clerical work, answering phones, producing and mailing the agency's newsletter, gardening, and painting.

Nature Conservancy

601 West Fifth Avenue
Suite 550
Anchorage, AK 99501
(907) 276-3133

Contact: Volunteer coordinator

This organization is committed to finding, protecting, and maintaining biological communities, ecosytems, and endangered species around the world. By controlling land and water resources, the Conservancy is able to preserve the plants and animals that inhabit them. Volunteers needed for projects both in the field and in the office.

Tanana Valley Special Olympics

909 First Avenue
Fairbanks, AK 99707
(907) 452-4595

Contact: Marg Nester
Provides sports training
and athletic competition
in a variety of
Olympic-type sports for
children and adults with
physical handicaps or
mental retardation.
Volunteers work with
athletes training for
athletic events.

***Tanana Valley State
Fair***
1800 College Road
Fairbanks, AK 99709
(907) 452-3750
Contact: Colleen Turner
  or Ann McBeth
Volunteers help at the
Fairgrounds in a number
of ways; they set up
exhibitions, distribute

flyers, and assist the
coordinators. At other
times, they help in the
office by filing or doing
other clerical tasks.
Minimum age 14.

Arizona

***Arizona Historical
Society***
949 East Second Street
Tucson, AZ 85719
(602) 628-5774

Contact: Geneva Cook

The Historical Society
collects and preserves
historical material from
the state of Arizona,
dating back to 1540.
Volunteers act as library
or education aides, help
with office work, or
serve as tour guides.
Minimum age 14.

***The Arizona Theatre
Company***
2828 North Central
Suite 1145
Phoenix, AZ 85004
(602) 234-2892

Contact: Geri Silvi

The Company puts on
high-quality theatrical
performances for the
entire population of
Arizona. Volunteers help
with special fund-raising
events, such as parties
and recreational
activities, and assist with
mass mailings and
general office duties.

***Make-a-Wish
Foundation of America***
1624 East Meadowbrook
Phoenix, AZ 85016
(602) 248-9474

Contact: Linda Anderson

The Foundation grants
wishes to terminally ill
children and tries to take
the whole family's needs
into account. Volunteers
under the age of 18 are
not permitted to work
directly with the children;
however, teenage
volunteers help with all
office activities and with
fund-raising.

March of Dimes
1616 East Indian School
  Road, Suite 200
Phoenix, AZ 85016
(602) 266-9933

Contact: Angie James

Provides leadership in
the prevention and
treatment of birth defects
and related health
problems. Volunteers
help with fund-raising,
phone-a-thons, and office
work.

***Ronald McDonald
House***
501 East Roanoke
  Avenue
Phoenix, AZ 85004
(602) 264-2654

Contact: Laura Pesciera

A home for the families
of children in the
hospital, usually with
long-term illnesses.
Volunteers act as house
or yard volunteers,
making up rooms or
assisting with yard
maintenance.

***Sunshine Rescue
Mission***
124 South San Francisco
Flagstaff, AZ
(602) 774-3512

Contact: Virginia Sterned

The Mission provides
dormitory
accommodations and
three meals a day for
men and women in
need, as well as
long-term residence
facilities for the
homeless. Volunteers
usually help sort clothes,
prepare meals, and clean

the dining area after meals.

Therapeutic Riding of Tucson
P.O. Box 30584
Tucson, AZ 85751
(602) 749-2360
Contact: Sandy Jahn

Provides therapeutic horseback-riding opportunities for handicapped children and adults. Volunteers help with the riders and assist with grounds work and stall cleaning. Ability to work outdoors is a must. Minimum age 14.

Tucson Children's Museum
300 East University Boulevard

Tucson, AZ 85705
(602) 792-9985
Contact: Sarah Congdon

Volunteers work on one-time projects or special events and assist with workshops and exhibits designed for children, such as dinosaur exhibits and story hours.

Tucson Council on Alcoholism and Drug Prevention
1230 East Broadway
Tucson, AZ 85719
(602) 620-6615
Contact: Hank Stewart

An outpatient treatment center for people who suffer from substance abuse. Teenage

volunteers work in the "Babes" program as instructional aides, teaching young children about substance abuse and its prevention by means of puppetry and storytelling.

United Nations Center
2911 East Grant Road
Tucson, AZ 85716
(602) 881-7060
Contact: Geneal Wilson

Provides community education about the United Nations and holds fund-raisers for UNICEF. Volunteers check out library books, order educational materials, and assist with inventory. Enjoyment of reading is helpful. Minimum age 16.

Arkansas

Advocates for Battered Women
P.O. Box 1954
Little Rock, AR 72203
(501) 376-3219
Contact: Beverly Lacefield

Provides shelter, advocacy, support groups, and counseling for women who are victims of violence. Volunteers help in all aspects of the operation.

Arkansas Rice Depot
8400 Asher
Little Rock, AR 72204
(501) 565-8855
Contact: Laura Rhea

The Depot began as an agency to distribute rice to various food pantries and kitchens throughout

Arkansas; it now collects many different commodities and makes them available to agencies statewide. Volunteers needed several times each month to help process the food or to work on the organization's newsletter.

Community Organization for Poverty Elimination (COPE)
3518 West Roosevelt
Little Rock, AR 72204
(501) 664-1265
Contact: Helen M. Sterley

COPE collects surplus food for distribution to poverty guideline households in Arkansas. The organization has several neighborhood

centers in and around Little Rock; volunteers help with both paperwork and the food. Minimum age 18.

Food Bank Network
3300 South Brown
Little Rock, AR 72204
(501) 666-6565
Contact: Inez Tunon

The Food Bank collects damaged and surplus foods. There are many opportunites for volunteers to participate. People 16 and over can help in the warehouse; the work (sorting, weighing, and repackaging food) can be dirty and difficult, but it is necessary and important. An option for those 14 and over is to work in the office. Special skills, such as carpentry, art, or writing, are always welcome.

Heifer Project International
Route 2, Box 33
Perryville, AR 72126-9695
(501) 889-5124

Contact: Arlene
Musselman

The organization supplies farm animals and training to poor families worldwide. Volunteers help on the ranch by mowing the lawn, painting fences, and performing other basic maintenance chores, as well as by grooming, feeding, and walking the animals.

Project for Victims of Family Violence
P.O. Box 2915
Fayetteville, AR 72702
(501) 442-9811

Contact: Susan Hartman

This agency stresses social *change,* as opposed to social *services,* for people whose lives are affected by family violence. Volunteers are directly involved with aiding families; they staff 24-hour crisis lines, work with the children, and provide community education and general services.

The Salvation Army
P.O. Box 1897
Little Rock, AR 72201
(501) 374-9296

Contact: Tina McBride

Works with the homeless, drug addicts, unwed mothers, prisoners, the poor, children, and senior citizens, supplying basic human necessities and counseling.

Youth Home, Inc.
5905 Forest Place
Suite 100
Little Rock, AR 72207
(501) 666-1960

Contact: Rosemary
Griffith

Youth Home operates two thrift shops in which volunteers help as sales clerks or stock clerks or work on drives to collect items for the store.

California

American Cetacean Society
Box 2639
San Pedro, CA 90731
(213) 548-6279

Contact: Patricia Warhol

Nonprofit organization established to gather information on and aid in the protection and preservation of marine mammals, especially whales, porpoises, and dolphins. Volunteers help with mailings, the Society's newsletter, and clerical duties in general.

American Oceans Campaign
725 Arizona Avenue
Suite 102
Santa Monica, CA 90401
(213) 576-6162

Contact: Darin Nellis

The goals of this organization include establishing marine areas on both the west and east coasts and ending pollution of the oceans caused by dumping and offshore oil drilling. Volunteers work in the agency's booths at events, assist in the office, and help with projects such as beach cleanup. The Campaign prefers volunteers 16 or older for booths and informational jobs.

Berkeley Free Clinic
2339 Durant Avenue
Berkeley, CA 94704
(415) 548-2570

Contact: Volunteer
coordinator

The Clinic has provided free medical, dental, and counseling and information referral services to the Bay Area for 14 years. All clinic services are free. Volunteers receive on-the-job training.

California Action Network (CAN)
P.O. Box 464
Davis, CA 95617
(916) 756-8518

Contact: Lewis Santer

CAN works to redefine the water allocation policy in California, especially with regard to the needs of the agricultural industry.

Volunteers work on an "on-call" basis, coming in when they are needed to set up and serve at press conferences, distribute literature, handle mailings, help with the newsletter, or sit at information tables.

Californians Against Waste Foundation

909 Twelfth Street
Suite 201
Sacramento, CA 95814
(916) 443-5422

Contact: John McCall

This organization works to implement recycling programs in communities throughout the state; it works both at the federal and local levels. Volunteers are asked to do research about recycling, including community and government involvement in and reaction to this issue. Volunteers also attend legislative hearings.

Direct Relief International

P.O. Box 30820
Santa Barbara, CA 93130-0820
(805) 687-3694

Contact: Kathy Davis

Donates medical supplies/services to health facilities in less developed parts of the world and provides emergency assistance to refugees and victims of disaster/civil strife. Volunteers assist with basic office or warehouse work.

Earth Island Institute

300 Broadway, Suite 28
San Francisco, CA 94133
(415) 788-3666

Contact: Frank Galea

Earth Island Institute sponsors dozens of ecological projects on the West Coast, such as the campaign to save the dolphins. Volunteers help the staff, especially with administrative/clerical work, and assist with special events, such as fairs.

Econet

18 de Boom Street
San Francisco, CA 94107
(415) 923-0900

Contact: Jillaine Smith

Econet is a clearinghouse of information on energy and the environment. Volunteers help with research that pertains to ecology.

The Humane Farming Association

1550 California Street
Suite 6
San Francisco, CA 94109
(415) 771-CALF (2253)

Contact: Debbie Williams

Works to prevent cruelty to farm animals; educates consumers regarding the misuse of drugs and chemicals in food production; protects small-scale family farmers from the threat of expanding factory farms. Volunteers help with a myriad of tasks, such as distributing literature, assembling information packets, data entry, and clerical work. Some work, like writing letters

to government officials, can be done at home.

The Humane Society of Santa Clara Valley

2530 Lafayette Street
Santa Clara, CA 95050
(408) 727-3383

Contact: Mark Marks

A shelter and pound for animals without homes. The Humane Society's mission is to promote respect for animal life. Volunteers are involved in a variety of jobs, such as adoption, fund-raising, hug-a-pet, humane education, kennel work, legislation, lost and found, wildlife preservation, and special events. A 5-hour training session is offered every sixth Saturday throughout the year.

In Defense of Animals

816 West Francisco Boulevard
San Rafael, CA 94901
(415) 453-9984

Contact: Ms. Doll Stanley

A national organization striving to end animal mutilation and cruelty at universities and laboratories across the nation. Coordinates the National World Laboratory Animal Liberation Week and conducts campaigns to end pound seizure. Volunteers provide assistance with mailings, answer phones, and handle clerical work.

Poverello House

412 F Street
Fresno, CA 93706
(209) 485-8002

Contact: Speak with anyone in office or just stop by

Poverello House is a rapidly expanding food kitchen, serving three meals per day; the center also provides free medical, dental, and social services. The House welcomes volunteers, who usually help in the kitchen or the office.

Project Concern International
3550 Alton Road
San Diego, CA 92123
(619) 279-9690

Contact: Kathy Drake

A health-care development organization interested in increasing child survival through disease prevention, improved nutrition, immunization, and mother/child health care by means of community health education. Volunteers in the United States are important as they raise the funds needed to make Project Concern's international programs possible. Youth committees are organized to work on various

benefits and events throughout the year.

Sea Shepherd Conservation Society
1314 Second Street
Santa Monica, CA 90401
(213) 394-3198

Contact: Peter Wallerstein

Concentrates on the protection of marine mammals and habitats. This is a direct-action operation that makes efforts to stop the killing of whales, dolphins, and seals throughout the world. The organization sends its ships out to sea to interfere with fishing practices that endanger those animals, but volunteers are also needed in the office to respond to letters and information requests as well as to help with general office work.

Starlight Foundation
10920 Wilshire Boulevard, Suite 1640
Los Angeles, CA 90024
(213) 208-5885

Contact: Lisa Sakata

Arranges and finances special trips (or fulfills other wishes) for chronically, critically, and terminally ill children. Volunteers work on

telephone, mailing, hospitality, and special events committees.

Surfrider Foundation
Box 2704, #86
Huntington Beach, CA 92647
(714) 960-8390

Contact: Diana Irizari

This organization works to protect and improve beaches in Southern California by organizing and mobilizing people who are interested in preserving California's shores. Volunteers can work either in the office, doing clerical work, or outside the office, selling T-shirts and distributing information. Surfrider needs help particularly in the summer months.

World Without War Council, Inc.
1730 Martin Luther King Jr. Way
Berkeley, CA 94709
(415) 845-1992

Contact: Randy Tift

This organization uses various means to promote world peace. Volunteers needed to help in the office with typing, word processing, mailings, and other clerical tasks.

Colorado

American Humane Association
63 Inverness Drive East
Englewood, CO 80112
(303) 792-9900

Contact: Joyce Davis

Provides material on animal care and training for animal care and

control agencies. Maintains files on anticruelty laws and other matters pertaining

150 Ways

to animal welfare. Works to promote high-quality standards for animal shelters and to reduce euthanasia in shelters.

Aspen Center for Environmental Studies
P.O. Box 8777
Aspen, CO 81612
(303) 925-5756
Contact: Jeanne Beaudry
The Aspen Center educates others about local nature and wildlife. Volunteers help take care of animals and work in the Center's garden.

The Center for Prevention of Domestic Violence
P.O. Box 2662
Colorado Springs, CO 80901
(719) 633-1462
Contact: Cynthia Zupanec
The Center's priority is the prevention of violence in the home/family; it also assists victims of domestic violence. The Center needs mature individuals to help with clerical tasks in its office.

Colorado Trail Foundation/Colorado Mountain Club
548 Pine Song Trail
Golden, CO 80401
(303) 526-0809
Contact: Trail crew coordinator
Builds and maintains trails in the national forests of Colorado. Volunteers work in crews during weekly sessions. Anyone in good physical condition is welcome; no

experience is required. Minimum age 16.

High Country News
P.O. Box 1090
Paonia, CO 81428
(303) 527-4898
Contact: Betsy Marsten
High Country News is a newspaper that focuses primarily on environmental issues in the northern Rockies area. It offers three-month-long volunteer internships; anyone interested should call for an application. Interns sort information received by the newspaper and put together hotlines and bulletins.

International Concerns Committee for Children
911 Cypress Drive
Boulder, CO 80303
(303) 494-8333
Contact: Anna Marie
Works to help those interested in the adoption of children from foreign countries. Provides personal counseling by adoptive parents. Volunteers needed for basic office work.

Morris Animal Foundation
45 Inverness Drive East
Englewood, CO 80112
(303) 790-2345
1-800-530-8765
Contact: Mark Mobley
Sponsors Ride for Research and Dog-a-Thon and animal health seminars. Volunteers organize and participate in county fairs

and also have the opportunity to turn their own fund-raising ideas into actual events. The money is used to fund veterinary school studies that research diseases and health problems of companion and zoo animals.

Nature Conservancy
1244 Pine Street
Boulder, CO 80302
(303) 444-2950
Contact: Sarah Claussen
This organization is committed to finding, protecting, and maintaining biological communities, ecosytems, and endangered species around the world. By controlling land and water resources, the Conservancy is able to preserve the plants and animals that inhabit them. Volunteers needed for projects both in the field and in the office.

Rocky Mountain Institute
1739 Snowmass Creek Road
Snowmass, CO 81654-9199
(303) 927-3851
Contact: Robbie Noiles
An educational and research foundation established to foster the efficient and sustainable use of natural resources through energy conservation and the use of renewable sources of energy. This agency has no regular volunteers. However, it is putting together a database of people willing to donate

their time when needed; these people can help outdoors in gardens and forests, especially in the summer.

Special Olympics
1400 South Colorado
 Boulevard
Suite 400
Denver, CO 80222
(303) 691-3339

Contact: Sally Thompson

Provides sports training and athletic competition

in a variety of Olympic-type sports for children and adults with mental retardation. Volunteers work with athletes who are training and preparing for the Special Olympics.

Western Colorado Congress
P.O. Box 472
Montrose, CO 81402
(303) 249-1978

Contact: Brenda Williams

A citizen-action group that runs community groups in ten towns in the west. The Congress deals with issues, mostly environmental and consumer, that are important to the communities. All members are volunteers.

Connecticut

Aid to Artisans
80 Mountain Spring Road
Farmington, CT
 06032-1613
(203) 677-1649

Contact: Clare Smith

Dedicated to creating employment opportunities for disadvantaged artisans in economically depressed areas of the United States and around the world. Volunteers help with fund-raising drives, write materials, and assist with program continuance.

Americares Foundation
161 Cherry Street
New Canaan, CT 06840
(203) 966-5195

Contact: Volunteer
 coordinator

Relief organization dedicated to saving lives and fulfilling emergency medical needs worldwide. Sponsors airlifts and sea shipments of food, vital medicines,

and medical supplies to provide immediate relief whenever and wherever needed.

Beyond War
995 Hopmeadow
Westminster School
Simsbury, CT 06070-1839
(203) 658-4543

Contact: Pam McDonald

An educational movement dedicated to informing people of the crises the world faces; promotes a way of thinking designed to avert war. Volunteers go through an orientation that introduces the organization and describes what functions volunteers will serve.

The Box Project
P.O. Box 435
Plainville, CT 06062
(203) 747-8182

Contact: Nancy Normen

Alleviates the suffering of the rural poor in the United States through the caring and support of

volunteer "helpers" who send care packages and necessities. Volunteers give friendship and aid through letters and boxes of goods sent directly to the family; they are also needed for office help.

Boy Scouts of America, Inc.
Long Rivers Council
70 Forest Street
Hartford, CT 06105-3297
(203) 525-1112

Contact: Robert S. Gary

A program for boys designed to promote character building, citizenship, and physical training through individual and group projects. High school girls can join the teenage Explorer program.

FIDELCO Guide Dog Foundation
P.O. Box 142
Bloomfield, CT
 06002-0142
(203) 243-5200

Contact: Carrie Tarca
This organization breeds and trains German Shepherd guide dogs that are later matched with blind individuals. Volunteer opportunities include raising a puppy for a year, helping to maintain the kennels, and grooming and exercising the dogs; volunteers also help with annual fund-raising event and other special events.

Thomas Merton House
43 Madison Avenue
Bridgeport, CT 06604
(203) 333-0332
Contact: Christina Wills
The House serves free breakfast and lunch for those in need and provides them with a place to rest and relax. Volunteers can help in the kitchen, preparing and serving food and cleaning up after meals. They may also assist in supervising and caring for the clients' children.

National Association for Drama Therapy
19 Edwards Street
New Haven, CT 06511
(203) 498-1515
Contact: Roberta Weatherby
Provides information about training programs,

sponsors conferences and workshops, conducts research, and publishes bibliographies, monographs, and books.

National Multiple Sclerosis Society
Greater Connecticut Chapter
74 Batterson Park Road
Farmington, CT 06032-2503
(203) 674-1995
Contact: Sue Dellow or Tina Grant
Seeks to prevent, treat, and cure the disease of multiple sclerosis and improve the quality of life of affected individuals and their families. Volunteers involved with all aspects of patient services and fund-raising events as well as general office duties.

Real Art Ways (RAW)
56 Arbor Street
Hartford, CT 06106
(203) 232-1006
Contact: Susan Perry
An arts center whose purpose it is to present arts programs in music, dance, theater, video, and the visual arts. Volunteers with an interest in these areas are welcome to help at

concerts, in the Gallery, and with office duties.

Save the Children Federation
54 Wilton Road
Westport, CT 06880
(203) 226-7271
Contact: Vicki Washington
Helps children through the process of community development. Operates programs in cities, towns, and remote villages in 41 countries around the world, including the United States. Volunteers participate in projects or special events that raise funds, educate, and/or build Save the Children's constituency.

Technoserve
49 Day Street
Norwalk, CT 06854
(203) 852-0377
Contact: Kimberly Fair
Teaches needy individuals the self-reliance necessary to run their own agricultural businesses—to produce their own food and income. Also helps rural and poor farmers in foreign countries. Volunteers participate in planning of relief packages and in office work.

Delaware

American Cancer Society
707 Walker Road
Dover, DE 19901
(302) 734-7431

Contact: Ask anyone for a volunteer application
Dedicated to eliminating cancer as a major health

problem through research, education, and service. Volunteers work on various committees, such as fund-raising and public information.

Casa San Francisco
P.O. Box 38
Milton, DE 19968
(302) 684-8694

Contact: Karen Malzone

The Casa is a crisis community center that provides shelter, food, medicine, adult education programs, and assistance with overdue bills for people in need. Volunteers help with cooking and cleaning in the shelter and also work in reception and adult education.

Delaware Special Olympics
Box 9591
Newark, DE 19714
(302) 368-6818

Contact: Call or stop by for an application

Provides sports training and athletic competition in a variety of Olympic-type sports for children and adults with physical handicaps or mental retardation. Volunteers can coach athletic teams (minimum age 16) or work on committees, events, or in the office.

Easter Seal Society of Delmar
61 Corporate Circle
Newcastle Corporate Commons
Newcastle, DE 19720-2405
(302) 324-4444

Contact: Phyllis Gordon

Identifies the needs of people with disabilities and provides them with appropriate rehabilitation. Volunteers help with office work and fund-raising.

Nature Conservancy
319 South State Street
Dover, DE 19903
(302) 674-3550

Contact: Robert McKim

This organization is committed to finding, protecting, and maintaining biological communities, ecosytems, and endangered species around the world. By controlling land and water resources, the Conservancy is able to preserve the plants and animals that inhabit them. Volunteers needed for projects in the field and in the office.

Salvation Army
P.O. Box 2390
Wilmington, DE 19899
(302) 656-1696

Contact: Brenda Williams

Works with the homeless, drug addicts, unwed mothers, prisoners, the poor, children, and senior citizens and supplies basic human services and counseling. Youth volunteers at this particular location can work in the after-school child-care program.

District of Columbia

Capital Area Community Food Bank, Inc.
2266 25th Place, NE
Washington, DC 20018
(202) 526-5344

Contact: John Schley

Stores and distributes food donated by Washington's charities, restaurants, food-service establishments. "Attacks hunger by attacking food waste." Volunteers sort, clean, and shelve food;

keep books and records; assist with public relations; contact food sources; and type, file, and answer telephones. Volunteers should be able to get along with all kinds of people. Minimum age 17.

Capitol East Children's Center
315 G Street, SE
Washington, DC 20003
(202) 546-6966

Contact: Judith Fischer

This organization provides child care and after-school programs for kids. Volunteers needed as bookkeepers and special interest consultants. Minimum age 15.

Capitol Hill Hospital
700 Constitution Avenue, NE
Washington, DC 20002
(202) 269-8000

Contact: Leslie Stubbs

A nonprofit, acute-care community hospital. Positions available as candy stripers; duties include office work and assisting nurses. Skills required: reading and writing. Minimum age 15.

Coalition for the Homeless

2824 Sherman Avenue, NW
Washington, DC 20009
(202) 328-1186

Contact: Karen Silberman

Nonprofit organization that operates transitional homes for the homeless in and around Washington, D.C. Assists homeless individuals in realizing an independent living status and in becoming contributing members of the community. Volunteers work in the office and in the transitional houses. Minimum age 18.

Community for Creative Non-Violence

425 Second Street, NW
Washington, DC 20009
(202) 393-4409

Contact: John Gibbs

Needs volunteers at several facilities: a drop-in center that operates seven days a week, a soup kitchen that provides hot meals every night, and a free food store, where hundreds of people receive groceries each day. Volunteers help in the soup kitchen, the shelter, and in community organizing

and other community work.

Cooperative International

Pupil-to-Pupil Program
3229 Chestnut Street, NE
Washington, DC 20018
(202) 529-2163

Contact: Mr. Green

Students in any grade can donate materials used in the classroom to students in Africa, Asia, and Latin America.

Fort Washington Park

National Capital Parks
East
1900 Anacostia Drive, SE
Washington, DC 20020
(301) 763-4600

Contact: James Phelps

Provides living history programs about a day in the life of a soldier. Volunteers (Fort Washington Guards) participate in "living history" demonstrations in the park or serve as park assistants and help with the maintenance of park trails. Minimum age 16.

Friends of the Vietnam Veterans Memorial

1224 M Street, NW
Washington, DC 20005
(202) 628-0726

Contact: Wanda Ruffin

A nonprofit organization of volunteers dedicated to serving visitors to the Memorial as well as friends and families around the country. Memorial assistants assist visitors at the Memorial in finding names, do name rubbings, and provide referral services.

Volunteers should be people-oriented.

Friendship House Association

619 D Street, SE
Washington, DC 20003
(202) 675-9050

Contact: Bill Johnson

The organization provides training for mentally disabled adults in personal, social, educational, recreational, and vocational skills. Young volunteers can be educational tutors, volunteer photographers, development volunteers, or arts and crafts assistants. A high school diploma is required.

National Park Service—Mall Operations

900 Ohio Drive, SW
Washington, DC 20242
(202) 485-9696

Contact: Jim Lance

Maintains and runs the Washington Mall. Volunteer information guides needed to distribute brochures about the Washington Monument and other memorials and to assist visitors at national memorials. A willingness to help others is required. Minimum age 16.

National Park Service—Old Stone House

3051 M Street, NW
Washington, DC 20007
(202) 426-6851

Contact: Cindy
  Donaldson

Provides recreational and historical services for the

community. Volunteer park aides talk to visitors about the history of the house and the Georgetown–Washington area. Skills required include the ability to speak about general history. Minimum age 16.

Travellers' Aid Society
National Airport
Washington, DC 20001
(703) 684-3472
Contact: Anne Ingram
A social service agency that deals with people who are away from home and their

resources. Tries to help people help themselves. Volunteers answer questions and offer assistance, referring people to professionals if necessary. Minimum age 14.

Florida

Adopt-a-Shore Program
Keep Florida Beautiful, Inc.
402 West College Avenue
Tallahassee, FL 32301
(904) 561-0700

Contact: Rosemary Prince

Groups, businesses, clubs, or community organizations take action by contracting to clean up litter from one mile of adopted shoreline (including lakes, streams, creeks, marshes, estuaries, and boat ramps) at least four times a year for two years. In return, Adopt-a-Shore erects a sign in their name at the adopted site.

Association for Retarded Citizens
P.O. Box 9658
Daytona Beach, FL 32120
(904) 274-4736

Contact: JoAnne Tobler

Provides workshops and programs for retarded adults. Volunteers work with mentally handicapped persons in a classroom or sheltered workshop setting.

Be a Friend, Inc.
1919 Beachway Road
Jacksonville, FL 32207
(904) 398-3209

Contact: Betty Tway

A visiting service to the elderly in all areas of Jacksonville, Orange Park, and the beaches. It places volunteers one-on-one with an older person or assigns them to yard cleanup and food collection/delivery.

Blind Rehabilitation Center
1111 Willis Avenue
Daytona Beach, FL 32114
(904) 254-3824

Contact: Debbie Armstrong

A state center that provides services for visually impaired adults. Volunteers assist in clients' development of recreational skills, read to blind clients, and accompany them on field trips.

Bridge-the-Gap, Inc.
561 West 25th Street
Jacksonville, FL 22209
(904) 354-9392

Contact: Yvonne Lane
Provides services and programs for the needy and disabled. Volunteers donate items or help the agency with special events.

Broward House
P.O. Box 350367
Fort Lauderdale, FL 33335
(305) 522-4749
Contact: Camille
A residential facility for people with AIDS who are not well enough to live on their own but are not ill enough to be hospitalized. Volunteers needed to be companions.

Central Florida Blood Bank
32 West Gore Street
Orlando, FL 32806
(407) 849-6100
Contact: Shirley Burke
The blood bank serves several counties in Florida. Volunteers needed to assist in the lab, in the office, and on the bloodmobile.

The City Rescue Mission
P.O. Box 114
Jacksonville, FL 32201
(904) 353-5565

Contact: Ms. Ellison

Provides hot meals, temporary shelter, and other emergency services to homeless men, women, and children. Volunteers act as supper servers and can work at the thrift store on-site.

Civic Theatre

1001 East Princeton Street
Orlando, FL 32803
(407) 896-7365

Contact: Merle Wilson

Presents plays in three different theaters. Volunteers learn how plays are put together, while helping with production, props, lights, sound, makeup, costumes, ushering, ticket sales, and special events.

Clean Up Orlando

1010 South
  Westmoreland Avenue
Orlando, FL
(407) 246-2752

Contact: Maude Fain

Orlando's local "Keep America Beautiful" affiliate. The program strives to improve the ecological value of the city, to keep the city green, and to promote beautification and recycling while reducing waste. Volunteers needed to participate in ongoing projects to clean up Orlando.

Covenant House

733 Breakers Avenue
Fort Lauderdale, FL 33304
(305) 561-5559

Contact: Kevin Callahan

The Covenant House not only provides housing for transient teens but

also cares for them, even after they leave the facility, by making available food, clothing, and various social services. Volunteers needed for many different jobs, such as food service, housekeeping, clerical assistance, data entry, escorting, switchboard operation, recreational aid, child care, and peer counseling.

Emergency Pregnancy Services

1842 King Street
Suite 109
Jacksonville, FL 32204
(904) 387-7510

Contact: Gerrie or Jan

This pro-life, crisis intervention center assists with any problems related to pregnancy and provides informational material and emotional support regarding pregnancy. Volunteers can work in the stock room, sorting baby clothes and other donated items, or can act as receptionist, greeting clients, answering phones, and disseminating literature and information. Interested volunteers are also trained to perform pregnancy tests at the center. Minimum age 14.

Extended Family: Alzheimer's Assistance Program

P.O. Box 10174
Daytona Beach, FL 32120
(904) 252-2489

Contact: Anne Cooper or
  Linda Schell

A respite center with Saturday programs during which volunteers can work directly with people afflicted with Alzheimer's disease. Volunteers assist participants in recreational and therapeutic activities, serve snacks and meals, and help with adult day care.

Food Bank of Jacksonville

1502 Jessie Street
Jacksonville, FL 32206
(904) 353-3663

Contact: Donna McTier

The food bank stores, sorts, and distributes items from its warehouse to agencies and individuals. Volunteers collect food, store it in the warehouse, stock shelves, take inventory, and clean in and around the facility.

Fort Caroline National Memorial

12713 Fort Caroline Road
Jacksonville, FL 32225
(904) 641-7155

Contact: Paul Ghioto

Fort Caroline is a historic site that preserves the memory of the French colonial presence in northeast Florida. The site needs volunteers for the visitor information desk, sales assistance, typing/word processing, trail maintenance, and special events, such as re-creation of colonial camps.

Florida Parks and Recreation
Wekiwa Springs State Park
1800 Wekiwa Circle
Apopka, FL 32712
(407) 884-2011
Contact: Karen Brillante

Provides recreational services to the community. Volunteers needed for ongoing positions with the department as field project assistants, for park service, and constructing nature trails. Those under age 18 must have parent/guardian consent.

Green Up Orlando
1206 West Columbia Street
Orlando, FL 32805
(407) 246-2287
Contact: John Sorensen

Effects direct improvements in public places and neighborhoods by means of volunteer efforts and contributions. Volunteers needed to plant trees and bushes in city parks, green spaces, and on parkways and traffic islands.

Gulf Coast Zoological Society
5899 Whitfield Avenue, #205
Sarasota, FL 34243
(813) 355-0000
Contact: Cherry Whitman

The Society goal is to become a world-class zoological conservation, observation, and research center. It is currently in a development phase and is working toward construction of its facility. Volunteer help is needed with office work, fund-raising, and special events.

Halifax Urban Ministries
215 Bay Street
Daytona Beach, FL 32114
(904) 252-0156
Contact: Olive Nelson

An emergency food pantry that offers free hot lunches to families and transients by preparing and distributing food, unloading boxes, and bagging food. When the weather drops below 40 degrees, the pantry becomes an overnight shelter. Volunteers prepare and serve food.

Headstart Child Development Program
123 West Indiana Avenue
Deland, FL 32720
(904) 736-5956
Contact: Sally Marshall

Provides comprehensive development services to children from economically disadvantaged families. Volunteers work with children in a classroom setting or one-on-one. Any skills a volunteer can provide are welcome.

Hospice of Volusia and Flagler Counties
655 North Clyde Morris Boulevard
Daytona Beach, FL 32114
(904) 257-6111
Contact: Susan Robinson

Helps persons with life-limiting illnesses live out their remaining months as fully, free of pain, and with as much dignity as possible. Volunteers help either by raising funds for this organization or by training to be a home volunteer.

Jacksonville Actors' Theatre, Inc.
P.O. Box 47584
Jacksonville, FL 32247-7584
(904) 642-5634
Contact: Del Austin

Offers a full season of contemporary adult and children's theater, as well as the annual Shakespeare at the Met Festival. Volunteers work in any area of theatrical production, such as lighting, properties, set construction, costuming, sound, publicity, and office work.

Life Care Center
989 Orienta Avenue
Altamonte Springs, FL 32701
(407) 831-3446
Contact: Marilyn Greemore

A skilled-care nursing home. Energetic people needed to operate the Center's ice cream parlor, take the hospitality cart around to residents' rooms, assist with arts and crafts, and spend time with older people.

Mana-Sota Lighthouse for the Blind, Inc.
7318 North Tamiami Trail
Sarasota, FL 34243
(813) 359-1404
Contact: Virginia Haug

Provides many services for the blind. The

Lighthouse provides several volunteer opportunities to work with the visually impaired. Volunteers are also needed to do some work in the office.

Museum of Science and History
1025 Gulf Life Drive
Jacksonville, FL 32207
(904) 396-7061 Ext. 225

Contact: Joy Hardaker

The Museum, which presents educational exhibits and programs based on science and history, needs volunteers to work as greeters on holidays and weekends, assist with exhibits, work with animals, and help with mailings.

Orlando Day Nursery
100 West Anderson Street
Orlando, FL 32801
(407) 422-5291

Contact: Andrea West

Helps care for children of low-income and homeless families. Volunteers read to children, play games, or teach crafts.

Orlando Police Department Explorers
P.O. Box 913
Orlando, FL 32802
(407) 246-2110

Contact: Officer Laura Blue

Volunteer explorers accompany officers on patrol and in training exercises. They learn about law enforcement and their community through weekly explorer meetings.

Orlando Science Center
810 East Rollins Street
Orlando, FL 32803
(407) 896-7151

Contact: Nancy Tallent

Runs programs to make science understandable to and enjoyable for everyone. Volunteers help with displays and events, and youth interns assist with office duties.

Rape Crisis Center
P.O. Box 63
Daytona Beach, FL 32115
(904) 254-4106

Contact: Monique Fulmore

Helps those who are in need of emergency assistance. Volunteers can participate in reception/phone work, organize the clothing bank, and work on special projects, such as conferences, Victims' Rights Week, and the public awareness program.

River Region Human Services, Inc.
330 West State Street
Jacksonville, FL 32202
(904) 359-6571

Contact: Anne Knight

Deals with drug abuse treatment, prevention, intervention, and education. Volunteers can help not only at the Teen Alliance Center but also at the agency's booth at community events.

Riverside Avondale Preservation
904 King Street
Jacksonville, FL 32205
(904) 389-2449

Contact: Carla Trautman

This agency is involved with the preservation of sites as well as historic character and economic stability in the Riverside Avondale historic district. Volunteers assist with clerical work, public relations/publicity, and production of the agency's newsletter.

Tree Hill Nature Center
7152 Lone Star Road
Jacksonville, FL 32211
(904) 724-4646

Contact: Lucy Heine

The Center works to preserve Tree Hill and provide environmental education to the Jacksonville community. Volunteers assist with trail maintenance, gardening, leading of group tours on nature walks, and summer camp activities.

Women's Resource Center
340 Tuttle Avenue
Sarasota, FL 34237
(813) 366-1700

Contact: Nancy Shoemaker

The Center provides many social and educational services for women. Teenage volunteers assist with clerical and reception duties.

Youth Alternatives
1386 Indian Lake Road
Daytona Beach, FL 32114
(904) 252-6550

Contact: Linda Van Wulfen

Works with physically, sexually, and emotionally abused adolescents, helping to increase independent-living skills; crisis counseling and behavior management are also offered. Volunteers help the residential specialist and talk and work with the children.

Georgia

Cherry Blossom Health Care Center
3520 Kenneth Drive
Macon, GA 31206
(912) 781-7553

Contact: Sarah Griffin

A nursing-care facility. Volunteers act as activity helpers, readers, and friendly visitors.

Children's Wish Foundation International
8825 Roswell Road
Suite 613
Atlanta, GA 30350
1-800-323-9474

Contact: Stephanie Smith

Seeks to fulfill the wishes of terminally ill children under 18 years old. Volunteers work on a variety of projects, often helping with the mail or donations or in the warehouse.

Columbus Humane Society
P.O. Box 6039
Columbus, GA 31907
(404) 563-3647

Contact: Mrs. Orkoch

A shelter and pound for animals without homes. The Humane Society's mission is to promote respect for animal life, and it needs people to help care for the animals. Training will be provided.

Freedom Park
3301 Ross Avenue
Macon, GA 31204
(912) 751-9248

Contact: Robert Worthy

Provides recreational services and programs for the community. Anyone who likes working with kids may volunteer as a camp counselor.

Georgia Legal Services
791 Poplar Street
Macon, GA 31201
(912) 751-6261

Contact: Meltonia Stephens

A nonprofit legal organization for individuals who cannot afford an attorney. Volunteers help with clerical work and in the legal library.

Girls' Club of Columbus
P.O. Box 4040
Columbus, GA 31904
(404) 322-5395

Contact: Janice DeMarsh

Holds programs for girls of all ages. Volunteers needed for arts and crafts, jazz, ballet, cooking, nutrition, and gymnastics and other sports; as tutors; as teachers for educational careers; and as summer camp counselors.

Harriet Tubman Museum
P.O. Box 6671
Macon, GA 31208
(912) 743-8544

Contact: Barbara Blount

The Museum provides an excellent opportunity to learn about an important figure in American history; it contains art, artifacts, Tubman's own works, and literature about her. Volunteers assist with reception and in the office; light clerical, phone, and garden work is involved.

Hay House
934 Georgia Avenue
Macon, GA 31201
(912) 742-8155

Contact: Georgia Bryant

Hay House is a historic house that is used now to educate people about the history of Georgia. Volunteers work as tour guides or help in the gift shop.

Macon Housing Authority
P.O. Box 4928
Macon, GA 31208
(912) 745-8634

Contact: Connie Smith

Provides housing assistance and recreational programs for residents of public housing. Volunteers, who must be at least 16, act as recreational assistants, helping with games, sports, arts and crafts, and tutoring.

Macon Little Theatre
4220 Forsythe Road
Macon, GA 31210
(912) 477-3342
Contact: Jerry
  Mittlehauser
A community theater. People are welcome to audition as well as volunteer for stagecraft positions.

Macon Outreach Program
267 First Street
Macon, GA 31202
(912) 743-8026
Contact: Carol Buccieri
Provides special events,

like collecting canned goods on Halloween, in which young people can participate. The agency needs volunteers to help with clerical work and in the food pantry—collecting, counting, and distributing food.

Metro Fair Housing Services, Inc.
P.O. Box 5467
Atlanta, GA 30307
(404) 221-0147
Contact: Maria Borowski
Promotes decent, safe, affordable housing on a nondiscriminatory basis and counsels tenants with financial difficulties.

Volunteers help with fund-raising, events, and general office work.

Seeds Magazine
222 East Lake Drive
Decatur, GA 30030
(404) 371-1000
Contact: F. L. Dwyer
An organization that encourages Christians to become involved in combating world hunger. Offers educational materials about the causes of and cures for hunger. To apply to Seeds, send a resume and cover letter. Send $3 for a list of current volunteer opportunities.

Hawaii

American Cancer Society
East Hawaii Unit
614 Kilauea
Hilo, HI 96720
(808) 935-9763
Contact: Roberta
  Cartwright
  or

American Cancer Society
Cameron Center
95 Mahalani Street
Wailuku, HI 96793
(808) 244-5553
Contact: Patricia Aiken
  or

American Cancer Society
Central District
98-027 Hekaha Street,
  Building #3, Unit 31
Aiea, HI 96701

(808) 486-8420
Contact: Mariett
  Bustamente
Dedicated to eliminating cancer as a major health problem through research, education, and service. Volunteers help with special events, fund-raising, office duties, public education, and canvassing.

American Lung Association
245 North Kukui Street
Honolulu, HI 96817
(808) 537-5966
Contact: Darlene Ching
An organization whose goal is the conquest of lung disease and the promotion of pulmonary health. Volunteers help

with special projects as needed.

American Red Cross
4155 Diamond Head
  Road
Honolulu, HI 96816-4417
(808) 734-2101
Contact: Diane Phillips
Works to improve the quality of human life, enhance self-reliance and concern for others, and help people avoid, prepare for, and cope with emergencies. Volunteers take part in most projects.

Castle Medical Center
640 Ulukahiki Street
Kailua, HI 96734
(808) 263-5337
Contact: Helen Waihee
A comprehensive medical treatment center. Volunteers work

one-on-one with patients, in special units, in various aspects of patient services, and in research and laboratory facilities.

Easter Seal Society
710 Green Street
Honolulu, HI 96813
(808) 536-1018
Contact: Linda Guess
Identifies the needs of people with disabilities and provides them with appropriate rehabilitation. Volunteers work on special projects and fund-raising events.

Hawaiian Humane Society
2700 Waialae Avenue
Honolulu, HI 96816
(808) 955-5122
Contact: Cindy Kantor
A shelter and pound for animals without homes. The Humane Society's mission is to promote respect for animal life. One service it provides is animal assistance therapy, in which volunteers take domestic animals to homes for the elderly and handicapped. Volunteers walk and groom animals. Minimum age 14.

Honolulu Zoo
151 Moanulua Road
Honolulu, HI 96819
(808) 834-9168
Contact: Eileen Kelleher
Has numerous facilities and exhibits, from

primates to birds. Volunteers work as junior zoo keepers and help with educational programs and special events.

Lyman House Memorial Museum
276 Haili Street
Hilo, HI 96720
(808) 935-5021
Contact: Kathleen Adams
The Museum is concerned with the preservation and teaching of the cultural history of Hawaii. There are many opportunities for a teenager to volunteer here, from answering phones to conducting research in the Museum's library.

National Tropical Botanical Garden
P.O. Box 95
Hana, HI 96713
(808) 248-8912
Contact: Nancy Bergau
This Garden is both educational and beautiful. Volunteers act as interns in the gardens or in their specific areas of interest.

Ronald McDonald House
1970 Judd Hillside Road
Honolulu, HI 96822
(808) 942-8183
Contact: Cathi Chun
A home for the families of children in the hospital, usually with

long-term illnesses. Volunteers don't have extensive contact with the families but assist with office duties and act as overall assistants.

Sea Life Park
Makapuu Point
Waimanalo, HI 96795
(808) 259-7933
Contact: Marilyn Lee
Has four main water shows, a whaling museum, a touch tank area, turtle lagoon, penguin exhibit, and much more. Volunteers help with all exhibits and work directly with animals.

Young Women's Catholic Association
Family Violence Shelter
3094 Elua Street
Lihue, HI 96766
(808) 245-6362
Contact: Karen Bacino
The Shelter is a resource for battered women and children. It offers not only services for women and their children who have been abused at home but also programs for abusive men, such as Alternatives to Violence (ATV). In addition to being involved with such general tasks as computer, office, and yard work, volunteers may interact with the children, providing a source of confidence and support.

Idaho

American Red Cross
5380 Franklin Road
Boise, ID 83705
(208) 342-4500
Contact: Becky Thomas
Works to improve the quality of human life, enhance self-reliance and concern for others, and help people avoid, prepare for, and cope with disaster. At this location, volunteers assist with clerical tasks in the office, work with nurses at blood drives, and participate in special events and projects.

Habitat for Humanity
521 Lakeside Avenue
Coeur D'Alene, ID
(208) 667-3116
Contact: Call and leave a message, and someone will get back to you.
Helps to eliminate homelessness through the construction of decent shelter for the economically disadvantaged. Volunteers work on housing construction and rehabilitation projects in the Coeur D'Alene area.

Idaho Conservation League
P.O. Box 844
Boise, ID 83701
(208) 345-6933
Contact: Joan Hummel
A statewide membership organization whose main focus is on environmental issues. The League has a water quality program, premium lands program, and lobbying services, and they need volunteers to help with clerical work and projects in the office.

Nature Conservancy
P.O. Box 64
Sun Valley, ID 83353
(208) 726-3007
Contact: Marla Easum
This organization is committed to finding, protecting, and maintaining biological communities, ecosytems, and endangered species around the world. By controlling land and water resources, the Conservancy is able to preserve the plants and animals that inhabit them. Volunteers needed for projects both in the field and in the office.

Peregrine Fund, Inc.
5666 West Flying Hawk Lane
Boise, ID 83709
(208) 362-3716
Contact: Nancy Freutel
Funds research on and preservation of falcons. Volunteers assist in the Fund's office and can work on everything from mailings to special projects.

Ronald McDonald House
101 Warm Springs Avenue
Boise, ID 83712
(208) 336-5478
Contact: Charlotte Combe
A home for families who have children in the hospital, usually with long-term illnesses. Volunteers help with anything from answering phones and doing clerical work to checking people in and out.

Snake River Alliance
P.O. Box 1731
Boise, ID 83701
(208) 344-9161
Contact: Jill Anderson
Aims to increase awareness of the dangers imposed on people and the environment by the production of nuclear weapons. Volunteers work on all projects both in and out of the office.

Special Olympics
8426 Fairhaven Avenue
Boise, ID 83704
(208) 323-0482
Contact: Mike Woodhead
Provides sports training and athletic competition in a variety of Olympic-type sports for children and adults with physical handicaps or mental retardation. People are welcome to join in the activities and train toward participation in the Special Olympics. The Partners Club, organized through local schools, matches Special Olympics athletes with non–physically challenged individuals.

Trout Unlimited, Upper Snake River Chapter
1387 Cambridge Drive
Idaho Falls, ID 83401
(208) 746-4956

Contact: Volunteer coordinator

Focuses on preserving, protecting, and enhancing primarily cold water fisheries, such as streams and rivers. This is done both by means of community awareness and lobbying and by actual restoration of in-stream flows. Volunteers help with clerical work in the chapter's office; nonmembers are also welcome to work at project sites. (A student membership costs $10.)

Illinois

Allendale Association
P.O. Box 277
Lake Villa, IL 60046
(708) 356-2351

Contact: Kenwar Singh

A residential treatment center for young children. Volunteers serve in the educational program as tutors.

The Anti-Cruelty Society
157 West Grand Avenue
Chicago, IL 60610
(312) 644-8338

Contact: Jean Jurczyk

Cares for and shelters abandoned pets. Volunteers assist with adoptions, take care of animals, assist with veterinary examinations, and visit nursing homes with pets.

Boys and Girls Clubs
625 West Jackson Boulevard
Suite 300
Chicago, IL 60661
(312) 648-1666

Contact: Carl Lavender

Provides city youth with attractive alternatives to life in the street. Fourteen units located in various neighborhoods offer volunteer opportunities in the areas of tutoring, field trips, adventure camp, physical education, and more.

Center for Street People
P.O. Box 409146
4455 North Broadway
Chicago, IL 60640
(312) 728-0727

Contact: Bishop Chears

Provides emergency and support services to the homeless, attempting to reintegrate them into society. Volunteers help make it possible for the agency to meet the growing and diverse needs of homeless clients.

Clearbrook Center for the Handicapped
2800 West Central Road
Rolling Meadows, IL 60008-2535
(708) 870-7711

Contact: Karen Spas

Provides a variety of services to developmentally delayed and high-risk children from birth to age 3. Volunteers serve children as big brothers/big sisters and teachers. Day and evening volunteers needed.

Dove, Inc.
788 East Clay
Decatur, IL 62521
(217) 423-2238

Contact: Patty Plato or Thelma Hentz

Supplies a variety of services for men, women, children, and seniors. The Women's Services division provides support for emotionally and physically abused women. Volunteers care for the clients' children, playing with them and reading to them. The Community Services department sponsors such activities as the Boys' Club and the Girls' Drill Team, where volunteers assist with activities and fund-raising.

Glenkirk
3504 Commercial Avenue
Northbrook, IL 60062
(708) 272-5111

Contact: Eleanor Mosely

An organization for mentally retarded and developmentally disabled persons from birth to adulthood. Volunteers serve as companions, teachers, and tutors.

Handy Camp Association for Handicapped Children
P.O. Box 1592
Homewood, IL 60430
(708) 799-8448

Contact: Thomas Vicek

Provides summer recreational day camp for handicapped children ages 5 to 15 years. Volunteers needed to act as Teen Buddies and help with fund-raising.

La Rabida Children's Hospital
East 65th Street at Lake Michigan
Chicago, IL 60649
(312) 363-6700

Contact: Michelle Fulton

A medical facility whose main focus is on ill children. Volunteers needed days and evenings to provide tender loving care to chronically ill children at the hospital.

Learning About Handicaps Program
3131 Sycamore Road
DeKalb, IL 60115
(815) 758-8616

Contact: Jan Mize

Offers educational programs in dealing with the handicapped for nondisabled elementary and junior high school students. Volunteers are trained to teach classes on disability awareness during a fall orientation. (A one-school-year commitment is preferred.)

Little Brothers—Friends of the Elderly
1658 West Belmont Avenue
Chicago, IL 60657
(312) 477-7702

Contact: Clara Collins

Seeks to combat the isolation often experienced by elderly people by providing friendship and other social services. Sponsors visiting programs, holiday and birthday parties, and summer vacations. Volunteers needed to visit and assist the isolated, lonely elderly in their own homes. Visits are arranged according to the volunteers' schedules. Orientation is held monthly.

National Easter Seal Society
Chicago Metropolitan Area
220 South State Street
Chicago, IL 60604
(312) 939-5115

Contact: Trish Wojcicki

Identifies the needs of people with disabilities and provides them with appropriate rehabilitation. Volunteers help with office projects and fund-raising events.

Opportunity House
P.O. Box 301
202 Lucas Street
Sycamore, IL 60178
(815) 895-5108

Contact: Program director

Offers programs for the elderly and for handicapped young adults. Volunteers serve in a variety of capacities, as education assistants, social aides, interpreters, or working for the special needs of the individuals.

Safe Passage
P.O. Box 621
DeKalb, IL 60115
(815) 756-7930

Contact: Cheryl Graham

Provides services for victims of domestic violence. Volunteers work on a 24-hour hotline (training required), as typists, data-entry processors, special projects assistants, fund-raisers, and children's program helpers.

Stop AIDS Chicago
2835 North Sheffield
Suite 238
Chicago, IL 60657-5051
(312) 871-3300

Contact: Michael Blackwell

Educates all communities in the Chicago area about AIDS. Volunteers work as office assistants, on phone teams, and in fund-raising.

Talk Line/Kids' Line
Box 1321
Elk Grove, IL 60009
(708) 981-1271

Contact: Heather Ogan

Callers to this help line are encouraged to work on problem solving on their own. Volunteers serve 3 hours per week.

World Relief International
450 Gunderson Drive
Carol Stream, IL 60189
1-800-535-5433

Contact: Romy
  Struckmeyer
Responds to immediate
needs created by
disasters, offering

follow-up programs to
give people means of
regaining independence.
Volunteers can get

involved in office work
or work with refugees,
depending on where
they live.

Indiana

**American Cancer
Society**
1011 West Franklin
Evansville, IN 47710
(812) 424-8281

Contact: Beth Woodruff

Dedicated to eliminating
cancer as a major health
problem through
research, education, and
service. Volunteers work
as office assistants and
help on special projects
and fund-raising events.

**American Diabetes
Association**
222 South Downey
  Avenue, Suite 320
Indianapolis, IN 46219
(317) 352-9226

Contact: Kelly Schaefer

Seeks to improve
standards of diabetes
treatment and promote a
cure for diabetes.
Volunteers work on
projects according to
their interests;
opportunities available
include computer work,
helping with special
events, and working in a
summer camp for
diabetic children.

**Angel Mounds State
Historic Site**
8215 Pollack
Evansville, IN 47715
(812) 853-3956

Contact: Peggy Brooks

Prehistoric Indian village
site uses volunteers aged
12 and over to prepare
for celebrations of Native
American holidays, make
craft items, garden, and
landscape.

**Association for
Retarded Citizens**
2542 Thompson Avenue
Fort Wayne, IN 46807
(219) 456-4534

Contact: Sue Schmidt

Helps those in need of
assistance because of
retardation. Teenage
volunteers help with
preschool classes for
mentally retarded
children, assist with
lunchtime and field trips,
and lend a helping hand
wherever needed. No
minimum age, but
volunteers should be
fairly mature.

**Friends of the Third
World**
611 West Wayne Street
Fort Wayne, IN 46802
(219) 422-6821

Contact: Marian Waltz

A group of individuals
concerned with the
environment and Third
World poverty.
Volunteers can work in a
recycling center, a craft
shop that displays and
sells art created by Third

World artisans, or a print
shop that creates a
neighborhood newsletter;
they can help maintain
the grounds and facilities;
they can help in the
office, updating mailing
lists and files.

Meals on Wheels
370 Bellemeade Avenue
Evansville, IN 47715
(812) 476-6521

Contact: Rebecca
  Browning

Provides hot meals to
hungry individuals.
Volunteers take meals to
the essentially
homebound and can
either drive or deliver the
meals.

Nature Conservancy
1330 West 38th Street
Indianapolis, IN 46208
(317) 923-7547

Contact: Jeffrey Maddox

Committed to finding,
protecting, and
maintaining biological
communities, ecosytems,
and endangered species
around the world. By
controlling land and
water resources, the
Conservancy is able to
preserve the plants and
animals that inhabit
them. Volunteers needed
for projects both in the
field and in the office.
Transportation may be
available.

Ozanam Family Shelter
713 Second Avenue
Evansville, IN 47710
(812) 423-4643

Contact: Karen Williams

Provides food and shelter
services for families
without homes. The
Shelter needs volunteers
at least 15 years old to
clean, cook, play with
children, answer phones,
make beds, and organize
storage areas.

Reitz Home Museum
P.O. Box 2478
Evansville, IN 47728-0478
(812) 426-1871
Contact: Tess Grimm
A historic Victorian
home. High school–aged
volunteers interested in
history can give tours
and provide public
information to visitors.

The Salvation Army
P.O. Box 566
South Bend, IN 46601
(219) 233-9471

Contact: Major Anderson
Works with the
homeless, drug addicts,
unwed mothers,
prisoners, the poor,
children, and senior
citizens and supplies
basic human necessities
and counseling.
Volunteers work
primarily with children,
playing games, doing
crafts, and so on.

Iowa

Arts and Recreation Council of Greater Des Moines
310 Shops Building, 8th
and Walnut
Des Moines, IA 50309
(515) 280-3222

Contact: Lee Ann Bakros

Holds festivals and
concerts; unites arts and
recreation organizations
and individual artists in
the Des Moines area.
Volunteers act as office
assistants, help artists at
festivals, and sell items
and distribute fliers at
concerts. Minimum age
15.

Children's Garden
2901 Grand Avenue
Des Moines, IA 50312
(515) 244-0651

Contact: Alice Nielson

Provides child care, field
trips, and educational
and recreational activities
for children under the
age of 10. Volunteers
help in all activities—
supervise field trips,

naps, and lunches; help
in kitchen and in garden;
help put together
classroom programs, and
so on. Minimum age 16.

The Children's Museum
533 16th Street
Bettendorf, IA 52722
(319) 344-4106

Contact: Cindy Bales

Has hands-on exhibits for
children, play areas, and
special facilities such as
the bubble room.
Volunteers act as TotSpot
Attendants, watching
over children and
assisting their parents or
care-givers at the TotSpot
exhibit.

Food Bank of Iowa
30 Northeast 48th Place
Des Moines, IA 50313
(515) 244-6555

Contact: Rob Ford

Gathers and stores food
products from donors to
be given to area soup
kitchens and shelters.
Volunteers sort, clean,

and weigh grocery
products and provide
clerical assistance when
needed. Orientation and
on-the-job training
provided. Minimum age
14.

Iowa East Central T.R.A.I.N.
2804 Eastern Avenue
Davenport, Iowa 52803
(319) 324-3236

Contact: Patricia A.
  Steiger

T.R.A.I.N. (Teach,
Rehabilitate, Aid Iowa's
Neglected) helps
lower-income people
with various services.
Volunteers assist teachers
and teachers' assistants in
caring for children,
prepare for and
participate in activities,
help supervise children,
and accompany groups
on field trips.

Ronald McDonald House
1441 Pleasant Street
Des Moines, IA 50314
(515) 243-2111

Contact: Barb Tankersley

A home for families with children in the hospital, usually with long-term illnesses. Volunteers help with light housework, check in donated goods, answer phones and provide office support, and help with food services.

Science Center of Iowa
4500 Grand Avenue
Des Moines, IA 50312
(515) 274-6868

Contact: Beverly Hummel

Provides scientific displays, exhibits, and demonstrations for the public. Volunteers help in gift shop, at admissions desk, in preschool, and with summer classes; present demonstrations; and help maintain exhibits.

Self Help Foundation
P.O. Box 88
Waverly, IA 50677
(319) 352-4040

Contact: Lou, Ext. 3130

Dedicated to alleviating malnutrition and hunger and replacing dependency with self-sufficiency in developing countries.

State Historical Society of Iowa
Capital Complex
Des Moines, IA 50319
(515) 281-8864

Contact: Cynthia Henderson

Holds documents and information on the history of Iowa. Volunteers assist in the library, guide tours, and help with research and cataloging.

Kansas

American Cancer Society
R.R. 2, Box 134A
Baldwin, KS 66006
(913) 843-0795

Contact: Jennie Macomber

Dedicated to eliminating cancer as a major health problem through research, education, and service. Volunteers help in the office with special projects, mailings, filing and typing, and with fund-raising events.

Camp Fire Girls and Boys
4301 Huntoon
Topeka, KS 66604
(913) 272-0601

Contact: Steve Halbett

Provides many services for youth. Volunteers act as counselors for recreational and educational programs; supervise children in arts and crafts and other activities; accompany children on outings and excursions.

Capper Foundation
3500 Southwest Tenth
Topeka, KS 66604
(913) 272-4060

Contact: Jeanette Waters

Summer programs for disabled persons include tennis, swimming, day camp, and field trips. Volunteers help the disabled with sports and outdoor experiences, guide wheelchairs around camp, assist in activities, and provide moral support.

Cerebral Palsy Research Foundation of Kansas, Inc.
20 North Old Manor
Wichita, KS 67202
(316) 688-1888

Contact: Susan Meyers

Sponsors programs for victims of cerebral palsy and supports medical research for the disease. Volunteers assist adults with physical disabilities in recreational actvities and exercises. For example, a volunteer might take someone swimming every other week during the summer.

Cross-Lines Cooperative Council
1620 South 37th Street
Kansas City, KS 66106
(913) 432-5497

Contact: Judy Atwood

Provides neighborhood services to the community of south Kansas City. Volunteers participate in housing repair, recycling projects, tutoring, or recreation. Minimum age 15.

Friendship Day Care Centers
500 East Sixth
Hutchinson, KS 67501
(316) 663-1801

Contact: Karen Maelzer

Serves lower-income families and holds various summer programs for school-age children at three centers. Summer volunteers needed, preferably with a minimum commitment of 3 months.

Good Neighbor Aging Program
1221 Southwest Seventeenth
Topeka, KS 66604
(913) 234-0568

Contact: Ann Burnett

Provides meals and other services for individuals over the age of 60. Volunteers needed to work at meal sites, help deliver meals, do office work, and, if able to drive, provide transportation for the elderly.

Habitat for Humanity
3133 Creekwood
Lawrence, KS 66049
(913) 841-2531

Contact: John Gingerich

Helps to eliminate homelessness through the construction of decent shelter for the economically disadvantaged. Volunteers work on construction and rehabilitation projects or help out in the office.

Helping Hands Humane Shelter
2625 Northwest
Rochester Road
Topeka, KS 66617
(913) 233-7325

Contact: Marcia Gitelman

Provides shelter and care services for animals. Volunteers needed to help care for animals and clean cages.

Kansas Museum of History
6425 Southwest Sixth
Topeka, KS 66615-1099
(913) 272-8681

Contact: Jennifer Thissen

Presents a chronological history of the state of Kansas. Volunteers needed to greet visitors at the front desk, conduct orientation sessions for groups, and help with hands-on activities. Minimum age 15.

Kansas Neurological Institute
3107 Southwest 21st
Topeka, KS 66604
(913) 296-5361

Contact: Lynne LeFils

Provides services for patients with neurological impairments. Many volunteer opportunities are available. For example, whirlpool aides assist with giving clients whirlpool baths; summer friends act as special buddies to nonverbal, nonambulatory clients; classroom assistants act as peers with students; and popcorn sellers pop, sack, and sell popcorn. Minimum age 15.

Mennonite Voluntary Service, General Conference
722 Main Street, Box 347
Neuton, KS 67114
(316) 283-5100

Contact: David Orr

Helps meet the needs of poor and disadvantaged people in North America. Works in 30 communities in the United States and Canada by assisting local communities as they confront social, economic, political, and spiritual problems. Most programs run for 2 years, although short-term programs (from 11 months to 1 year) are available.

Omnisphere and Science Center
220 South Main
Wichita, KS 67202
(316) 264-3174

Contact: Ron Tibbits

Aims to make learning about science fun for both young and old alike. Volunteers run hands-on science exhibits and help provide information to the public.

Sedgwick County Zoo and Botanical Garden
5555 Zoo Boulevard
Wichita, KS 67212
(316) 942-2213

Contact: Renee Cooley

Has several programs for volunteers. There are Saturday programs for young people 11 to 15. Fourteen- and fifteen-year-olds can be a "shadow" to zookeepers, following them and helping them with their work. Those 16 or older are considered adult volunteers, and may feed and care for animals, including newborns and those in incubators.

Wichita Center for the Arts
9112 East Central
Wichita, KS 67206
(316) 634-2787

Contact: Jane Eby

Runs a gallery, school, and theater open to the public. Volunteers help lead tours of the museum and assist teachers with classes and programs during the summer day camp.

Wichita Children's Museum
435 South Water
Wichita, KS 67202
(316) 267-2281

Contact: Beth VanHorn

Invites children of all ages to come and view its exhibits. Volunteers prepare, design, and construct museum exhibits or assist with children's parties. Minimum age 14.

Kentucky

American Cancer Society
2229A New Hartford Road
Owensboro, KY 42303-1308
(502) 683-0425

Contact: Jeanette Woodward

Dedicated to eliminating cancer as a major health problem through reserch, education, and service. Volunteers help plan, organize, and raise funds through special events such as parties and "a-thons." They also help with general office work, such as answering phones, taking messages, typing, and alphabetizing and updating donor cards.

Camp Kennedy and Woodland Day Camp
Division of Parks and Recreation
545 North Upper Street
Lexington, KY 40508
(606) 255-0835

Contact: Evelyn Bologna

Provides tennis courts, supervised playgrounds, tennis, swimming, programs for the handicapped, and arts programs. Volunteers work in camp as companions, help with crafts, and teach and supervise swimming, hiking, games.

Central Adult Day Care Center
P.O. Box 1459
Lexington, KY 40591
(606) 254-5300

Contact: Sherri Harkless

Provides a wide range of services, including therapeutic activities, for individuals over the age of 60 or individuals with Alzheimer's disease. People aged 14 and older assist with recreational programs and outdoor activities and act as companions.

Christian Appalachian Project (CAP)
322 Crab Orchard Road
Lancaster, KY 40446
(606) 792-3051

Contact: Kathy Klusner

Christian service organization that helps the people in eight counties in eastern Kentucky. Runs child development centers, workshops for the handicapped, programs for the elderly, home repair programs, summer camp services for the deaf, rummage stores, and a school from kindergarten to 12th grade. Long- and short-term volunteers needed to help out in all areas. Minimum age 17.

Green River Therapeutic Riding Program
4530 Highway 1514
Utica, KY 42376
(502) 785-4033

Contact: Donna Baldridge

Offers therapeutic and recreational riding program for mentally, emotionally, and physically handicapped youth and adults in the tri-state area. Volunteers assist individuals with mounting and dismounting and while riding; provide friendship and support to the riders; help prepare horses for the riders; and prepare, clean, and maintain equipment.

Kentuckiana Girl Scout Council

#1 Executive Boulevard, LL7
Owensboro, KY 42301
(502) 684-9481

Contact: Deanna Miller

Girl Scouts gives girls the opportunity to understand and take action on personal, community, and global issues and gives them a chance to make friends and develop their leadership capabilities. Volunteer opportunities for young people go beyond being a Girl Scout, such as working on summer programs for young girls in conjunction with the Parks Department, helping in the office or library, or working in public relations and special events.

Lexington Child Abuse Council: NEST

530 North Limestone Street
Lexington, KY 40508
(606) 259-1974

Contact: Michele Martin

NEST is a respite care center where parents who feel they will abuse their children can leave them for a while, until they cool off and regain control of their temper. Volunteers, who must be at least 16, and help with clerical work and act as companions to the children.

March of Dimes Birth Defects Foundation

Western Kentucky Chapter
920 Frederica Street
Suite 108
Owensboro, KY 42301
(502) 683-2410

Contact: Becky Stegenberger

March of Dimes is dedicated to the prevention of birth defects, low birth weight, and infant deaths. Volunteers help coordinate special events and work as clerical assistants, helping the office secretary with such tasks as data entry. Training is provided for all positions.

OASIS

P.O. Box 140
Owensboro, KY 42302
(502) 685-1843

Contact: Jeannie Kirk

Provides services to victims of verbal, psychological, and physical domestic violence. OASIS has many volunteer opportunities, but teenage volunteers most often work as child-care assistants, providing basic care to children from violent homes. Volunteers should love children and be patient, flexible, and dependable.

Rolling Heights Child Care

2161 East 19th Street
Owensboro, KY 42301
(502) 683-5573

Contact: Roxie Roby

Provides high-quality day-care and child-development programs for children from low-income families. Volunteers work as care-givers, helping with breakfast and assisting in the infants' and toddlers' rooms, playing games with the children, and so on. Training is provided.

Louisiana

Acadiana Open Channel
P.O. Box 5159
124 East Main Street
Lafayette, LA 70501
(318) 232-4434
Contact: Sharon Warren
This production facility for a public access television station will train volunteers 14 years of age or older to be camera operators.

AIDS Task Force of Acadiana
307 Jefferson Street
Lafayette, LA 70501
(318) 232-2624
Contact: Dana Brignac
Provides a variety of services for persons with AIDS or those interested in AIDS education. Volunteers help out with mailings, light typing, envelope stuffing, and computer work.

Arthritis Foundation
3955 Government Street
Suite 7
Baton Rouge, LA 70806
(504) 387-6932
Contact: Jean R. Baron
An organization whose goal is to support research, find a cure for and prevent arthritis, and improve the quality of life of those with arthritis. Volunteers help with office work and special projects. Minimum age 15.

American Red Cross
Orleans Service Center
1523 St. Charles Avenue
New Orleans, LA 70130
(504) 587-1551

Contact: Bill Williams

Works to improve the quality of human life, enhance self-reliance and concern for others, and help people avoid, prepare for, and cope with emergencies. Volunteer positions available in the following areas: office work, transportation of supplies, maintenance of disaster vehicles, swimming and health instruction, and disaster communications. Minimum age 13.

Audubon Zoo
P.O. Box 4327
New Orleans, LA 70178
(504) 861-2537

Contact: Kathy LeBlanc

Volunteers assist with Zoo Corps, Safari Cart, Children's Village, and Edzoocator programs. Group orientation plus training sessions required. Minimum age 14, except for Zoo Corps, which is 16.

Baton Rouge General Medical Center
Office of Volunteer
  Service
3600 Florida Boulevard
Baton Rouge, LA 70806
(504) 387-7079

Contact: Lynn S. Weill

A general medical facility. Volunteer opportunities of all kinds available. Minimum age 14.

Center for Displaced Homemakers
1304 Bertrand Drive
Suite C-1
Lafayette, LA 70506
(318) 265-5191

Contact: Janet Melancon

Provides workshops and counseling for women in need. Volunteers who are at least 16 years of age needed as clerical assistants, to help with light typing, produce monthly calendar, and get out mailings.

Friends of City Park
#1 Dreyfouss Avenue
City Park Casino Building
New Orleans, LA 70124
(504) 483-9377

Contact: Peggy Conley or
  Jane Kreisman

Volunteer jobs available as storyland, garden, and concession assistants, carousel cleaners, and telephone receptionists. Volunteers gain experience in the arts, botany, retail sales, antique upkeep, and office procedures. Minimum age 13.

Louisiana Arts and Science Center
P.O. Box 3373
Baton Rouge, LA 70821
(504) 344-9463

Contact: Ann Hubbard

Runs a planetarium, Egyptian gallery, space shows, and a hands-on children's room. Volunteers needed on weekdays and weekends as workshop teachers' assistants. Minimum age 13.

Louisiana Council on Child Abuse
333 Laurel, Suite 875
Baton Rouge, LA 70801
(504) 346-0222
Contact: Jay Settoon

Provides services and programs relating to child abuse. Children's Program Assistants needed to work with children in a group setting. Training is provided. Volunteers should be 16 or older.

Louisiana Nature and Science Center
P.O. Box 870610
New Orleans, LA 70187
(504) 246-5672
Contact: Laura Reynolds

Has outdoor and indoor facilities and runs a recycling program and summer camp. Volunteer jobs include summer camp assistant, exhibit guide, young astronaut assistant, and greenhouse guide. Minimum age 14.

Ollie Steele Burden Nursing Home
4200 Essen Lane
Baton Rouge,LA 70809
(504) 926-0092

Contact: Ed Picard

A live-in facility for the elderly, in need of volunteers to take on sewing projects and to help with activities, such as Bingo. Minimum age 15.

The Parker House
578 Caddo Street
Baton Rouge, LA 70806
(504) 928-9398

Contact: Darlene Abbott

Provides services to children who have been removed from their families because of abuse and neglect. Needs volunteers to help with yard work and house cleaning, in addition to set-up and maintenance of the Centers for Children and organization of donated items. Minimum age 15.

Saint Joseph's Diner
403 West Simcoe
Lafayette, LA 70507
(318) 232-8434

Contact: Lou Gauthier

Needs people to help prepare and serve the one meal per day it serves to homeless and disadvantaged people.

Volunteers should be prepared to slice, dice, and peel vegetables, wash and dry dishes, and clean up after meals.

Volunteers in Public Schools
Valley Park
  Administrative Center
4510 Bawell Street
Baton Rouge, LA 70808
(504) 929-5484

Contact: Liz Connor

Junior high schools with opportunities for volunteers to tutor students in sixth, seventh, and eighth grades. Minimum age 16.

Young Women's Christian Association
2549 Priscilla Lane
Baton Rouge, LA 70809
(504) 926-3820

Contact: Monica
  Gatreaux

The YWCA provides many services for the community. Anyone 13 or older can volunteer in the children's summer camp or as a Child Development volunteer. Those who are 18 can train to be Phone Friend Counselors.

Maine

Cerebral Palsy Center
331 Veranda Street
Portland, ME 04103
(207) 874-1125

Contact: Betty Morrison

Sponsors programs for victims of cerebral palsy and supports medical research for the disease.

Volunteers help with preschool and adult programs.

Habitat for Humanity of Greater Portland, Inc.
15 Pleasant Avenue
Portland, ME 04101
(207) 772-2151

Contact: Richard LeBlanc

Helps to eliminate homelessness through the construction of decent shelter for the economically diasdvantaged. Volunteers help with construction projects in the field or with office work.

Maine Audubon Society
118 U.S. Route 1
Falmouth, ME 04105
(207) 781-2330

Contact: Gretchen Blickle

Provides opportunities to appreciate and learn about nature. During the summer, volunteers lead guided walks and canoe tours at the Scarborough Marsh location and work in the shop and at rental services. During the rest of the year, regular volunteer opportunities include sanctuary cleanup on weekends and office work and mailings.

Maine Center for the Blind
89 Park Avenue
Portland, ME 04102
(207) 774-6273

Contact: Nancy Bennett

Provides many services for the blind, including a residence program, community service program, a rehabilitation center, and a computer access program. Sighted volunteers accompany

the residents, take them to the beach, and participate in various activities with them.

Nature Conservancy
122 Main Street
Topsham, ME 04086
(207) 729-5181

Contact: Suzanne Drew

This organization is committed to finding, protecting, and maintaining biological communities, ecosytems, and endangered species around the world. By controlling land and water resources, the Conservancy is able to preserve the plants and animals which inhabit them. Volunteers needed on an on-call basis for projects both in the field and in the office.

Refugee Resettlement Program
107 Elm Street
Portland, ME 04101
(207) 871-7437

Contact: Eli Dale

Aims to ease the process of integration into American culture and society for refugee immigrants, relying

heavily on the contributions of volunteers and donors. Youth volunteers are especially encouraged to act as big brother/sister to refugee children. Help is also needed in the donation center, picking up, sorting, storing, and soliciting donated items. Interested volunteers may also be assigned to caseworkers, who assist people in adjusting to life in the United States and in becoming self-sufficient members of society.

State Parks
Two Light State Park
Cape Elizabeth, ME
  04107
(207) 799-5871

Contact: John Scott

Maintains state park facilities and provides many services for the community. Volunteers help with maintenance of the park grounds, may be involved with interpretative work or statistical analyses, or assist with such projects as painting.

Maryland

Adventure Theatre
7300 MacArthur
  Boulevard
Glen Echo Park, MD
  20812
(301) 320-5331

Contact: Volunteer
  coordinator

Provides performances, classes, and workshops

for children in the Washington area. Volunteers can help increase public awareness of the theater.

Alliance for the Mentally Ill
10414 Detrick Avenue
Kensington, MD 20895
(301) 572-5524

Contact: Elsie Painter

Operates a thrift shop that raises funds and provides job opportunities for those who are mentally ill or recovering. Volunteer positions as cashier or store manager are available.

ARC/Calvert County
P.O. Box 1860
Prince Frederick, MD
  20678
(301) 535-2413
Contact: Maureen Ecker
Provides residential and vocational services to individuals with mental retardation and developmental disabilities. Volunteers needed for fund-raising.

Association for Retarded Citizens
1300 Mercantile Lane
Suite 200
Landover, MD 20785
(301) 925-7050
Contact: Margie
  Dickmann
Holds support groups for parents of retarded individuals, provides residential services and many family services. Volunteers needed for assistance with fund-raising projects.

Baptist Home for Children
Greentree Shelter
6301 Greentree Road
Bethesda, MD 20817
(301) 365-2190
Contact: Carla Nadeau
This residence and shelter for children and women can use administrative aides. Those 16 or older can also become a big brother/sister at the residence.

Bethesda–Chevy Chase Rescue Squad
5020 Battery Lane
Bethesda, MD 20814
(301) 652-0077

Contact: Lewis German
Provides emergency rescue service for the Bethesda area. Those at least 17 can volunteer as rescue squad technicians or paramedics. Training is provided.

Bethesda Interfaith Housing Coalition
20910 Clarksburg Road
Boyds, MD 20841
(301) 972-4310
Contact: Maureen
  Herndon
A transitional housing facility for economically underprivileged families. Volunteers assist with all services and give support to the families.

Bethesda Youth Services
4700 Norwood Drive
Bethesda, MD 20815
(301) 652-2820
Contact: Jeannie Gipple
Provides many services for young adults. People are needed to tutor students, help with their homework, and assist with reception and clerical work in the office.

Children's Development Clinic
301 Largo Road
Largo, MD 20772-2199
(301) 322-0519
Contact: Kathy Hinkle
An educational facility for children. Volunteers act as clinicians to help children improve their motor, language, and reading skills. Training is provided. Volunteers should be at least 16.

Community Services
Richard R. Clark Senior
  Center
1210 East Charles Street
LaPlata, MD 20646
(301) 934-5423
Contact: Susan E. Beaver
Provides special events, classes, recreation, and information for the senior citizens of Charles County. Volunteer activity instructors lead classes in various programs for seniors.

Center for Children
P.O. Box 329
LaPlata, MD 20646
(301) 870-3446
Contact: Debbie Moore
Offers child-abuse prevention, treatment, and education programs for children. Volunteers assist with office duties and fund-raising events. Minimum age 16.

Christmas in April
5910 Onondaga Road
Bethesda, MD 20816
(301) 320-9466
Contact: Volunteer
  coordinator
Sponsors housing rehabilitation and clean-up projects for run-down neighborhoods. Volunteers work in large teams on weekends to clean up designated areas.

Environmental Conservation Organization
1211 North Student
  Stamp
College Park, MD 20742
(301) 314-8345

Contact: Greg Bazakas

A recycling center in need of volunteers to sort and move recyclables.

Great Oaks Center

3100 Gracefield Road
Silver Spring, MD 20904
(301) 595-5000, Ext. 340

Contact: Rita Hinkle

A center for the developmentally disabled. Volunteers at least 14 can be sponsors, visiting patients and providing entertainment and emotional support.

Harriet L. Hunter Government Center

Office of Volunteer Work
Department on Aging
6420 Allentown Road
Camp Springs, MD 20748
(301) 248-6606

Contact: Lasandra Bell

Provides many services for the elderly, including insurance counseling and other programs. Volunteers are often needed for help with special events.

Historic Saint Mary's City

P.O. Box 39
Saint Mary's City, MD 20686
(301) 862-0979

Contact: Marie Goldsmith

Directs the preservation and interpretation of Maryland's 17th-century capital. Will teach anyone at least 14 about pre-Colonial Native American culture and way of life in preparation for being a volunteer.

Home Energy Services Center

3704 Decatur Avenue
Kensington, MD 20895
(301) 942-7475

Contact: Diane Pellicori

Provides area residents with information and services regarding energy conservation. Volunteers assist the office staff in various capacities.

Hotline and Suicide Prevention Center

9300 Annapolis Road
Suite 100
Lanham, MD 20706
(301) 731-4922

Contact: Richard Reap

A crisis-intervention center that needs volunteers to work the telephone hotline any time of day. Training is provided. Minimum age 16.

Hughesville Regional Shelter for Women

P.O. Box 613
Hughesville, MD 20637
(301) 274-0683

Contact: Dana Powell

An emergency shelter for women and children. Volunteers provide after-school care for children, help with phones, and assist with dinner and meal services.

Kensington Volunteer Fire Department

P.O. Box 222
Kensington, MD 20895
(301) 929-8000

Contact: Personnel Division

Accepts the volunteer assistance of those 16 and older, although no training is provided.

Long-term commitment necessary for beginners.

Literacy Council

4307 Jefferson Street, Room 608
Hyattsville, MD 20781
(301) 864-6107

Contact: Joyce Charles

Provides tutoring and reading assistance for persons wishing to learn how to read. Volunteers 17 and older can tutor adults in basic reading and writing skills. Training is provided.

The Lord's Table Soup Kitchen

201 South Frederick Avenue
Gaithersburg, MD 20877
(301) 330-5812

Contact: Mary Canapary

Provides services for needy individuals. Those 16 and older can help in the kitchen and serve food to the hungry.

Maryland NARAL

911 Silver Spring Avenue
Suite 3
Silver Spring, MD 20910
(301) 565-4154

Contact: Anyone in the office

Dedicated to keeping abortion safe, legal, and accessible in Maryland. Volunteers act as office assistants and get involved with special projects.

Merkle Wildlife Sanctuary

Department of Natural Resources
11704 Fenno Road
Upper Marlboro, MD 20772
(301) 888-1410

Contact: Michael Gregor

Provides a home to wildlife. Volunteers participate in the maintenance of the sanctuary's various gardens.

Metropolitan Washington Ear
35 University Boulevard, East
Silver Spring, MD 20901
(301) 681-6636
Contact: Nancy Knauss

Provides services for the visually impaired, blind, and print-handicapped in the Washington area. Needs volunteers for such tasks as accompanying the visually impaired to the theater and reading newspapers, magazines, and books to the blind over the air from a studio in Silver Spring.

Montgomery County Historical Society
111 West Montgomery Avenue
Rockville, MD 20850
(301) 340-6534
Contact: Karen Yaffe

Can use volunteers to give tours at its two museums and to do research on various projects.

Montgomery Housing Opportunities
10400 Detrick Avenue
Kensington, MD 20895
(301) 929-6776
Contact: Valerie Chilewski

Volunteers act as companions to isolated seniors at this facility for

persons of low and moderate income. Training is provided. Minimum age 16.

National Capital Park and Planning
9500 Brunnett Avenue
Silver Spring, MD 20901
(301) 495-2504
Contact: Jane Hench

Run's the capital's nature centers. Volunteer aides care for animals, maintain exhibits, and work on projects and events. Minimum age 16.

National Chamber Orchestra
15209 Frederick Road
Suite 207
Rockville, MD 20850
(301) 762-8580
Contact: Diane Souder

Puts on musical events and concerts for the community. Volunteers are ushers, distributing programs and escorting people to their seats.

Planned Parenthood
4701 Randolph Road
Suite 209
Rockville, MD 20852
(301) 468-7678
Contact: Laura Feinberg

Provides medical services and counseling for women. Volunteers needed to help in the office. Training is provided.

Prince George's Arts Council
6611 Kenilworth Avenue
Suite 215
Riverdale, MD 20737
(301) 864-4093

Contact: Sarah Rodman

Provides technical assistance to artists, grants to agencies and individuals, and arts advocacy. Volunteers work on various projects and activities within the county's arts community.

RICA–Southern Maryland
9400 Surratts Road
Clinton, MD 20735
(301) 372-1881
Contact: Mary Hasler

A center for emotionally disturbed young people. Volunteers coordinate activities or tutor students.

Shady Grove Adventist Hospital
Office of Volunteers
9901 Medical Center Drive
Rockville, MD 20850
(301) 279-6111
Contact: Carol Necker

Volunteers help with patient care and provide general assistance to the hospital staff.

WUMCO (Western Upper Montgomery County) Help
P.O. Box 247
Poolesville, MD 20837
(301) 972-8481
Contact: Volunteer coordinator

Provides emergency food, transportation, and financial assistance for anyone in need. Volunteers especially needed around holidays to work on holiday projects, such as packaging or delivering food baskets.

Massachusetts

ACCION International
130 Prospect Street
Cambridge, MA 02139
(617) 492-4930

Contact: Cheryl Klein

Works against poverty and hunger throughout Latin America by providing job training and other services. Volunteers work in the office on fund-raising and various special projects.

Atlantic Center for the Environment
39 South Main Street
Ipswich, MA 01938
(508) 752-7868

Contact: Internship
  coordinator

The Center covers the Atlantic region, from northern New England through Atlantic Canada. Internships are available in the areas of water resources, wildlife management, resource management, conservation education, natural history, and investigative journalism. Interns work as a team and participate in camps, canoe trips, research projects, workshops, and publications. Minimum age 16.

Big Brothers/Big Sisters of Worcester County
50 Franklin Street
Worcester, MA 01608
(508) 752-7868

Contact: Benedict Ticho

Seeks to match young boys and girls from single-parent homes with positive role models. New Directions selects high school juniors to provide positive role models for younger children. Training provided.

Friendly House, Inc.
36 Wall Street
Worcester, MA 01604
(508) 792-1799

Contact: Debbie Novia

A multiservice center, including health, social services, education, recreation, and community organization for all ages. Volunteer opportunities are available in every unit of Friendly House, including the Little Folks program (for children 4 to 6), elderly programs, meals, recreation and sports, mental health, and medical assistance.

Heifer Project International
Overlook Farm
216 Wachusett Street
Rutland, MA 01543-2099
(508) 886-2221

Contact: Dale Perkins

A worldwide self-help organization that provides livestock, poultry, training, and related agricultural services to people in developing areas, including sections of the United States. Volunteers are vital to the success of HPI, performing clerical and agricultural work, acting as tour and work group leaders. Minimum age 14.

Mail for Tots
25 New Chardon Street
P.O. Box 8699
Boston, MA 02114
(617) 242-3538

Contact: Ed Burns

Distributes a list of children and adults who are chronically ill, hospitalized, or shut-in and who need pen pals and gifts to cheer them up. Volunteers needed on a part-time basis or to work on special projects.

Massachusetts Association for the Blind
51 Harvard Street
Worcester, MA 01609
(508) 791-8237

Contact: Carol Polizoti

Provides a variety of services for the blind. Prospective volunteers attend a two-hour orientation dealing with the responsibilities of volunteering, vision loss, and the skills needed to work with a visually impaired individual. Volunteer roles include escorting individuals to appointments, on shopping trips, or to leisure-time events and reading and visiting.

Massachusetts Audubon Society
Laughing Brook
  Education Center and
  Wildlife Sanctuary
789 Main Street
Hampden, MA
  01036-5034
(413) 566-8034

Contact: Frances Dutille

A 259-acre wildlife sanctuary that holds programs and maintains exhibits designed to cultivate appreciation of nature and the environment. Volunteers care for resident wildlife, assist with Sanctuary maintenance, and help in the gift shop or with special events.

Muscular Dystrophy Association
415 Boston Turnpike
Shrewsbury, MA 01545
(508) 842-8106

Contact: Julie Leary

Performs research into the causes and cures of different categories of neuromuscular disease.

This branch offers patient care, provides equipment and services, and operates a clinic at a local hospital. Volunteers needed for clerical work and special events. Minimum age 16.

New England Assistance Dog Service
Box 213, 6 Green Street
West Boylston, MA 01583
(508) 835-3304

Contact: Sheila O'Brien

Trains guide dogs for the deaf. Dogs are taught to respond to certain sounds (doorbell, smoke alarm, baby crying) and to alert the deaf person to these sounds. Volunteer positions available as kennel attendants, and in

maintenance work, clerical, and public relations. Minimum age 15.

Summer's World Center for the Arts, Inc.
70 Piedmont Street
Worcester, MA 01610
(508) 756-1921

Contact: Kathleen Corcoran

Provides year-round programs: art classes, art shows and exhibits, festivals, and crafts, drama, and music workshops. Volunteers perform light office work and during the summer aid staff members at concerts, art and drama classes, and senior citizens' events. Minimum age 15.

Michigan

The Art Center
125 Macomb Place
Mt. Clemens, MI 48043
(313) 468-8666

Contact: Kay Betke

Sponsors exhibitions, art fairs, workshops and classes, promotes the visual arts. Volunteers needed in the areas of office work, crafts, and cultural arts.

Casa Maria Family Services
1500 Trumbull Avenue
Detroit, MI 48216
(313) 962-4230

Contact: Rosaana Pardo

Provides youth with counseling, guidance, runaway services, and recreational and cultural

opportunities. Volunteer opportunities available in education, friendship, guidance, and recreation.

Center for Independent Living
3375 South Division
Grand Rapids, MI 49548
(616) 243-0846

Contact: Beth Harvey or Jan Whisner

Works with individuals who have a physical limitation and provides a variety of services from housing to counseling. Volunteers assist with clerical work, special events, and the agency's newsletter or television station.

Detroit Zoological Parks
8450 West Ten Mile Road
Royal Oak, MI 48068
(313) 398-0903

Contact: Kim Sneden

Offers educational tours of the Detroit Zoo, Belle Isle Zoo, and Belle Isle Aquarium. Work sites include Detroit, Macomb, Out-Wayne, and Oakland. Volunteers needed in public relations, education, and recreation.

God's Kitchen
203 South Division
Grand Rapids, MI 49503
(616) 454-4110

Contact: Barbara Raaymakers

Provides two services: Meals-on-Wheels and an on-site meal program. Younger volunteers needed to clean the dining area and the tables. Older teens help prepare, serve, and deliver food.

Habitat for Humanity
38 West Fulton, Suite 80
Grand Rapids, MI 49503
(616) 774-2431
Contact: John Kuiper

Helps to eliminate homelessness through the construction of decent shelter for the economically disadvantaged. Volunteers must be at least 16 years old to help with jobs like painting, landscaping, house construction, the planning of banquets, and office work.

HAVEN
92 Whittemore
P.O. Box 787
Pontiac, MI 48342
(313) 334-1284
Contact: Jane Balouski

Offers counseling, guidance, shelter, and a crisis line for victims of domestic violence and sexual abuse. Volunteer opportunities include administration, child care, guidance, and education.

The Holiday Project
P.O. Box 4396
Centerline, MI 49015
(313) 585-8659
Contact: Deborah Cieslak

Provides benefits to the needy public. Volunteers

needed for administrative functions, crafts, friendship, and public relations.

Kids in Need of Direction
11000 West McNichols Rd., Suite 205
Detroit, MI 48221
(313) 341-5463
Contact: Amy Devone

Works with families to build self-esteem and improve poor attitudes. Work sites available in Detroit, Macomb, and Oakland. Volunteers needed for child care, friendship, guidance, and program development.

Mothers Against Drunk Driving (MADD)
15195 Farmington Road
Suite #D1
Livonia, MI 48152
(313) 422-MADD
Contact: Chris Schonfeld

Informs the public that drunk driving is unacceptable and criminal. Volunteers needed for administrative functions, advocacy, criminal justice, education, and guidance.

Michigan Cancer Foundation
110 East Warren
Detroit, MI 48201
(313) 833-0710
Contact: Mary Mulligan

Funds cancer research and provides services for cancer patients and their families. Work sites include Detroit as well as Macomb, Out-Wayne, and Oakland. Volunteers needed for office duties,

friendship, guidance, and public relations.

Michigan Commission for the Blind
1200 Sixth Street, 15th Floor
Detroit, MI 48226
(313) 256-1524
Contact: Leamon Jones

Offers rehabilitation activities for anyone legally blind residing in Michigan. Work sites include Detroit, Macomb, and Out-Wayne. Volunteers needed to befriend the disabled, run errands, assist with crafts, and provide clerical assistance.

Michigan Opera Theatre
6519 Second Avenue
Detroit, MI 48202
(313) 874-7850
Contact: Diane Windom

Nonprofit opera company committed to providing the Detroit community with opera and musical theater. Clerical volunteer opportunities available.

Nature Conservancy
2840 East Grand River
Suite 5
East Lansing, MI 48823
Contact: Pam Shank

Committed to finding, protecting, and maintaining biological communities, ecosytems, and endangered species around the world. By controlling land and water resources, the Conservancy is able to preserve the plants and animals that inhabit them. Volunteers needed for projects both in the field and in the office.

Older Persons Commission
312 Woodward Street
Rochester, MI 48307
(313) 656-1403

Contact: Ruth Hartler

Provides the elderly with a broad range of activities and services. Volunteers needed for crafts and clerical duties.

Paws with a Cause (Ears for the Deaf)
1235 100th Street Southeast
Byron Center, MI 49315
(616) 698-0688

Contact: Mike Sapp

Provides dogs that "hear" for the deaf. The minimum age for volunteers is about 16, and typically they work with the dogs and help in the kennel and in the office.

Special Olympics
860 Crahen Road, NE
Grand Rapids, MI 49506
(616) 942-5614

Contact: Shirley Bevins

Provides sports training and athletic competition in a variety of Olympic-type sports for children and adults with physical handicaps or mental retardation. Volunteers act as coaches and "huggers" for contestants.

Welcome Home for the Blind
1953 Monroe Northwest
Grand Rapids, MI 49505
(616) 363-9088

Contact: Anne Griffioen

Provides many services for the visually impaired. Volunteers 14 and older can work with the clients, helping them with activities and arts and crafts, reading to them, and taking them on walks.

Minnesota

American Cancer Society
23 Seventh Street, Northeast
Rochester, MN 55906
(507) 287-2044

Contact: Lynn Brummer or Bette Forberg

Dedicated to eliminating cancer as a major health problem through research, education, and service. Volunteers needed for various office duties and, if volunteer is qualified, data entry. Groups of volunteers are welcome (an entire local Boy Scout troop has volunteered).

American Red Cross
11 Dell Place
Minneapolis, MN 55403
(612) 871-7676

Contact: Peggy Lathrop

Works to improve the quality of human life, enhance self-reliance and concern for others, and help people avoid, prepare for, and cope with disaster. Office assistants needed to type and stamp Red Cross course certificates, file, sort, and perform varied office functions. Teenage volunteers also take part in instructor training for AIDS awareness and CPR, as well as youth leadership development training.

Association for Retarded Citizens
903 West Center
Rochester, MN 55902
(507) 287-2032

Contact: Cherie Hales

Provides services for retarded individuals. Volunteers bake for bake sales; bag corn for corn sales; assist at race and triathlon water stations, first aid stations, and concession stands; volunteers accompany disabled young adults to movies.

Charter House
211 Second Street, NW
Rochester, MN 55901
(507) 286-8572

Contact: Bonnie Hintz

A senior citizens' high-rise. Volunteers act as readers, notetakers, crafts aids, snack assistants, companions, and game leaders and also help with public education, outreach, and support groups.

A.M. Chisholm Museum
506 West Michigan Street
Duluth, MN 55802
(218) 722-8563
Contact: Bonnie Cusick

Encourages interest in the arts, humanities, technology, and nature through its collections, programs, and exhibits. Volunteer opportunities include guiding tours, clerical work, participation in the Folk Festival, collection research and inventory, and acting as Back in Time Players.

CHUM Drop-In Center
125 North First Avenue West
Duluth, MN 55802
(218) 726-0153
Contact: Kim Seitz

Provides services for people suffering from social isolation, drug or alcohol dependence, mental illness, and poverty by means of referrals and provision of food, clothing, and temporary shelter. Volunteers can help in the laundry facility, in the food pantry, with special events, and by developing conversational relationships with needy individuals.

Courage Center, Duluth
205 West Second Street, #451
Duluth, MN 55802
(218) 727-6874

Contact: Mary Lou Donovan

Enables persons with physical disabilites to participate in both competitive and noncompetitive athletic and recreational activities. Volunteers needed to provide assistance for sports programs, clerical work, transportation, photography, and maintenance of facilities.

Duluth Community Garden Program (Plant-a-lot)
206 West Fourth Street
Duluth, MN 55806
(218) 722-4583
Contact: John Durward

Provides garden plots, seeds, tilling, and fertilizers for (and loans tools to) local, low-income gardeners. Volunteers assist in sale of seeds, make posters and banners, help at the Harvest Dinner, and participate in gardening projects.

Duluth Public Library
520 West Superior Street
Duluth, MN 55802
(218) 723-3814
Contact: Janet Niemi

Volunteers serve as store clerks and deliver books to homebound patrons.

Glensheen
3300 London Road
Duluth, MN 55804
(218) 724-3041
Contact: Pat Browman

A self-supporting museum owned by the University of Minnesota. Volunteers conduct or

assist with tours, work in the museum shop, and help with special events.

Kids' Network
Lake Superior Area Family Services
1000 Torrey Building
314 West Superior Street
Duluth, MN 55802
(218) 722-5326
Contact: Cynthia Marxen

Offers a variety of services for both children and parents affected by family violence. Volunteer duties include child care, transportation, reception, clerical tasks, data entry, library work, and participation in special events.

March of Dimes
4940 Viking Drive
Minneapolis, MN 55435
(612) 835-3033
Contact: Kim Olsen

Dedicated to the prevention of birth defects, low birth weight, and infant deaths. Teenage volunteers provide overall office assistance—stuffing envelopes, helping with fund-raisers, basic computer work. Kim Olsen is in charge of a special program called Chain Reaction, which enables teens to help other teens through group discussions and activities.

Moose Lake Regional Treatment Center
1000 Lakeshore Drive
Moose Lake, MN 55767
(218) 485-4411, Ext. 253
Contact: Donald Jensen

This state residential facility serves mentally ill,

developmentally disabled, chemically dependent, and psycho-geriatric patients. Volunteers can work directly with patients by visiting, tutoring, transporting, and entertaining them, and by taking part in crafts and recreational activities. Assistance is also needed in garden and facility maintenance.

National Multiple Sclerosis Society

2344 Nicollet Avenue
Suite 280
Minneapolis, MN
  55404-3381
(612) 870-1500

Contact: Colleen O'Fallon

Seeks to prevent, treat, and cure the disease of multiple sclerosis and improve th quality of life of affected individuals and their families. Volunteers dispense food and beverages at recreational fund-raisers and assist in the office.

North Country R.I.D.E.

P.O. Box 312
Esko, MN 55733
(218) 879-7608

Contact: Nancy Melander

Nonprofit organization that offers differently abled persons (in Duluth, Cloquet, and surrounding areas) horseback riding as a means of therapy and rehabilitation. Volunteers may lead or walk next to horses,

work with the differently abled, and help with carpentry or clerical duties.

Park and Recreation Department

403 East Center Street
Rochester, MN 55904
(507) 281-6160

Contact: Beth Asfahl

Provides recreational programs for the physically challenged. Volunteer recreation assistants assist with various activities such as horseback riding, field trips, and swimming for children and adults with mental and/or physical disabilities. Minimum age 16.

Rochester Public Library

11 First Street, Southeast
Rochester, MN
  55904-3743
(507) 285-8000

Contact: Nancy Jo
  Leachman

Volunteers are involved in a variety of projects and assist with book mending, keep shelves and documents orderly, and help in the children's room.

Soil Conservation Service

4850 Miller Trunk
  Highway, Suite 1-B
Duluth, MN 55811
(218) 720-5209

Contact: Paul Sandstrom

Works with individuals and governments on the

local level, providing leadership in the conservation and wise use of soil, water, and related resources. Volunteers can help with computer work, soil surveys, and clerical work.

Surf and Sand Health Center

3910 Minnesota Avenue
Duluth, MN 55802
(218) 727-8933

Contact: Debbie Aho

Offers its clients nursing care, physical and oxygen therapy, recreation programs, and social services. The numerous volunteer opportunities include visiting patients, helping with crafts, "adopting" a grandparent, providing entertainment or hair and nail care, and participating in activities, outings, and special events.

Women's Coalition

P.O. Box 3558
Duluth, MN 55803
(218) 728-6481

Contact: Mary Ness

Provides shelter and social services for battered women and their children. Volunteer assistance is needed for advocacy, clerical work, answering crisis calls, transportation, and finding affordable housing.

Mississippi

American Red Cross/V.A. Center
145 North Shelby
Greenville, MS 38701
(601) 378-3245

Contact: Nancy Riddle

Works to improve the quality of human life, enhance self-reliance and concern for others, and help people avoid, prepare for, and cope with disaster. Volunteers interested in assisting with disaster services should contact the agency to find out more about disaster training class schedules.

Jackson County Senior Companion Program
P.O. Box 8723
Moss Point, MS 39562
(601) 769-3318

Contact: Tommye Nelson

Provides companionship and recreational program for senior citizens. The program can always use younger people to socialize with senior individuals, work in ceramics, provide transportation, or participate in various activities.

Mental Health Association of the Capital Area
5135 Galaxie Drive
Suite 302 C
Jackson, MS 39206
(601) 982-4003

Contact: Alicia Thames

Provides a wide range of services for those affected by mental illness, including advocacy, a foster grandparent program, and a monthly newsletter. This agency needs volunteers, usually 16 or older, to answer phones, make copies, prepare mailings, and help with special events. Lunch and commutation expenses will be covered.

Mississippi Food Network
P.O. Box 411
Jackson, MS 39205
(601) 353-7286

Contact: Alan Henderson

Collects and distributes "distressed merchandise"—food whose packaging or appearance may be damaged. The items are carefully sorted, and any usable products are repackaged, cataloged, and made available to agencies and individuals in need of food. Volunteers can work either in the warehouse or in the office.

Mississippi Museum of Art
201 East Pascagoula
Jackson, MS 39201
(601) 960-1515

Contact: Anna Walker

Volunteer opportunities include clerking in the gift shop, playing the piano in the restaurant, working in the education department, and working on special events and projects in general.

Mynelle Gardens
4736 Clinton Boulevard
Jackson, MS 39209
(601) 960-1812

Contact: Fran Leber

Five acres of gardens and two homes available for tours. Volunteers needed to work in the new garden library and in the garden itself.

The Salvation Army
P.O. Box 448
Jackson, MS 39204
(601) 968-3999

Contact: Major David Singletary

Works with the homeless, drug addicts, unwed mothers, prisoners, the poor, children, and senior citizens to supply basic human necessities and counseling. Volunteers needed to work in the office and on special events.

Singing River Mental Health Services
4507 McArthur Street
Pascagoula, MS 39567
(601) 769-1793

Contact: Elizabeth Hudspeth

Provides marital and family counseling, children's services, alcohol and drug services, and outpatient treatment services. Volunteers needed to work in the offices.

Stewpot, Inc.
1100 West Capitol Street
Jackson, MS 39203
(601) 353-2759

Contact: Matt Devenney
Serves lunch daily to
those in need. Volunteers
needed during the meal,
in the office, and to help
with pickup of donated
food.

**The Warren County
Children's Shelter**
Route 6, Box 279
Vicksburg, MS 39180
(601) 634-0640
Contact: Anita Lefan or
 Susan Chatham
Provides many services

for children. Volunteering
involves some office
work, in addition to
kitchen duties, arts and
crafts, light cleaning, and
recreational activities.

Missouri

American Red Cross
211 West Armour
 Boulevard
Kansas City, MO 64111
(816) 931-8400

Contact: Karna Converse

Works to improve the
quality of human life,
enhance self-reliance and
concern for others, and
help people avoid,
prepare for, and cope
with disaster. Volunteers
are involved as members
of the disaster action
team or with other
services the Salvation
Army provides.

**Battered Women's
Shelter**
P.O. Box 27067
Kansas City, MO 64110
(816) 861-3460

Contact: Fran Cobb

Provides food, shelter,
transportation, court
advocacy,
housing-assistance
referrals, support groups,
counseling, and
employment information
for women who have
been victims of domestic
violence. Needs
volunteers for all of its
services, including
telephone hotlines.

**Good Neighbor for the
Elderly**
1900 Northeast
 Englewood Road
Kansas City, MO 64118
(816) 452-2553

Contact: Connie Brennan

Provides a variety of
programs and services
for the elderly.
Volunteers periodically
visit the elderly and
provide services and
companionship.

**Greater Kansas City
Greens**
P.O. Box 30353
4509 Walnut
Kansas City, MO 64111
(816) 753-7552

Contact: Gabriel Weeks

Grass-roots movement
that emphasizes political,
environmental, and
nonviolent action;
cooperative world order;
and self-reliance. Holds
monthly orientation
meetings. Volunteers
help mail newsletters,
send thank-you letters,
and work with group
workshops.

Harvesters
1811 North Topping
Kansas City, MO 64120
(816) 231-3173

Contact: Sherri Hooper
Acts as a food bank for
12 counties, collects
donated food, runs a
food drive for people in
need, runs a
prepared-food program,
and distributes food to
shelters. Volunteers help
collect, record, and
distribute donated food
items.

**Muscular Dystrophy
Association**
1301 Vandiver Drive
Suite U
Columbia, MO 65202
(314) 442-5154
Contact: Darrell Smith
Performs research into
the causes and cures of
different categories of
neuromuscular disease
and provides services for
patients with these
diseases. Needs
volunteers to assist with
special events,
fund-raising, and patient
services.

Nature Conservancy
2800 South Brentwood
 Boulevard
St. Louis, MO 63144
(314) 968-1105
Contact: Suzanne
 Greenley
Committed to finding,
protecting, and

maintaining biological communities, ecosytems, and endangered species around the world. By controlling land and water resources, the Conservancy is able to preserve the plants and animals that inhabit them. Volunteers needed for projects in the field and in the office.

Physicians' Home Health Network
619 North Providence
Columbia, MO 65203
(314) 449-0206

Contact: Mary Ann Speckhals or Judy Hubbard

Provides home health care. Needs helpers for the elderly and disabled. Volunteers assist with

errands, laundry, and shopping.

Teen Connection
1333 South 27th Street
Kansas City, MO 66106
(913) 677-2999

Contact: Lisa Castro

Has volunteer opportunities in six different areas. It particularly needs volunteers to work on its hotlines; volunteers do not need to be in an office, as calls are forwarded to them during their shift.

Transitional Housing Agency Services
1010 Fay Street
Columbia, MO 65201
(314) 443-0405

Contact: Michelle Cleaveland

Provides services for those in need. Volunteers help make supplies and furnishings for the apartments of the chronically mentally disabled.

The Whole Person, Inc.
6301 Rock Hill Road
Suite 305 E
Kansas City, MO 64131
(816) 361-0304

Contact: Shannon Jones

Provides peer counseling, personal-care assistance, technical assistance, support groups, a loan program for the disabled, and independent-living assistance. Prospective volunteers should request the newsletter.

Montana

Alliance for the Wild Rockies
Box 8731
Missoula, MT 59807
(406) 721-5420

Contact: Dan Funsch

A new group dedicated to preserving wilderness in the Wild Rockies Bioregion. Works hard at the local, state, and national levels to educate the public through slide shows, press articles, and a publication called *The Networkers*. Volunteers can work in their area of interest—some help out in the office, and others conduct research and

review forest service projects.

Alternative Energy Resources Organization
44 North Last Chance Gulch #9
Helena, MT 59601
(406) 443-7272

Contact: Al Kurki

Helps Montana food producers reduce their dependence on pesticides. Sponsors community task forces that work on conservation issues. Volunteers help organize literature in the resource library and work on

other projects that come up.

Big Brothers/Big Sisters
405 West Park
Butte, MT 59701
(406) 782-9644

Contact: Phyllis Costello

Seeks to match young boys and girls from single-parent homes with positive role models. Each volunteer is interviewed, evaluated, and given a training program. Big Brothers and Big Sisters spend time together in recreational and educational activities.

March of Dimes Foundation
7 East Airport Road
Billings, MT 59105
(406) 252-7480

Contact: Retta Benner

Dedicated to the prevention of birth defects, low birth weight, and infant deaths. Volunteers help with office mailings, phone work, and office duties.

Montana Nature Conservancy
P.O. Box 258
Helena, MT 59624
(406) 443-0303

Contact: Brian Kahn

Committed to finding, protecting, and maintaining biological communities, ecosystems, and endangered species around the world. By controlling land and water resources, the

Conservancy is able to preserve the plants and animals that inhabit them. The Conservancy maintains a 40,000-acre sanctuary along the front range of the Rocky Mountains. Volunteers needed in the field and in the office, depending on skills and interests.

The Salvation Army
P.O. Box 1307
Bozeman, MT 59771
(406) 586-5813

Contact: Don Bowman

Works with the homeless, drug addicts, unwed mothers, prisoners, poor children, and senior citizens to supply basic human necessities and counseling. Volunteers help with all services.

Special Olympics
3300 Third Street
Northeast
Great Falls, MT 59404
(406) 791-2368

Contact: Ann Waitt

Provides sports training and athletic competition in a variety of Olympic-type sports for children and adults with mental retardation. Volunteers serve as coaches, trainers, and "huggers" for athletes and help with special events.

St. Vincent de Paul
500 Central Avenue West
Great Falls, MT 59403
(406) 761-0870

Contact: Alan Reavley

Provides services for the economically disadvantaged. Teenage volunteers sort donated clothes, make soup, do yard work, and work in the thrift store.

Nebraska

American Diabetes Association
2730 South 114 Street
Omaha, NE 68144
(402) 333-5556

Contact: Lynne Senn

Seeks to improve standards of treatment and promote a cure for diabetes. Volunteers help with bulk mailings and special events and assist with overall clerical duties.

American Red Cross
3838 Dewey Avenue
Omaha, NE 68105
(402) 341-2723

Contact: Joan Jensen

Works to improve the quality of human life, enhance self-reliance and concern for others, and helps people avoid, prepare for, and cope with emergencies. Volunteers help assemble blood collection bags,

serve beverages and snacks to donors, and assist with clerical work and bulk mailings.

Arthritis Foundation
4600 Valley Road
Suite 310
Lincoln, NE 68510
(402) 486-3266

Contact: Meg Johnson

An organization whose goal is to support research into the prevention and cure of arthritis and to improve the quality of life of those with arthritis. Volunteers help with special events (such as golf tournaments and parties), overall fund-raising, and office assistance.

Eastern Nebraska Council on Aging
885 South 72nd Street
Omaha, NE 68114
(402) 444-6444

Contact: Joyce Luben, 444-6584

Works to keep the over age 60 population independent in their own homes. Volunteer opportunities available for friendship with the elderly—visiting, letter writing, reading, and accompanying the elderly on walks. People also needed to work in the public information department and for holiday meal delivery. Minimum age 14.

Girls Incorporated of Omaha
3706 Lake Street
Omaha, NE 68111
(402) 457-4676

Contact: Volunteer coordinator

Provides recreational, tutoring, and self-esteem-building services and a variety of educational programs for girls ages 6 through 18. Volunteers teach or coach volleyball, soccer, softball, or basketball. Some sports experience is required, along with the ability to interact well with this age group.

Greater Omaha Association for Retarded Citizens
3610 Dodge Street
Suite 101
Omaha, NE 68131
(402) 346-5220

Contact: Dena Launderville

Sponsors a variety of programs for retarded individuals. Volunteers are matched for friendship with mentally retarded teenagers (match is based on interests, age, and home location). On-the-job training is provided; minimum age 13.

March of Dimes
1618 L Street
Lincoln, NE 68508
(402) 476-0117

Contact: Mindy Rupprecht

Dedicated to the prevention of birth defects, low birth weight, and infant deaths. Volunteers help with office mailings, phone work, and assist with special events.

Muscular Dystrophy Association
9233 Bedford Avenue
Omaha, NE 68134
(402) 571-1885

Contact: Rebecca Scott

Performs research into the causes of and cures for different categories of neuromuscular disease and provides services for patients with these diseases. Volunteers help with dance marathons, bowl-a-thons, telethons,

and summer camp. Minimum age 16.

National Kidney Foundation
2212 North 91 Plaza
Omaha, NE 68134
(402) 397-9234

Contact: Marie Applebee

Seeks to eradicate diseases of the kidney and urinary tract and makes grants to kidney disease researchers. Provides services to patients with kidney disease. Volunteer opportunities include clerical work, mailings, counting, and helping with special events.

Nebraska Nature Conservancy
418 South 10th
Omaha, NE 68102
(402) 342-0282

Contact: Jane Moody

Committed to finding, protecting, and maintaining biological communities, ecosystems, and endangered species around the world. By controlling land and water resources, the Conservancy is able to preserve the plants and animals that inhabit them. Volunteers needed to work in the office and in the field, according to skills and interests.

Nebraska Special Olympics, Inc.
P.O. Box 7569
Omaha, NE 68107
(402) 731-5007

Contact: Raeanna Larson or Margaret Lageschulte

Provides sports training and athletic competition in a variety of

Olympic-type sports for children and adults with mental retardation. Volunteers help the mentally retarded in all aspects of their sports competition—coaching, hugging, inspiring, providing friendship. Minimum age 12.

Omaha Children's Museum
500 South 20th Street
Omaha, NE 68102
(402) 342-6164

Contact: Lindy Bull

Has art exhibits and special programs for children. Volunteer opportunities available for exhibit workers and guides. Minimum age 12.

Urban League of Nebraska
3022–24 North 24th Street
Omaha, NE 68111
(402) 455-6571

Contact: Chris Wiley

A learning center for low-income individuals. Volunteer opportunities available to tutor young children in reading, math, and computers. Minimum age 16.

Nevada

American Heart Association
1135 Terminal Way
Suite 105
Reno, NV 89502
(702) 322-7064

Contact: Vicki Erickson

A health organization with over 2 million volunteers that raises money for scientific research on heart disease. Volunteers work in the office to update mailing lists, file, type, answer telephones, and help with inventory.

Children's Miracle Network
2040 West Charleston Boulevard
Las Vegas, NV 89102
(702) 383-2388

Contact: Colleen Courtney

Holds special events to raise money for the pediatric ward of University Hospital. Volunteers help as runners for the hosts of

telethons and assist as needed with other events such as duck races and a 5K run.

F.I.S.H. (Friends in Service Helping)
232 South Tenth
Elko, NV 89801
(702) 738-3038

Contact: Dee Waters

Provides special services for those in need, including travelers in the Elko area whose vehicles have broken down or run out of gas. Also runs a thrift shop for local residents. Volunteers help with travelers' aid, sort donated items for the thrift store, and help with fund-raising projects.

National Easter Seal Society
1455 East Tropicana
Suite 660
Las Vegas, NV 89119
(702) 739-7771

Contact: Trish Marsh

Identifies the needs of people with disabilities

and provides them with appropriate rehabilitaton. Volunteers don't have one-on-one contact with clients, as those individuals work solely with the speech and occupational therapists. However, volunteers do work on a number of special events, such as golf tournaments and bike-a-thons, and they also help with large mailings.

Help Them Walk Again Foundation
5300 West Charleston
Las Vegas, NV 89102
(702) 878-8360

Contact: JoAnne Toadvine

Provides recreational services for victims of spinal cord injuries. Volunteers help mainly with special events such as the Western Hoedown Banquet, an annual fund-raiser. Volunteers work one-on-one with the clients.

National Kidney Foundation
4100 Boulder Highway
Las Vegas, NV 89121
(702) 456-0026

Contact: Gary Davis

Seeks to eradicate diseases of the kidney and urinary tract, and makes grants to kidney disease researchers. Provides services to patients with kidney disease.

Washo Association for Retarded Citizens
790 Sutro Street
Reno, NV 89512
(702) 333-8253

Contact: Leon Merchant

Serves to help the mentally retarded function in society through numerous self-help training programs. Volunteers can either work directly with the retarded individuals or can help with office administration.

New Hampshire

Boys and Girls Club
555 Union Street
Manchester, NH 03104
(603) 625-5031

Contact: Ken Neil

Seeks "to promote the health, social, educational, vocational, and character development of young people." Volunteers work on projects depending on their interests, from arts and crafts to coaching a sports team.

Clamshell Alliance
P.O. Box 734
Concord, NH 03301
(603) 224-4163

Contact: Billy Donovan or Paul Gunter

Opposes nuclear energy; goal is to stop construction of nuclear energy plants in New England. In addition to canvassing, which is paid by commission (40 percent), volunteers work in the office, organize meetings and events, work on the newsletter, or put together pamphlets and other literature regarding nuclear energy. Volunteers within a 10-mile radius of the Seabrook Nuclear Facility distribute leaflets along the shore.

National Easter Seal Society
555 Auburn Street
Manchester, NH 03103
(603) 623-8863

Contact: Debbie Weymouth

Identifies the needs of people with disabilities and provides them with appropriate rehabilitation. Volunteers help with mailings and other office activities and help organize and staff fund-raising events and parties.

The Visiting Nurse Association
194 Concord Street
Manchester, NH 03104
(603) 622-3781

Contact: Kim Williams

Sends nurses to sick individuals' bedsides and runs a day-care center in the Greater Manchester area. High school–age volunteers generally don't have contact with the children or the patients but help with office work (filing, typing, photocopying).

William J. Moore Regional Services
132 Titus Avenue
Manchester, NH 03103
(603) 668-5423

Contact: Bob Mazzola

An agency for the mentally and physically handicapped, from birth through adult. Sponsors day programs, workshops, and recreational activities. Volunteers help with all aspects of the organization, from office help to one-on-one contact with clients.

New Jersey

American Cancer Society
20 Mercer Street
Hackensack, NJ 07601
(201) 343-2222
Contact: Frances Lando
Dedicated to eliminating cancer as a major health problem through research, education, and service. Volunteers help with special events such as the George Washington Bridge Bike-a-thon and assist with mailings and office work.

Boys and Girls Club
P.O. Box 1748
317 North Pennsylvania Avenue
Atlantic City, NJ 08404
(609) 347-2697
Contact: Jacqueline Preston
Seeks "to promote the health, social, educational, vocational, and character development of young people." Volunteers work based on their interests and skills. For example, the computer literate can teach a computer class. Other options include coaching sports or helping with such indoor activities as arts and crafts.

Camp Fatima of New Jersey
P.O. Box 612
Livingston, NJ 07039
(201) 992-5251
Contact: Beth Duthie
The state's only all-volunteer camp for the handicapped. Sixty-five handicapped individuals per week (for the month of August) participate in recreation, arts and crafts, games, and leisure activities. Volunteer counselors work one-on-one with the handicapped. For those who are interested in special education, this is a good opportunity to get some first-hand experience. Minimum age 17.

Cape May County Park Zoo
Route 9, Pine Lane
Cape May Courthouse, NJ 08210
(609) 465-5271
Contact: Phil Judyski or George Konopka
A zoo located within the county park that provides a number of exhibits and educational programs. Volunteers can act as junior zoo keepers and work in their area of interest, such as with the primates or cats.

Hi Tops
21 Wiggins Street
Princeton, NJ 08540
(609) 683-5155
Contact: Sandi Mahmet
An educational program on sexuality for adolescents. A council of teen volunteers is trained in peer leadership and sex education in order to give workshops to their peers on such topics as sexually transmitted diseases and contraception.

Hyacinth Foundation
103 Bayard Street
New Brunswick, NJ 08901
(908) 246-0204
Contact: Karl Manger
Provides people with AIDS with buddies, support groups, advocacy, counseling, and legal services. Serves the counties of southern and central New Jersey, as well as Pennsylvania and Delaware. Volunteers can provide much needed office support or go through training to become a volunteer who works closely with a person with AIDS.

James Street Neighborhood House
c/o Protestant Community Centers
19 James Street
Newark, NJ 07102
(201) 621-2273
Contact: Tony Peele or Dorothy Knauer
This center for Newark residents holds programs in art, music, recreation, and drama and sponsors trips and cultural activities. After-school hours are flexible. Most volunteers make a six-month commitment.

New Jersey Buddies
P.O. Box 413
Teaneck, NJ 07666
(201) 837-8126
Contact: Frank Smith
Conducts fund-raising for AIDS research, provides a newsletter, a hotline, and one-on-one buddies

for people with AIDS. A seven-week training session is required of all volunteers. Volunteers are matched up with a person with AIDS in Bergen County.

New Jersey Nature Conservancy
17 Fairmount Road
P.O. Box 181
Pottersville, NJ
  07979-0181
(201) 439-3007
Contact: Linda Range
Committed to finding, protecting, and maintaining biological communities, ecosystems,

and endangered species around the world. By controlling land and water resources, the Conservancy is able to preserve the plants and animals that inhabit them.

New Jersey Special Olympics
242 Old New Brunswick
  Road
Piscataway, NJ 08854
(908) 562-1500
Contact: Brenda
  Goldman
Provides sports training and athletic competition in a variety of

Olympic-type sports for children and adults with mental retardation. Volunteers act as coaches, chaperones, and friends to athletes at all sporting events.

One to One New Jersey
494 Broad Street
Newark, NJ 07102
(201) 242-1142
Contact: Brenda Beavers
Provides youth services, such as mentoring and development, for youth at risk. Teenage volunteers are mentors to younger children.

New Mexico

American Cancer Society
839 Paseo de Peralta
Santa Fe, NM 87501
(505) 988-5548
Contact: Mattie
  Santistevan
Dedicated to eliminating cancer as a major health problem through research, education, and service. Volunteers stamp brochures, keep the stockroom updated, work with files, and help with special events.

Animal Humane Association
615 Virginia, Southeast
Albuquerque, NM 87108
(505) 255-5523
Contact: Evelyn Blissard
Works for the rights of animals; runs an

adoption program and a thrift shop. Volunteers become familiar with the goals of the organizaton, help answer the public's questions, work at the front desk with the adoption programs, and help in the thrift shop.

Commission on the Status of Women
4001 Indian School Road
  Northeast, Suite 220
Albuquerque, NM 87110
(505) 841-4662
Contact: Yolanda Roybal
A referral and advocacy service for women that sponsors support groups and conferences. Volunteers help with all administrative and planning services.

New Mexico Environmental Law Center
1709 Paseo de Peralta
Santa Fe, NM 87501
(505) 989-9022
Contact: Conci Bokum
A public interest law firm dedicated to protecting New Mexico's natural environment through litigation, public education, and awareness. Provides legal services without charge to individuals and organizations for environmental causes; publishes a newsletter for the public. The Center uses volunteer attorneys and paralegals; however, there is a need for nonprofessional volunteer help as well to

work on the newsletter, fund-raising, and special projects.

New Mexico Nature Conservancy

107 Cienega Street
Santa Fe, NM 87501
(505) 988-3867
Contact: Bill Waldman

This organization is committed to finding, protecting, and maintaining biological communities, ecosystems, and endangered species around the world. By controlling land and water resources, the Conservancy is able to preserve the plants and animals that inhabit them. Volunteers needed both in the office and in the field, according to interests and skills.

Santa Fe Community Foundation

P.O. Box 1827
Santa Fe, NM 87504
(505) 988-9715
Contact: Lorraine Goldman or Margaret Gray

Sponsors community activities and tutoring programs for children. Also at this address is Santa Fe Partners in Education, through which volunteers can serve either as tutors in the Partners in Education program or as office assistants (data entry, typing, filing).

New York

ACCORD, A Center for Dispute Resolution, Inc.

The Cutler House
834 Front Street
Binghamton, NY 13905
(607) 724-5153
Contact: Karen Monaghan

A private, nonprofit community dispute-resolution center. Mediators are trained to assist people in identifying and focusing on a problem in order to find a solution. Volunteers act as mediators or help in the office.

Action for Older Persons, Inc.

144 Washington Street
Binghamton, NY 13901
(607) 722-1251
Contact: Cherie Morrison Davis or Natalie Thompson

Provides many services for older people. AOP volunteers work in the center on a variety of projects. Good Neighbors visit isolated elderly people in their homes once a week to share friendship and similar interests. Positions are available as an AOP volunteer and as a Good Neighbor; training is provided for both.

Adirondack Nature Conservancy

P.O. Box 188
Elizabethtown, NY 12932
(518) 873-2610
Contact: Timothy Barnett

Committed to finding, protecting, and maintaining biological communities, ecosystems, and endangered species around the world. By controlling land and water resources, the Conservancy is able to preserve the plants and animals that inhabit them.

Alley Pond Environmental Center

228-06 Northern Boulevard
Douglaston, NY 11363
(718) 229-4000
Contact: Irene Scheid

A nature center that offers trails and houses small animals in cages, and provides educational workshops and after-school programs. Volunteers help teachers; work with small animals; maintain trails, trees, and wildlife; and assist with natural science research.

Alzheimer's Association

Southern Tier Chapter
Box 562 Union Station
Endicott, NY
(607) 785-6926
Contact: Jenny Pasquale, 785-7852

Serves Alzheimer's victims and their families through educational programs, information, family support groups, and a newsletter. Volunteers work with the staff and assist with a variety of clerical tasks, including mailing lists and the quarterly newsletter.

American Cancer Society
Broome County Unit
57 Front Street
Binghamton, NY 13905
(607) 722-6471
Contact: Marjorie Schreier
Dedicated to eliminating cancer as a major health problem through research, education, and service. Volunteers can help with office duties, fund-raising, and special events.

American Cancer Society
Tioga County Unit
23 Lake Street
Owego, NY 13827
(607) 687-1255
Contact: Karen Koskela
Volunteers needed to organize and publicize events and fund-raisers, to act as drivers, and to help in the office.

American Civil Liberties Union (ACLU)
132 West 43rd Street
New York, NY 10036
(212) 944-9800
Contact: Chu Moy
A national organization whose purpose is to protect Americans' rights to freedom of expression, belief, and association and to fairness, privacy, and equal treatment before the law. Both the main office and local

branches need volunteers to help with mailings, fund-raising campaigns, and promotional efforts.

American Red Cross
Building 7, 3rd Floor
75 Vanderbilt Avenue
Staten Island, NY 10304
(718) 447-7160
Contact: Gladys Schweiger
Works to improve the quality of human life, enhance self-reliance and concern for others, and help people avoid, prepare for, and cope with emergencies. The Red Cross seeks student volunteers to work in hospitals and blood banks, to do clerical work, to receive first-aid training, and to help with Saferides and fund-raising and in the office.

Boys' and Girls' Brigade, Inc.
P.O. Box 1055
Woodside, NY 11377
(718) 639-9827
Contact: Edward Fowley
Provides recreational, educational, and social activities for children from 6 to 13. Volunteers help with the events and with the annual food drive and fund-raising projects.

Brooklyn Children's Museum
145 Brooklyn Avenue
Brooklyn, NY 11213
(718) 735-4400
Contact: Laverne Shipp
Houses hands-on exhibits for kids from preschool through junior high.

Exhibits include an artificial stream that runs through the museum, a greenhouse, a bone yard with human and animal bones, a music studio, an early learning center, and more. Volunteers help with informational tours and assist with exhibits and special events.

City Volunteer Corps
838 Broadway, 3rd Floor
New York, NY 10003
(212) 475-6444
Contact: Anne Williamson
Volunteer teams work on projects such as tutoring, renovation of housing, care of homebound elderly and blind, supervision in shelters, and conservation work in parks and on beaches. Volunteers work on a full-time basis. Minimum age 17.

Congress of Racial Equality (CORE)
2111 Nostrand Avenue
Brooklyn, NY 11210
(718) 434-3580
Contact: Roy Innis
Works toward true equality for all people throughout the world and sponsors programs in community development, substance abuse, housing, and education. Volunteers help with all activities at the local level and can help in the Summer Youth Program.

Coalition for the Homeless
105 East 22nd Street
New York, NY 10010
(212) 460-8110

Contact: Ceci Scott, 996-4166

Provides food, shelter, advocacy, rental assistance, and many more services for the homeless in New York City. Volunteers serve in all capacities, from food distributors to shelter monitors to office volunteers to home visitors.

Emmaus House/Harlem

2027 Lexington Avenue
New York, NY 10035
(212) 410-6006

Contact: Mamie Moore

"A center where homeless people build new lives through Work, Community, and Service." Volunteers work with the homeless in the offices, the night shelter, the kitchen, a woodwork shop, and an AIDS ministry. There is a need for an office typist, cook/kitchen manager, fund-raiser/proposal writer, and carpenter/woodworker.

Food for Survival

Hunts Point Co-op
 Market
Building F
Bronx, NY 10474
(212) 991-4300

Contact: Jasmine Mendez

Distributes slightly damaged canned goods to soup kitchens and shelters throughout the New York area. Volunteers help process canned goods that will go to the needy. Office positions also available.

God's Love We Deliver

P.O. Box 1776
Old Chelsea Station
New York, NY
 10113-0954
(212) 865-4900

Contact: Greg Lettau

Provides homebound people with AIDS with free four-course gourmet meals four days a week and on holidays. Volunteers deliver meals to clients, help with food preparation, and provide office support.

Green Chimneys Children's Services, Inc.

Putnam Lake Road
Brewster, NY 10509
(914) 279-2996
(212) 892-6810

Contact: Lillian Roode

An agency dedicated to basic education and daily living skills for children and adults so as to strengthen their emotional health and well-being. Programs involve day camps, horse camps, a farm center, a swimming pool, and much more. Volunteers work in most recreational and educational programs, according to their skills and interests.

Laubach Literacy International

P.O. Box 131
Syracuse, NY 13210
(315) 422-9121

Contact: Volunteer
 coordinator

Laubach volunteers teach about 60,000 adults per year. Resource center has information about education and illiteracy. Volunteers help with tutoring, information distribution, and office support.

The Nature Conservancy—Long Island Chapter

P.O. Box 2694
Sag Harbor, NY 11963
(516) 725-2936

Contact: Sara Davison

This organization is committed to finding, protecting, and maintaining biological communities, ecosystems, and endangered species around the world. By controlling land and water resources, the Conservancy is able to preserve the plants and animals that inhabit them. Volunteers needed in the field and in the office.

New York Special Olympics Program

211 East 43rd Street, 12th
 Floor
New York, NY 10017
(212) 661-3963

Contact: Karen Green

Provides sports training and athletic competition in a variety of Olympic-type sports for children and adults with physical handicaps or mental retardation. Volunteers train as coaches or provide moral support during various sports activities.

Open Door Student Exchange

250 Fulton Avenue
P.O. Box 71
Hempstead, NY 11551
(516) 486-7330

Contact: Howard
Berthental
Cooperates with
thirty-four countries to
bring international
students to the U.S. and
send American students
abroad. Volunteers help
with office duties
pertaining to the student
exchanges, a good way
to get exposure to
international programs.

Project P.A.W.
127 Bevier Street
Binghamton, NY 13904
(607) 724-2241
Contact: E. Wickizer or
D. Kocan
A low-cost neutering

program for animals of
low-income families.
Sponsors an adopt-a-pet
program for cats and
dogs and runs a thrift
store to raise funds for
animal programs.
Volunteers work with the
animals as kennel
assistants—grooming the
animals, cleaning cages,
and working on other
animal-related chores.

**Staten Island Center
for Independent Living**
150 Walker Street
Staten Island, NY 10302
(718) 720-9016

Contact: Dorothy Doran
Provides aid and services
to individuals with any
kind of disability, with an
emphasis on helping
them to become
self-sufficient and
independent. Volunteers
can provide such services
as reading to visually
impaired persons, and
they can provide office
support.

North Carolina

American Red Cross
Asheville Area Chapter
100 Edgewood Road
Asheville, NC 28804
(704) 258-3888
Contact: Christi Hurd
Works to improve the
quality of human life,
enhance self-reliance and
concern for others, and
help people avoid,
prepare for, and cope
with emergencies.
Volunteers needed as
blood pressure screeners,
canteen assistants, and
registration desk
assistants at blood drives;
they also assist with
office mailings and
telephones.

**Greensboro Mental
Health Association**
338 North Elm Street
Suite 303
Greensboro, NC 27401
(919) 373-1402

Contact: Patti Hanna
Seeks to educate the
public about the issues
concerning mental
health. Volunteers can
help with special projects
and educational
programs.

Habitat for Humanity
9 Biltmore Avenue
P.O. Box 18058
Asheville, NC 28814
(704) 251-5702

Contact: Joan Cooper
Helps to eliminate
homelessness through
the construction of
decent shelter for the
economically
disadvantaged. This
branch also has an outlet
store. Volunteers help at
on-site Habitat housing
projects or sell furniture
and other items in the
outlet store.

**Humane Society of
Winston-Salem**
P.O. Box 15605
61 Miller Street
Winston-Salem, NC 27113
(919) 721-1303
Contact: Ashley
Doughton
A shelter and pound for
animals without homes.
The Humane Society's
mission is to promote
respect for animal life.
Volunteers care for and
play with the animals
and help keep the
animals clean.

Mountain Geri-Care
P.O. Box 848
Asheville, NC 28802
(704) 258-1183
Contact: Jim Lenhart
Adult care center that
provides numerous
recreational activities for
senior citizens.
Volunteers needed as

senior citizen aides, to assist the elderly with leisure activities and meals.

North Carolina Museum of Life and Sciences

433 Murray Avenue
Durham, NC 27704
(919) 220-5429

Contact: Ida Phillips

Houses a nature center with native animals from North Carolina, an outdoor music center, a farm yard with domestic animals, a discovery room with hands-on exhibits, a "bodytech" center that explains the way the body works, a maze, a geology exhibit, and more. Volunteers work mainly in the discovery room, located in the nature center, helping with the hands-on exhibits.

North Carolina Nature Conservancy

Carr Mill Mall, Suite 223
Carrboro, NC 27510
(919) 967-7007

Contact: Ida Phillips

This organization is committed to finding, protecting, and maintaining biological communities, ecosystems, and endangered species

around the world. By controlling land and water resources, the Conservancy is able to preserve the plants and animals that inhabit them. Volunteers needed in the office and in the field, according to skills and interests.

Presbyterian Peacemaking Center

Box 5635
Raleigh, NC 27650
(919) 834-5184

Contact: Alan Proctor

Affiliated with North Caroline State University, a ministerial organization with peacemaking as its major concern. Though most volunteers are college students, high school students can help with publicity and administration.

Samaritan Soup Kitchen

1243 Patterson Avenue
Winston-Salem, NC 27101
(919) 748-1962

Contact: Diane Gainous

An interdenominational Christian ministry that stresses acceptance and commitment in its volunteers, who work in the preparation of food, service, and clean-up

Sycamore Center

301 East Washington Street, Suite 101
Greensboro, NC 27401
(919) 333-6860

Contact: Leslie Jackson

Operates a 24-hour crisis service to help with issues such as rape and other physical abuse, spouse abuse, AIDS, substance abuse, and suicide. Volunteers who work on the switchboard crisis line undergo a 9-week training program that meets once or twice per week. Other volunteers needed in the office and on a project basis.

Western North Carolina AIDS Project

P.O. Box 2411
Asheville, NC 28802
(704) 252-7489

Contact: Elaine Ferguson

The project provides a number of services and educational programs for people with AIDS or anyone interested in AIDS education. Volunteers work in a number of capacities, including in the office and in helping to put together programs. The buddy program matches volunteers with clients and requires 20 hours of training.

North Dakota

AID, Inc.

314 West Main Street
P.O. Box 922
Mandan, ND 58554

(701) 663-1274

Contact: Lois Walz

A private, nonprofit agency that helps

lower-income individuals and families with their rent, utilities, food, or other concerns.

Volunteers work in the thrift store or food pantry and help with holiday dinners and other projects.

The Center for Adolescent Development

P.O. Box 7370
Bismarck, ND 58502
(701) 258-9945

Contact: Patty Silk-Hartze

A drug- and alcohol-abuse prevention program for adolescents. Volunteers lead workshops and small-group discussions, develop substance-abuse prevention programs, and plan activities.

Dakota Boys Ranch Thrift Store

2017 DeMers Avenue
Grand Forks, ND 58201
(701) 775-7805

Contact: Cindy Benson

A thrift store whose proceeds go to a nearby Boys Ranch for juvenile delinquents. Proceeds help to purchase books and educational materials for the boys. Volunteers needed to organize shelves, unload merchandise, and hang or shelve clothing as needed. Some counter work is required.

Grand Forks City Mission

420 Division Avenue
Grand Forks, ND 58201
(701) 772-6609

Contact: Dwain
Steinkuehler

Provides food and shelter services for the needy. Volunteers needed to help sort, fold, stock, and hang up merchandise. Volunteers should like working with people.

Humane Society of Grand Forks

Route #2, Box 48
Grand Forks, ND 58203
(701) 775-3732
(701) 775-0858

Contact: Cathy Snodgrass

A shelter and pound for animals without homes. The Humane Society's mission is to promote respect for animal life. Volunteers distribute pet toys, walk dogs, and maintain, groom, and play with the cats and dogs. On-the-job training provided.

North Dakota School for the Blind

500 Stanford Road
Grand Forks, ND 58203
(701) 777-4144

Contact: Janice
Sowakonos

Volunteers needed to assist teachers and work

one-on-one with blind campers. Office assistants also needed to scan records and books and perform computer date entry. No prior computer skills necessary. Volunteers should be of junior high school age or older.

The Village Family Service Center

415 East Avenue A
Bismarck, ND 58501
(701) 255-1165

Contact: Kathy File

Matches up boys and girls with an older role model. Volunteers work in a big brother/big sister capacity, spending time with their new "siblings," taking them on such outings as the zoo or the movies.

Youthworks

311 North Washington
Bismarck, ND 58501
(701) 255-6909

Contact: Lynette Bosch

Has thirteen programs for youth at risk. Programs include runaway, emergency shelter, and crisis intervention. Volunteers work as counselors and friends to high-risk peers.

Ohio

American Cancer Society

3372 Central Parkway
Cincinnati, OH 45225
(513) 559-1050

Contact: Vicki Reese

Dedicated to eliminating cancer as a major health problem through research,

education, and service. Special-events volunteers and office assistants needed for mailings, typing, and telephone work.

Association for the Developmentally Disabled
1395 West Fifth Avenue
Columbus, OH 43212
(614) 486-4361
Contact: Nancy Tela
Runs group homes and provides a variety of services for disabled individuals. Volunteers help with creative programs and special events. Minimum age 12.

Battered Women's Shelter
P.O. Box 9074
Akron, OH 44305
(216) 836-7404
Contact: Sarabeth Mahusky
A shelter facility and advocacy group for women. Runs a hotline, a legal advocacy program, and other support services for women. Volunteers not skilled in public speaking or legal advocacy do general work in child care, housekeeping, transportation, or donation sorting.

Big Brothers/Big Sisters Residential Camp
2104 Tuller Street
Columbus, OH 43201
(614) 294-4423
Contact: Dave Schirner
Open camp for young children. Volunteers act as counselors-in-training, assisting with hiking, camping, and other recreational activities. Minimum age 15.

Booth House/Salvation Army
624 South Main Street
Dayton, OH 45402
(513) 228-8210
Contact: Jane Benner
An emergency shelter for homeless men. Volunteers provide overall assistance with clerical work, help serve meals, and help social workers with paperwork.

Community Drug Board
725 East Market Street
Akron, OH 44305
(216) 996-5110
Contact: Kristen Baysinger
A drug-prevention and drug-intervention program that holds camps and seminars for both young people and adults. Project Panda, a summer camp with the goal of drug prevention, uses a volunteer youth staff. Volunteers must have attended the camp for one previous summer. Minimum age is 11. Child-care volunteers (minimum age 13) are needed in the day-care center.

CYO Recreational Program for Disabled Youth
404 Elbon Avenue
Akron, OH 44306-1500
(216) 773-0426
Contact: Tricia Hunt
Sponsors programs and services for disabled youth. Volunteer groundskeepers, student aides, and recreational

counselors needed. Minimum age 16.

Friends Disaster Service
241 Keenan Road
Peninsula, OH 44264
(216) 650-4975
Contact: Dean Johnson
Volunteer group of individuals who work within the Quaker ethic to provide cleanup and restoration services to communities devastated by natural disasters.

Good Samaritan Hunger Center
P.O. Box 5753
Akron, OH 44372
(216) 864-8520
Contact: Marjory Norman
Provides services for those in need. Volunteers serve, distribute, and cleanup food at shelter site or prepare food at kitchen sites. Prefer age 16 and above.

Happy Canine Helpers
16277 Montgomery Road
Johnstown, OH 43031
(614) 965-2204
Contact: Linda Allaby-Bidwell
Trains and cares for dogs that will eventually assist people with physical disabilities. Volunteers help with everything from cleaning the kennels and feeding the dogs to answering the phone. A volunteer who works on a regular basis can get involved in the actual training process.

Toward Independence
46 South Detroit Street
Xenia, OH 45385
(513) 426-9542

Contact: Pat Thoerner

Provides housing and support services for mentally retarded persons. Volunteers spend time with the residents and help them with their activities.

United Cerebral Palsy and Services for the Handicapped
326 Locust Street
Akron, OH 44302
(216) 762-9755

Contact: Cheryl Ford

Provides a large number of services and programs for the handicapped, such as an employment service, in-home and out-of-home care, and

transportation. Volunteers work one-on-one with the handicapped on most of these programs.

YWCA Shelter Services
141 West Third Street
Dayton, OH 45402
(513) 461-5550

Contact: Carolyn Osborn

Provides the needy with "anything they would get at home," such as clothing, food, shelter, legal referrals, educational groups, and personal-growth seminars. Volunteers help in many ways, including child care, shelter maintenance, and picking up donations. Minimum age 15.

Western Reserve Girl Scout Council
108 Fir Hill
Akron, OH 44304
(216) 376-6876

Contact: Jean Hinkson

Girl Scouts gives girls the opportunity to understand and take action on personal, community, and global issues and a chance to make friends and develop their leadership capabilities. Girl Scouts get involved with many community service projects, but those who do not participate as Girl Scouts can volunteer for clerical work in the offices. Minimum age 13.

Oklahoma

Brass Ring Society of Oklahoma
2121 South Columbia
#LL1
Tulsa, OK 74114-3512
(918) 747-0200

Contact: Leanna Mangum

Grants wishes to terminally ill children. The Society is a very small organization and does not regularly use volunteers; however, from time to time office help is needed. The most frequent type of volunteer work by students is fund-raising with school groups. Some classes sponsor candy sales, dances, pizza parties, and other such events to raise money.

Center for the Physically Limited
815 South Utica
Tulsa, OK 74104
(918) 584-8607

Contact: Beth Venus

Provides recreational programs and exercise facilities for physically challenged children, young adults, and older adults. Volunteers provide a variety of services, including working one-on-one with handicapped individuals and assisting them in activities at the Center.

Gateway to Thrift
113 North Main
Broken Arrow, OK 74012
(918) 251-4683

Contact: Camelia Baker

A thrift store run by the Gateway Foundation, which provides services to the mentally handicapped. Volunteers work directly with customers, as well as sort, price, and arrange donated items. Volunteers also needed at the Gateway Foundation.

Habitat for Humanity—Tulsa
76 North Zunis
Tulsa, OK 74110
(918) 582-5108

Contact: Jim Robinson

Helps to fight homelessness through the construction of decent shelter for the economically disadvantaged. Either builds homes from scratch or renovates existing structures. Volunteer needs range from general cleanup to skilled labor, as well as clerical assistance.

March of Dimes
5147 B South Harvard
Tulsa, OK 74135
(918) 742-0333
Contact: Kathy Brown
Dedicated to the prevention of birth defects, low birth weight, and infant deaths. Volunteers help with fund-raisers, such as the March of Dimes WalkAmerica, including mailings and publicity.

Menno House Repair
504 Northeast Sixteenth Street
Oklahoma City, OK 73104
(405) 232-6277

Contact: Volunteer coordinator

Provides home repair services for low-income families, the elderly, or the handicapped. Volunteers help with roofing, weatherization, carpentry and remodeling, and minor plumbing.

Up with Trees
2435 South Peoria
Tulsa, OK 74114
(918) 747-4219
(918) 446-TREE

Contact: Sid Patterson

Volunteers plant and maintain trees along highways in the Tulsa area. The trees are "sponsored" by organizations, which each receive a highway sign with their name on

it. Volunteers also help to make those signs.

Ye Old Farm Therapeutic Riding
27560 East 77th Street
Broken Arrow, OK 74014
(918) 357-3622

Contact: Melinda Stevenson

Provides riding therapy for children with physical and mental disabilities. Volunteers can help in all aspects of grooming and caring for the horses and help lead the horses when the clients arrive. Volunteers with any experience working with people who have disabilities can work as spotters.

Oregon

Cascade AIDS Project
408 Southwest Second
Suite 412
Portland, OR 97204
(503) 223-5907

Contact: Ronnie Pacini

Provides services for persons with AIDS, including a hotline, a pal program, and various educational programs. Volunteers work in many capacities, and hours are

flexible. Training for the hotline and the pal program is required.

Food For Lane County
255 Madison
Eugene, OR 97402
(503) 343-2822
Contact: Freddie Tryk
A warehouse that stores donated food goods to be distributed to the needy. Volunteers sort the items and bag them

into smaller quantities for distribution. Large groups of volunteers welcome.

Meadowood Springs Speech Camp
P.O. Box 1025
Pendleton, OR 97801
(503) 276-2752
Contact: Amy Veliz
A residential camp for children with speech or hearing impairments. Volunteers are placed

wherever they are needed most, usually in the activities program in which they act as supervisors during the indoor and outdoor activities. Volunteers work for one week and are provided with room and board. Minimum age 16.

Native Forest Council
P.O. Box 2171
Eugene, OR 97402
(503) 688-2600

Contact: Markus Casale

An educational organization devoted to making the public aware of the state of national forests. Volunteers help with basic computer work, mailings, research, and filing of information. Minimum age 16.

Northwest Environmental Advocates
408 Southwest Second Avenue
Suite 406
Portland, OR 97204
(503) 295-0490

Contact: Eugene Rosolie

Seeks to maintain, through litigation, the media, and public education, the quality of fish and wildlife habitats along the Columbia and Willamette rivers. Sponsors Riverwatch, a boat tour, that familiarizes the public with the conditions of the rivers. Volunteers can work on the boat as tour guides or help with public awareness programs.

Washington Park Zoo
4001 Southwest Canyon Road
Portland, OR 97221-2799
(503) 226-1561

Contact: Pam Vick

Teenage volunteers can work directly with the animals in the children's zoo or in special events and planning. During the summer months, volunteers are asked to work two 4-hour shifts per week. The summer program fills up very quickly, so applications should be in by February or March.

Pennsylvania

The American Anti-Vivisection Society
Noble Plaza, Suite 204
801 Old York Road
Jenkintown, PA 19046-1685
(215) 887-0816

Contact: Laura Yanne

A 10,000-member organization that works for the minimization of animal use in laboratory research. Members of the organization regularly participate in protests, boycotts, and letter-writing campaigns to further the cause of animal rights. Volunteers needed to hand out brochures, file, and work on small projects in the office.

Asbury Woods Nature Center
4105 Asbury
Erie, PA 16506
(814) 835-5356

Contact: Rob Keys

Holds a nature camp and other nature-related programs, houses animals, and runs a store. Volunteers help in many aspects of the Center, from its upkeep to working in the store or gardens.

Braddock's Field Historical Society
419 Library Street
Braddock, PA 15104
(412) 351-5356

Contact: Jeannette Carolina

A group of local volunteers whose goal is to save the Carnegie Library, the oldest library in the nation. Volunteer library assistants needed to help with cataloging, shelving books, and clerical work. Minimum age 14.

Buhl Science Center
Allegheny Square
Pittsburgh, PA 15212-5363
(412) 237-3300

Contact: Norman Downey

An advanced science center that houses an interactive planetarium, educational facilities, theaters, demonstrations, a discovery lab, a miniature railroad, and more. Volunteers give tours of a World War II submarine, perform demonstrations, help build and run the railroad, explain exhibits, and act as teachers' aides. Minimum age 15.

Citiparks Therapeutic Recreation
400 City-County Building
Pittsburgh, PA 15219
(412) 422-6556

Contact: Diane Horstman

Assistants for therapeutic recreation program needed to work on recreational programs for handicapped children ages 10 through 15. Minimum age 16.

Friends Weekend Work Camps
1515 Cherry Street
Philadelphia, PA 19102
(215) 241-7236

Contact: Katherine Maleney

Holds weekend work camps that serve as seminars for those wanting to learn more about inner-city living and the causes and effects of poverty. Participants spend weekends in a house in West Philadelphia. Individuals from outside the area are also encouraged to apply. Minimum age 16.

Hans Herr House
1849 Hans Herr Drive
Willow Street, PA 17584
(717) 464-4438

Contact: Martin Franke

Educates the public about the Mennonite experience in Lancaster County from 1719 to 1750. Volunteers can catalog, conduct historical research, garden, be a tour guide, or work in the gift shop.

Hearing Conservation/Deaf Services Center
630 Janet Avenue
Lancaster, PA 17601
(717) 397-4741

Contact: Eleanor Green

Provides services to the hearing-impaired. Volunteers maintain and develop a mailing list, help with hearing screenings at nursery schools, and assist with the telephone system for the hearing-impaired.

Help, Inc.
638 South Street
Philadelphia, PA 19147
(215) 546-7766

Contact: William Bruce

An organization run by youths to help youths. It sponsors a 24-hour telephone counseling line and free legal, psychological, medical, and referral help. Operates a free general medical clinic and offers runaways a place to stay.

Lutheran Service Society
604 West North Avenue
Pittsburgh, PA 15212
(412) 231-1540

Contact: Jean Zundel

Provides a Meals-on-Wheels service to those in need. Teams of volunteers—1 driver, 1 deliverer—bring 10 to 18 meals to private homes. The deliverer spends no more than 5 minutes at each home while the driver remains in the car. Minimum age 14.

Operation Liftoff
1171 Kings Avenue
Bensalem, PA 19020
(215) 639-1586

Contact: Ernest Bischoff

Fulfills the wishes of terminally ill children. Volunteers help with arrangements for those trips (mostly to Disney World) and with transportation and correspondence with the sick children.

Pearl S. Buck Foundation
Green Hills Farm
Perkasi, PA 18944
(215) 249-0100

Contact: Nancy Lelli

Matches more than 6,000 Amerasian children with American sponsors who pay $24 per month to sustain a child's education, medical care, and other expenses. Volunteers help with office work and publicity through brochure distribution. There is also a national network of "ambassadors," who work on the Foundation's behalf in many states. Volunteers can also work as tour guides in the Pearl S. Buck House, which has been preserved as an educational attraction.

Shelter for Abused Women
P.O. Box 359
Lancaster, PA 17603
(717) 299-1240

Contact: Donna Glover

Program for abused women and their children with a 24-hour hotline, shelter, individual and group counseling, and child-care services. Volunteers serve as postive role models for children at the shelter, help with entertainment and holiday parties, and help permanent staff in various ways.

Sunshine Foundation
4010 Levick Street
Philadelphia, PA 19135
(215) 335-2622

Contact: Kathy Crowther

Volunteers help fulfill the wishes of chronically or terminally ill children, most of whom suffer from kidney disease, leukemia, or cancer. Teenage volunteers work on a team basis and plan many fund-raising events, such as pizza bowls, under adult staff supervision. The funds raised are used to send children and their families on vacations together and for other activities for the children to enjoy.

Trevor's Campaign for the Homeless
137–139 East Spring Avenue
Ardmore, PA 19003
(215) 642-6452

Contact: Valerie Smith

Provides shelter and frequent food delivery for the homeless in Philadelphia. Volunteers work in many capacities—in the shelter, in the thrift store run by the campaign, in food preparation, or in delivering the food.

The World Game Institute
University City Science Center
3508 Market Street
Suite 361
Philadelphia, PA 19104
(215) 387-0220

Contact: Gianna Tripodi

The Institute conducts research and provides services meant to increase global awareness. Volunteers help with research and computers, set up workshops, sell or distribute at events, and work in other areas according to their interests.

Rhode Island

Big Brothers of Rhode Island
100 Lafayette Street
Pawtucket, RI 02860
(401) 722-6300

Contact: Volunteer coordinator

Matches young boys from single-parent homes with positive role models. Volunteers provide guidance and companionship to fatherless boys. Minimum age 18.

Children's Museum of Rhode Island
58 Walcott Street
Pawtucket, RI 02860
(401) 726-2591

Contact: Nancy Worthen

A museum for children providing hands-on exhibits, fun activities, and birthday parties. Volunteers work as exhibit guides, help with birthday parties, and do whatever they can to make children's visits to

the museum more enjoyable.

Foster Parents Plan
155 Plan Way
Warwick, RI 02887
(401) 738-5600

Contact: Beth Bowen

Assists 500,000 children and families in over twenty developing countries through self-help programs for child survival, education, and family income. Volunteers help with special events and office work, including helping in the letters department, which receives 7,000–10,000 letters per week from children in developing countries.

Insight
43 Jefferson Boulevard
Warwick, RI 02888
(401) 941-3322
Contact: Paula Olivieri
The agency is devoted to rehabilitation for the blind; it offers a vision clinic and a radio station that features readings of current books and magazines for the blind. Volunteers work as readers at the clinic or do whatever they can to help the clients.

Literacy Volunteers of America—Rhode Island
260 West Exchange Street
Suite 315
Providence, RI 02903
(401) 351-0511
Contact: Deborah
  Venator
Provides one-on-one tutors for those who want to learn how to read. Volunteers are generally required to have a high school

diploma, but some exceptions are made. Tutors undergo approximately 15 hours of training. Various locations across Rhode Island.

Martin Luther King Center
20 West Broadway
Newport, RI 02840
(401) 846-4828
Contact: Diane Ferrar
A community center that provides day-care services, a breakfast program for the nutritionally deprived, and educational and recreational programs for the community. Volunteers help with all of these programs, particularly in the supervision of children and in serving meals.

Meals on Wheels
145 Oakland Avenue
Providence, RI 02908
(401) 351-6700
Contact: Kate Fairchild
Delivers noontime meals to elderly, disabled, and shut-in individuals. Volunteers with cars, driver's licenses, and auto insurance are

needed. Pre-made meals are picked up at the hospital and delivered to the needy individuals. Work is done in teams. Local routes statewide.

Rhode Island Shakespeare Theater
P.O. Box 1126
Newport, RI 02840
(401) 849-7892
Contact: Michelle Roche
Provides theater performances for the community. Volunteers assist the house staff with evening performances, build sets and scenery, sew costumes, work on props, work in the box office, or provide support in the main office.

Save the Bay
434 Smith Street
Providence, RI 02908
(401) 272-3540
Contact: Dana Cross
Works to inform the public about pollution problems in the area. Volunteers work on fund-raising events, write letters, call legislators, perform library research, and help with office mailings and data entry.

South Carolina

Association for the Blind
41 Pitt Street
Charleston, SC 29401
(803) 723-6915
Contact: Isabel Ewing
Provides recreational programs for the blind.

Volunteers help with activities such as ceramics and bowling, serve as walking guides, and provide transportation.

Boys and Girls Club
P.O. Box 21387

Charleston, SC 29403
(803) 577-5545
Contact: Rodney Collins
Seeks to promote the health, social, educational, vocational, and character development of young

people. Volunteers help kids with educational computer games, homework, and arts and crafts and assist in the library on-site.

C. M. Tucker Jr. Human Resources Center
2200 Harden Street
Columbia, SC 29203
(803) 737-5354
Contact: Maria Barrera

A state-run nursing home with many Alzheimer's patients. Volunteers become "family members" to the residents, acting as friendly visitors, playing Bingo, bringing their own pets to the Center for the residents to enjoy, and providing entertainment such as singing and dancing if they have special talents. Volunteers have been as young as 5 years old.

Columbia Urban League
1400 Barnwell Street
Columbia, SC 29201
(803) 799-8150
Contact: Cynthia Pryor

The League provides many services for the citizens of Columbia. Volunteers help the permanent staff with office-related duties.

Concerned Citizens for Animals
3627 Fork Shoals Road
Simpsonville, SC 29681
(803) 243-4222
Contact: Betty Way, 243-2235

A shelter that also provides pet-neutering

services for lower-income families. Volunteers take animals for walks, help clean cages, and make the pets as happy and comfortable as possible.

Harvest Home
1875 Harden Street
Columbia, SC 29204
(803) 252-9522
Contact: Elaine Frick

Provides food services for those in need. Volunteers fill bags with groceries, help stock shelves, and work on agency relations.

Jewish Community Center
1645 Wallenberg Boulevard
Charleston, SC 29407
(803) 571-6565
Contact: Blanche Siesstein

Provides many services for the community, including recreational and educational programs. Volunteers needed for child-care, office work, and as recreational counselors for summer camp.

Salvation Army
88 Simmons Street
Charleston, SC 29403
(803) 723-3658
Contact: Mrs. Captain Worthy

Works to supply basic necessities and counseling to the homeless, drug addicts, unwed mothers, prisoners, the poor, children, and senior citizens. At this particular center there is a youth

group for individuals ages 7 through 18, whose aims are education, fellowship, service, and worship. The youth group meets weekly and is involved with a number of community service activities.

Teenline Hotline
P.O. Box 71583
Charleston, SC 29415-1583
(803) 747-3007
Contact: Marcia Alterman

A hotline that kids can call to talk to a peer about anything on their minds. Volunteers are screened and receive 35 hours of training. They work on three shifts per month and commit to working for a minimum of nine months. Minimum age 15.

United Ministries
606 Pendleton Street
Greenville, SC 29601
(803) 232-6463
Contact: Vivian Williams

Sponsors a program called Spend The Day, which sends groups of teenagers out for one day at a time to homes of people in need to help with cleanup and chores.

Zoo Camp
c/o Greenville Zoo
150 Cleveland Park Drive
Greenville, SC 29601
(803) 240-4310
Contact: Kathy Taylor

Allows teenagers to become junior zookeepers for either a five- or a two-day session during the summer. Volunteers get a behind-the-scenes glimpse of what goes on at the zoo and help with everything from animal care to games and crafts programs. The goal is to help build appreciation of animals. Minimum age 16.

South Dakota

American Red Cross
P.O. Box 941
Pierre, SD 57501
(605) 224-8163

Contact: Bonnie Zebroski

Works to improve the quality of human life, enhance self-reliance and concern for others, and help people avoid, prepare for, and cope with emergencies. This branch focuses mainly on disaster relief, usually fires. It also provides services to military families. Volunteers can work on any number of projects, such as babysitting training and ordering materials for swimming classes.

The Banquet
c/o Southeast United Church
2315 East Park
Pierre, SD 57501
(605) 224-6785

Contact: Eileen Herrin

Provides meals for anyone in need. Volunteers fix and serve nutritious meals that are usually sponsored by groups of volunteers, such as church or youth groups. The food is served at a church facility.

Cornerstone Rescue Mission
30 Main Street
Rapid City, SD 57709
(605) 341-2844

Contact: Joyce Picotte

Provides meals and overnight services for anyone in need. Teenage volunteers often come with their school class; however, individuals are also welcome. Volunteers prepare food, serve meals, and do anything to make the residents' stay more pleasant.

Countryside Hospice
800 East Dakota
Pierre, SD 57501
(605) 224-3214

Contact: Holly Hoing

Volunteers don't work one-on-one with patients but are needed to run errands and work on the many fund-raising events, such as the Turkey Supper and the Duck Race.

Missouri Shores Women's Resource Center
c/o Hughes County Courthouse
104 East Capitol
Pierre, SD 57501
(605) 224-0256

Contact: Millie Thielen

Provides shelter and services for battered women. Teenage volunteers help with child-care and shelter maintenance.

Ronald McDonald House
2001 South Norton
Sioux Falls, SD 57105
(605) 336-6398

Contact: Diane Ishmael

A home for the families of children in the hospital, usually with long-term illnesses. Volunteers help mainly with office work, checking people in and out and helping to maintain order.

Sioux Falls Humane Society
2001 North Third
Sioux Falls, SD 57104
(605) 338-4441

Contact: Ronnie Fish

A shelter and pound for animals without homes. The Humane Society's mission is to promote respect for animals. This shelter houses over 300 animals, from horses to cats. Volunteers take the animals out for walks, give puppies baths, help with the adoption program, help clean cages, and if accompanied by an adult, take the pets to a local nursing home to visit the elderly.

St. Francis Homeless Shelter
1301 East Austin
Sioux Falls, SD 57103
(605) 334-3879

Contact: Dick Torney
Provides services for the needy. Volunteers do any number of things, including food

preparation, serving and cleaning up, playing with children staying in the shelter, and helping with laundry.

Tennessee

American Diabetes Association
317 Oak Street, Room 103
Chattanooga, TN 37403
(615) 756-8709
Contact: Wendy Deitch

Seeks to improve standards of diabetes treatment and promote a cure for the disease. Volunteers help in the office (typing, filing, answering telephones) and assist with special fund-raising events.

Bethlehem Center
1417 Charlotte Avenue
Nashville, TN 37203
(615) 329-3386
Contact: Kim Troup

A United Methodist community center that offers many services, including a day camp, alcohol- and drug-abuse prevention programs, senior citizens' programs, and literacy tutoring. Volunteers become camp counselors or tutors or assist in the after-school or day-care programs. Minimum age 14.

Children's Museum
2525 Central
Memphis, TN 38104
(901) 458-2678

Contact: J. J. Doughtie
Provides hands-on exhibits, presentations, and educational programs for young schoolchildren. Volunteers help in many aspects of the Museum operation, including exhibit demonstrations and supervision of children.

Lichterman Nature Center
5299 Quince Road
Memphis, TN 38119
(901) 767-7322
Contact: Bob Barney

A nature center on 65 acres with 3 miles of trails through natural habitat. Also houses a wildlife rehabilitation center that takes in injured wildlife. Volunteers serve as junior staff members in the rehabilitation center and work on various projects on the grounds.

Nashville Humane Association
112 Harding Place
Nashville, TN 37205
(615) 352-4030
Contact: Cheri Boyte
Provides shelter for animals. Volunteers help

with the animals, walk and play with the dogs, and help keep cages clean. Minimum age 16.

Social Action Group on Aging
2102 21st Avenue
Nashville, TN
(615) 297-2391

Contact: Tracy Carman

Provides nursing-home services for the elderly. Volunteers receive brief training and are asked to make a commitment to be a "friendly visitor" to an elderly person at least once a week.

Tennessee Teen Institute for Alcohol and Drug Abuse Prevention
P.O. Box 4737
Nashville, TN 37216
(615) 227-9041

Contact: Ann Brown-Tunstall

Provides preventive services for substance abuse. Volunteers help with light typing, filing, answering phones, and other duties assigned by the coordinator. Minimum age 16.

Texas

American Cancer Society
2222 Montgomery Street
Fort Worth, TX 76107
(817) 737-3185

Contact:Julie Dieter

The nationwide voluntary health organization dedicated to eliminating cancer as a major health problem through research, education, and service. Volunteers help with special events and fund-raising drives, mailings, and basic office duties.

American Diabetes Association
8008 Slide Road #25
Lubbock, TX 79424
(806) 794-0691

Contact: Martha Atwood

Seeks to improve standards of treatment and promote a cure for diabetes. Volunteers help with bulk mailings and special events and assist with clerical duties.

American Heart Association
1615 Stimmons Freeway
Dallas, TX 75207
(214) 748-7212

Contact: Lorraine Lee

A voluntary health organization with over 2 million volunteers that raises money for scientific research on heart disease. Office opportunities available include filing, fund-raising, and telephone and clerical work.

American Red Cross
3620 Admiral
El Paso, TX 79925
(915) 592-0208

Contact: Carmen Ruiz

Works to improve the quality of human life, enhance self-reliance and concern for others, and to help people avoid, prepare for, and cope with emergencies. Volunteer opportunities are available in community CPR and first-aid classes, at local hospitals, and as office assistant/receptionists in the branch office.

AMIGOS de Las Americas
5618 Star Lane
Houston, TX 77057
1-800-231-7796

Contact: Steve Kirk

An organization dedicated to community health and rehabilitation education overseas. Volunteers who travel abroad are charged a fee that covers airfare and meals. However, internships are available at the Houston office in the areas of finance, recruiting, and field programs.

Animal Rights Association
4201 Canyon Drive
Amarillo, TX 79110
(806) 353-6697

Contact: Annie Miller or Beth Blankenship

Provides shelter for animals. Volunteers give attention to the dogs and cats and make them feel loved and cared for. The only requirement is that the volunteer be strong enough to walk a dog. No cage cleaning required.

Boys Club of Corpus Christi
3902 Greenwood Drive
Corpus Christi, TX 78465
(512) 853-2505

Contact: Joe Garza Jr.

Provides free lunches and many recreational and educational activities for boys. Volunteers help supervise in the game room, during lunch, in the gym, and with all other activities.

Catholic Family Services
1422 South Tyler
Amarillo, TX 79105
(806) 376-4571

Contact: Kay Kennedy

Provides many community services and programs. Teenage volunteers can become a friend to a runaway or abused child or assist the elderly and handicapped with meals.

Circle T Riding Center
9560 Hildebrandt Road
San Antonio, TX 78222
(512) 633-0678

Contact: Barbara Billingsley

Gives riding instruction and riding therapy for handicapped individuals. Always need an extra hand to help clean, work on tack, groom and clip the horses, and help the instructors. Minimum age 14.

Friendship House
620 West Fourth
Texarkana, TX 75501
(903) 792-1301

Contact: Steven Cane

A mission affiliated with the Southern Baptist Church that provides food and essentials for people in need. The center is run almost entirely by volunteers, who help in the kitchen, the pantry, the clothes department, and with office and reception work.

Good Samaritan Center
1600 Saltillo
San Antonio, TX 78207
(512) 434-5531

Contact: Gloria Kehl

Holds a summer program for children, including recreation, games, field trips, swimming, and movies. Volunteers act as counselors for the youth groups. Minimum age 14

Habitat for Humanity
1329 Seventh Street
Corpus Christi, TX 78704
(512) 884-2340

Contact: John Creedon

Helps in the fight against homelessness through the construction of decent shelter for the economically disadvantaged. Volunteers help on construction projects in the Corpus Christi area. Office help is also needed.

March of Dimes Birth Defects Foundation
2345 50th Street, #109
Lubbock, TX 79412
(806) 797-6771

Contact: Linda Ellis

Provides leadership in the prevention and treatment of birth defects and related health problems. Volunteers answer phones, photocopy, file, organize materials, and help with the planning and organization of fund-raising events.

Muscular Dystrophy Association
3505 Olsen, Suite 203
Amarillo, TX 79109
(806) 359-3141

Contact: Karen Lane

Performs research into the causes and cures of different categories of neuromuscular disease and provides services for patients with these diseases. Volunteers work on a variety of special projects including bowl-a-thons and other fund-raising drives; they also stuff packets and help with general clerical work.

Ronald McDonald House
1501 Streit Drive
Amarillo, Texas 79106
(806) 358-8177

Contact: Anyone on duty

A home for the families of children in the hospital, usually with long-term illnesses. Volunteers help children, run errands, work in the office, and visit the children in the hospital.

Texas Special Olympics
11442 North Interstate 35
Austin, TX 78753
(512) 835-9873

Contact: Deborah Pittala

Provides sports training and competition in a variety of Olympic-type sports for children and adults with mental retardation. Volunteers can help with all of the sports programs or in the office.

Texans' War on Drugs
11044 Research Boulevard
Building D, Suite 200
Austin, TX 78759
(512) 343-6950

Contact: Judy Price

Sponsors a number of public awareness campaigns about substance abuse and programs such as the "red ribbon" campaign, in which people tie ribbons to their cars to indicate that they are against drunk driving.

Texas Fine Arts Association
3809-B West 35th Street
The Gatehouse
Austin, TX 78703
(512) 453-5312

Contact: Elizabeth Earle

A service organization for artists. Volunteers usually help with office duties but can also become involved in special arts-related projects as assigned.

Utah

Animal Caring Team
P.O. Box 520444
Salt Lake City, UT
    84152-0444
(801) 565-1282
(801) 969-6015

Contact: Rebecca Turner

Animal shelter for homeless, abandoned, and abused pets. Volunteers sponsor a dog or cat that is in need of temporary shelter until a permanent home is found or answer phone calls from their homes on a 24-hour basis one day per week.

Canyonlands Field Institute
P.O. Box 68
Moab, UT 84532
(801) 259-7750

Contact: Marian Ottinger

A nonprofit educational organization that promotes understanding and appreciation of the natural and cultural heritage of the Colorado Plateau region. Volunteers are involved with office and field work as well as special events and fund-raising activities.

The Children's Center
1855 East Medical Drive
Salt Lake City, UT 84112
(801) 582-5534
    or
5242 South 4820 West
Kearns, UT 84118
(801) 966-4251

Contact: Martha Smith
    Taylor

Serves emotionally and behaviorally disturbed children from the ages of 2 to 7. Volunteers help with activity-therapy groups and care for and play with children in residential treatment.

The Children's Museum of Utah
840 North 300 West
Salt Lake City, UT 84103
(801) 328-3383

Contact: David Miller

Provides museum services and hands-on exhibits for over 90,000 families and children who visit the museum each year. Volunteers explain exhibits to visitors, perform demonstrations and create demonstration exhibits, interact with visitors, and work in the gift shop.

Indian Walk-In
120 West 1300 South
Salt Lake City, UT 84115
(801) 486-4877

Contact: Madeline
    Greymountain

Provides a variety of services for Native Americans and low-income individuals and families. Volunteers work as tutors, help with powwows and a holiday dinner, answer phones, and stock shelves.

Make-a-Wish Foundation of Utah
1399 South 700 East #2
Salt Lake City, UT 84105

Contact: Christine Sharer
(801) 485-6842

Provides services to grants wishes for Utah children under the age of 18 who have life-threatening or terminal illnesses. Volunteers help with special events and fund-raising projects, train as Wish Granters, and help with office projects.

Park City Handicapped Sports Association
P.O. Box 680286
1425 Lowell Avenue, 500
    Resort Center
Park City, UT 84068
(801) 649-3991

Contact: Meeche White

Holds programs for mentally and physically handicapped children and adults. Volunteers work with year-round activities such as snow skiing, snowmobiling, waterskiing, horseback riding, swimming, fund-raising events, and office duties.

Pioneer Trail State Park
2601 East Sunnyside
    Avenue
Salt Lake City, UT 84108
(801) 584-8392

Contact: Ken Kohler or
    Ghia Burch

A state park that holds many programs for visitors. Volunteers help recreate pioneer skills and crafts for the public and act as tour guides in the houses in the park.

Southern Utah Wilderness Alliance

15 South 300
West Cedar City, UT 84720
(801) 586-8242

Contact: Shelly Sullivan

Works to preserve the canyonlands and desert wilderness of Utah. Volunteers help with data entry and general office duties.

Utah Wilderness Coalition

P.O. Box 11446
Salt Lake City, UT 84147
(801) 532-5959

Contact: Jerry Forsdick

A coalition of environmental groups working to protect the 5.7 million acres of wilderness in Utah; publishes a guide to wilderness areas to inform and educate the public about the benefits of wilderness. Volunteers help with public events, as well as with phone calls and mailings. They do "a little bit of everything."

Very Special Arts Utah

P.O. Box 526244
Salt Lake City, UT 84152
(801) 328-0703

Contact: Cary Stevens Jones

Holds recreational and artistic programs for individuals with disabling conditions, including those with physical or mental disabilities, the hearing- or sight-impaired, "youth at risk," and those with AIDS. Volunteers help plan and coordinate arts festivals or help in the office or with fund-raising events.

The Work Activity Center for Handicapped Adults

1275 West 2320 South
West Valley, UT 84119
(801) 977-9779

Contact: Rania George

Serves adults with cerebral palsy, Down syndrome, mental retardation, and severe multiple disabilities. Volunteers conduct art classes; work on computers with nonverbal clients; become "volunteer friends" and take one client, one day per month, to an activity; and assist clients who have limited use of their hands to eat during mealtime.

Vermont

Catamount Trail Association

P.O. Box 897
Burlington, VT 05402
(802) 864-5794

Contact: Ray Auger

The association is developing a cross-country ski trail in the state of Vermont. Volunteers who are active outdoors can help on the trail in the fall and winter, brushing the trail and putting up the blazes. In the spring and summer, volunteers help with fund-raising and wilderness conservation.

Champlain Valley Agency on Aging

P.O. Box 158
Winooski, VT 05404
(802) 865-0360

Contact: Sue Chase

Provides home services, as well as advocacy, information referral, legal services, and housing, for the elderly. Volunteers needed to act as friendly visitors with the elderly and help them to run errands.

Discovery Museum

51 Park Street
Essex Junction, VT 05452
(802) 878-8687

Contact: Kris Crouchley

A museum for children that provides hands-on exhibits and a wildlife center. Volunteers help with the small animals, such as ferrets, turtles, and rabbits. They also help in the wildlife center, work on demonstrations, or act as tour guides.

Green Mountain Club

P.O. Box 889
Montpelier, VT 05601
(802) 223-3463

Contact: Kathryn
  Borchert

Dedicated to preserving the high mountains and forest lands of the northeast and maintaining a hiking trail. Volunteers under the age of 18 can work in the office; those over 18 can work on the trail.

Recycle North
P.O. Box 158
Burlington, VT 05401
(802) 658-4143

Contact: Ron Krupp

A giant flea market with a social and environmental purpose. Everything at the market has been donated.

Volunteers needed to do anything and everything—some possibilities are working as front-desk staff, running the store, answering phones, tagging and selling items, or fixing equipment.

Vermont Institute of Natural Science
P.O. Box 86
Woodstock, VT 05091
(802) 457-2779

Contact: Cassie Horner

A small private research and education organization that sponsors environmental education programs, natural-science research,

and bird rehabilitation. Volunteers can do a variety of jobs, depending on their interests. They can give guided tours, help care for the birds, assist with research, or help on the grounds.

Volunteers for Peace
43 Tiffany Road
Belmont, VT 05730
(802) 259-2759

Contact: Meg Brook

A group of volunteers who work on camps overseas for two to three weeks. Projects include helping villagers with food, water, agriculture, and medical supplies.

Virginia

AIDS Project of Southwestern Virginia
P.O. Box 598
Roanoke, VA 24004
(703) 982-2437

Contact: Ellen Whitt

Provides information and education programs, a buddy program, and a hotline number for persons with AIDS or anyone interested in AIDS information. Volunteers who are over the age of 18 can volunteer to be buddies or to work on the hotline. Two weekends of training are required.

American Indian Heritage Foundation
6051 Arlington Boulevard
Falls Church, VA 22044
(703) 237-7500

Contact: Zainab Algibouri

Educates the public about the culture and needs of Native Americans, distributes emergency food and necessities to Native Americans in need, and coordinates events such as American Indian Heritage Week and July 4 Powwow. Volunteers work on special events, provide office support, and act as liaisons with Native American reservations across the country.

Children's Hospice International
700 Princess Street
Suite #3
Alexandria, VA 22314
(703) 684-0330

Contact: Patricia Dailey

Promotes hospice support in pediatric-care facilities and encourages hospices around the country to make themselves available to children. Volunteers needed to help answer letters, send out brochures, and help with general office work.

Conservation and Research Center
National Zoological Park
Front Royal, VA 22630
(703) 635-6500

Contact: Sharon Leathery

Conducts research projects and field work pertaining to animals. Most volunteers are over the age of 18 and interested in gaining research experience in the area. Prospective volunteers should submit their resume to the volunteer coordinator, who will circulate it to specific researchers.

Cousteau Society
930 West 21st Street
Norfolk, VA 23517
(804) 627-1144
Contact: Peggy Fooks

The main headquarters of the national organization dedicated to the study and exploration of oceans. Focuses attention on the fragile sea environments and wildlife threatened by pollution and development. Many volunteers come in with school groups and help with merchandising, packaging, and filing; however, individuals are welcome. Minimum age 16, unless with a school-sponsored group.

Freedom House
P.O. Box 12144
Richmond, VA 23241
(804) 649-9791
Contact: Judy Allen

An ecumenical ministry for the homeless that provides an evening meal, shelter, and transitional housing. Volunteers mainly help with the preparation, serving, and cleanup of the evening meal but are welcome to help in any way possible.

Gunston Hall Plantation
10709 Gunston Road
Lorton, VA 22079
(703) 550-9220

Contact: Susan Borchardt

Gunston Hall was the home of George Mason, the author of the Virginia Declaration of Rights. It is now a historical attraction. Volunteers available during the school year can work on tours given primarily to schoolchildren. Summer volunteer opportunities are available in the gardens.

Hopkins House Association
1224 Princess Street
Alexandria, VA 22314
(703) 549-4232

Contact: Roxanne Caple

A social services agency that provides programs for preschoolers, youth 6 through 12, teenagers, the elderly, and persons in crisis. Provides programs such as tutoring and an AIDS outreach group. Volunteers can help in most programs for youth.

Office of Refugee Resettlement
811 Cathedral Place
Suite E
Richmond, VA 23220
(804) 355-4559

Contact: Nancy Sieford

Sponsors programs to assist refugees with education and resettlement. Volunteers do everything from tutoring children in English to helping people learn to shop or registering children in schools. Many hands-on opportunities available.

Science Museum of Virginia
2500 West Broad
Richmond, VA 23220
(804) 367-6796
Contact: Jean White

Provides scientific exhibits, a planetarium, and displays. Teenage volunteers act as teachers' assistants, primarily during the summer, in a science program for children.

Shenandoah Valley Independent Living Center
21 South Kent Street
Winchester, VA 22601
(703) 662-4452
Contact: Cathy Legge

An independent-living center for the physically challenged that provides peer counseling and support-group sessions as well as other programs. Volunteers help in the office as well as with transportation for the clients.

Tidewater AIDS Crisis Task Force
P.O. Box 6267
Norfolk, VA 23508
(804) 423-5859
Contact: Teresa Roberts

A crisis center that provides support and counseling for persons with AIDS. Volunteers can help in the office with mailing and computer work, on the grounds with landscaping and maintenance, or with AIDS patients, providing transportation to the hospital and other support.

150 Ways

Trout Unlimited
800 Follin Lane, SE Suite 250
Vienna, VA 22180-4906
(703) 281-1100

Contact: Neal Emerald

An international organization that focuses on preserving, restoring, and enhancing rivers and freshwater streams to maintain trout fisheries. All volunteers are members of Trout Unlimited. This is an active organization in which volunteers take matters into their own hands. Volunteers can work anywhere in the country.

The Virginia Discovery Museum
P.O. Box 1128
Charlottesville, VA 22902
(804) 977-1025

Contact: Jan Jennings

A hands-on museum for children from 1 through 13. Volunteers help with tours, greet people and answer phones, or help with exhibits and demonstrations.

The Virginia Rehabilitation Center for the Blind
401 Azalea Avenue
Richmond, VA 23227
(804) 371-3059

Contact: Mrs. Carol Roger

Provides a large number of services for the visually impaired. For daytime volunteers, most tasks are office-related and include filing and typing. Evening volunteers help with the recreation program, for which they take clients into the community for such activities as bowling and swimming.

Virginia Treatment Center
515 North 10th Street
Richmond, VA 23219
(804) 786-7871

Contact: Lee Bloxom

A treatment center for children. Volunteers who wish to work directly with the children must be over the age of 18. Younger volunteers needed in both the business office and the on-site library.

Volunteers in Mission
Southern Baptist Foreign Mission Board
P.O. Box 6767
Richmond, VA 23230
(804) 353-0151

Contact: Barbara Apps

Sends volunteers overseas to work on everything from construction projects to Bible school. Volunteers must have completed the 10th grade, and projects run from one week to four months.

Washington

Alzheimer Society of Washington
P.O. Box 4104
Bellingham, WA 98227
(206) 671-3316

Contact: Josselyn Winslow

Provides information, education, advocacy, and support groups for those with Alzheimer's disease and their families. Volunteers help out in all areas, including fund-raising and working directly with afflicted individuals.

Birch Bay State Park
5105 Helwig Road
Blaine, WA 98230
(206) 371-2800

Contact: Mike Zimmerman

A state park that provides public outdoor recreational opportunities for individuals of all ages. Volunteers serve as information officers, help with research and educational programs, and assist with park maintenance.

Council on Child Abuse and Neglect
P.O. Box 1233
Walla Walla, WA 99362
(509) 522-2824

Contact: Cordy Nowogroski

Provides educational program, promotes public awareness, and supports legislative action pertaining to child abuse and neglect. Volunteers can help with all educational programs and with public awareness booths at local events.

Council for the Prevention of Child Abuse and Neglect
1305 Fourth Avenue
Suite 202
Seattle, WA 98101
(206) 343-2590

Contact: Dawn Rains

An organization dedicated to the elimination of child abuse. Volunteers provide office assistance, help with the newsletter, conduct research, and participate in fund-raising and other special events.

Foundation for the Handicapped
West 829 Broadway
Spokane, WA 99201
(509) 326-4577

Contact: Donna Hulme

An organization that provides a wide range of services for the handicapped and emphasizes the importance of helping handicapped individuals to become independent. Some of the clients are in group homes or institutions, but a large number live in their own homes. Volunteers can act as friendly visitors to these individuals, helping around the house and with shopping and transportation.

Habitat for Humanity
316 East 24th Avenue
Spokane, WA 99203
(509) 456-0335

Contact: Grace Harris

Helps to eliminate homelessness through the construction of decent shelter for the economically disadvantaged. Volunteers can work on construction and renovation projects and can also help with organizational and office work.

HOSTS (Help One Student to Succeed)
Box 279
Everson, WA 98247
(206) 966-7561

Contact: Tres Kamphouse

Located within a school, this is a program to teach reading to elementary school students in grades 3 through 6. Volunteers work as one-on-one reading tutors.

Inland Empire Public Lands Council
West 315 Mission
Spokane, WA 99201
(509) 327-1699

Contact: Tracy Sedlacek

Sponsors a forest watch program, which monitors sales of timber in the area and works with local Ranger Districts. Volunteers are needed for office help and bulk-mail preparation; field workers are also needed.

International Snow Leopard Trust
4649 Sunnyside Avenue North
Suite 342
Seattle, WA 98103
(206) 632-2421

Contact: Roberta Gunn

Dedicated to the conservation of the snow leopard and its equally endangered habitat. Volunteers help with special events, both fund-raising and educational, such as talks to the public about the conservation issue. Volunteers can also help with mailings and telephones.

The Literacy Council of Seattle
4318 First Avenue, Northeast
Seattle, WA 98105
(206) 633-5570

Contact: Dorothy Collias

Trains teenagers as well as adults to become tutors. Tutors work one-on-one with individuals who wish to learn to read. The organization matches the tutor with the individual.

March of Dimes Birth Defects Foundation
West 222 Mission
Suite 120
Spokane, WA 99201
(509) 328-1920

Contact: Heidi Wohl

Dedicated to the prevention of birth defects, low birth weight, and infant deaths. Volunteers help with special events and office work, such as mailings and computer entry.

North Cascades Institute
2105 Highway 20
Sedro Woolley, WA 98284
(206) 856-5700
Contact: Robin duPre
The Institute offers a number of environmental education programs, including Elderhostel programs based on natural history education, summer camps, and three-day field camps for schoolchildren. The work done by volunteers is flexible and based on their interests and skills. Some work in the office; others enjoy working on specific programs.

The Pacific Science Center
200 Second Avenue North
Seattle, WA 98109
(206) 443-2868
Contact: Marcia Livingston
Has a number of educational programs, exhibits, and a planetarium. Volunteers help with mailings, demonstrations, and exhibit set-up and act as summer interns.

Pure Sound Society
P.O. Box 526
Vashon Island, WA 98070
(206) 463-5607

Contact: Brad Wetmore
Offers environmental awareness courses and sponsors many conservation projects. Volunteers act as interns and help either in the office or in the field, helping to run the outdoor education programs and promoting the organization at public events.

The Teen Drug and Alcohol Helpline
P.O. Box 18317
Seattle, WA 98118-0317
(206) 722-4222

Contact: Bob Conroy
Teenagers go through training to work on a hotline helping other teens with substance-abuse questions.

Washington Environmental Council
5200 University Way, NE
Suite 201
Seattle, WA 98105
(206) 527-1599

Contact: Meghan Dahl or Laurie Scinto
An organization concerned with environmental initiatives and education. Volunteers' duties depend on their interests

and when they are available. Weekend work might include staffing a table at a fair; office work and research help are also needed.

Wishing Star Foundation
West 539 West Sharp
Spokane, WA 99201
(509) 325-9803

Contact: Doug Raper
This foundation grants wishes to children with life-threatening diseases. Volunteers help with fund-raising and with clerical work and can work on a project basis, such as a Fun Run on a weekend afternoon.

World Concern
22314 70th West
Mount Lake Terrace, WA 98043
(206) 771-5700

Contact: Mary Lou Burris
The organization gives aid to the poor and seeks to restore the health and self-sufficiency of the world's impoverished people. This center packages medicine, clothing, and seed packets to be sent to the needy overseas. (Teenage volunteers do not work with medicine.)

West Virginia

Alderson Hospitality House
P.O. Box 579
Alderson, WV 24910
(304) 445-2980
(304) 445-2769

Contact: Bob or Vita Shively
Welcomes individuals who visit prisoners at the nearby federal women's

prison. Not funded by the government or part of the federal prison system. Volunteers help with transportation, administrative work, and general household chores, such as cooking and cleaning. Driver's license required; openness to strangers helpful.

American Lung Association

415 Dickinson Street
P.O. Box 3980
Charleston, WV
  25339-3980
(304) 342-6600

Contact: Shawn Chillag

An organization whose goal is the conquest of lung disease and the promotion of pulmonary health. Volunteers can get involved with special fund-raising events.

The Community Care Center

500 Fourth Street
St. Albans, WV 25177
(304) 727-4357

Contact: Judy Kinkaid

The Center provides individual, group, and family counseling; job placement; and other services. Volunteers can help in the newspaper office or with such programs as the child-care clinic, reading stories to the children, or helping them with flashcards.

Covenant House

1109 Quarrier Street
Charleston, WV 25301
(304) 344-8433

Contact: Barbara Ferraro

Provides food and shelter, clothing, showers, mail receipt, and emergency assistance for the homeless. (Not affiliated with Covenant House in New York.)

The Humane Society

P.O. Box 392
Parkersburg, WV 26101
(304) 422-5541

Contact: Mary Suffin

A shelter and pound for animals without homes. The Humane Society's mission is to promote respect for animals. Volunteers over 18 can participate in the Pet Therapy program, taking the animals to visit the elderly. Volunteers under 18 can walk the dogs and play with the pets.

Huntington Center for Independent Living

914½ Fifth Avenue
Huntington, WV 25701

Contact: Jody Cox

Provides services for those with any kind of disability, either mental or physical. Many volunteers who work are part of the transition program and are handicapped themselves. However, nondisabled volunteers are welcome; they help with the organization of parties and dances and help in the office.

Junior Achievement

708 Bigley Avenue
Charleston, WV 25302
(304) 346-9753

Contact: Monica Pitman

Teenage junior achievement volunteers go into fifth- and sixth-grade classrooms and present the business principles that they themselves have learned from adult volunteers. They work with the children and show them how to make and sell a product.

Manna Meal

1105 Quarrier Street
Charleston, WV 25301
(304) 346-0359

Contact: Brenda Darien

Serves breakfast and lunch to anyone who needs a meal, every day of the year except Thanksgiving. Volunteers help with food preparation, service, and cleanup and do whatever they can to help make the meal more enjoyable.

Muscular Dystrophy Association

1409 Greenbrier Street
Charleston, WV 25311
(304) 344-9807

Contact: Stacey Grounds

Performs research into the causes of and cures for different categories of neuromuscular disease and provides services for patients with these diseases. Volunteers help with special events and fund-raising, including the telethon.

Wisconsin

Alliance for Animals
111 King Street
Madison, WI 53703
(608) 257-6333
Contact: Denise
Provides services and advocacy for animal rights. Volunteers can help with newsletter articles, fund-raising and promotions, and graphic design for promotional activities.

American Players Theatre
P.O. Box 819
Spring Green, WI 53588
(608) 588-7401
Contact: Valerie
  Ewing-Metz
Provides theater performances for the community. Volunteers needed as ushers, delivery persons, or to help with costumes and sewing.

American Red Cross
Route 3
Ashland, WI 54806
(715) 682-3362
Contact: Betty Chambers
Works to improve the quality of human life, enhance self-reliance and concern for others, and help people avoid, prepare for, and cope with emergencies. Volunteers needed for the various services and programs provided by the American Red Cross.

Bethesda Lutheran Home
700 Hoffman Drive
Watertown, WI 53094
(414) 261-3050

Contact: Janet Simon
Provides services for the mentally retarded and the developmentally disabled. Volunteers work at a summer camp for disabled individuals, helping with arts and crafts and with various classroom projects.

Big Brothers/Big Sisters
2059 Atwood Avenue
Madison, WI 53704
(608) 249-7328
Contact: Information is provided as to the next scheduled orientation session for potential volunteers (sessions are held approximately every two weeks)
The organization seeks to match young boys and girls with positive role models. Each volunteer is interviewed, evaluated, and given a training program. Big Brothers and Big Sisters spend time in recreational and educational activities with their "siblings."

Center Project AIDS Clinic
P.O. Box 1874
Green Bay, WI 54304
(414) 437-7400
Contact: Laurie Cotter
Provides educational counseling and programs for persons being tested for the HIV virus or for persons with AIDS. Volunteers can work on a newsletter, undergo training to provide counseling for those

individuals being tested, or become a "buddy" to a person with AIDS.

Central Wisconsin Center
317 Knutson Drive
Madison, WI 53704
(608) 249-2151
Contact: Merlen Kurth
A home for developmentally disabled children and adults. Volunteers help with knitting, crocheting, and crafts for bazaars; play instruments/sing, help in the summer recreation program; and escort residents on-site. Minimum age 16.

The Chequamegon Theatre
P.O. Box 225
Ashland, WI 54806
(715) 682-5554
Contact: Kathy Logan,
  682-2256
A community theater group, run by volunteers, that puts on performances for the community several times per year and holds a children's theater during the summer. Volunteers can work in all aspects of the productions, including costumes and the box office.

Computers to Help People
1221 West Johnston
  Street
Madison, WI 53715
(608) 257-5917
Contact: Carl Durocher
Provides computer services for the hearing-impaired, the

visually-impaired, and persons with other disabilities. One service includes the scanning of books to be printed in Braille. Volunteers conduct research, work as interpreters and signers, perform clerical and typing duties, work on marketing and promotions, and work on computers. Minimum age 13.

Habitat for Humanity
P.O. Box 1172
Green Bay, WI 54305
(414) 433-6766

Contact: Charles Vanzig

Helps to eliminate homelessness through the construction of decent shelter for the economically disadvantaged. Volunteers help work on on-site Habitat housing construction or

renovation projects or, if they prefer to be in an office, help with administrative duties.

Lake Wissota State Park
Route 8, Box 360
Chippewa Falls, WI 54729
(715) 382-4574

Contact: Allen Middendorp

A state park with various recreational facilities. Volunteers can help with park maintenance and special projects.

International Crane Foundation
E-11376 Shady Lane Road
Baraboo, WI 53913-9778
(608) 356-9462

Contact: Marianne Wellington

Protects cranes and crane habitats all around the world and houses a

crane farm that has 14 of the 16 species of crane, including the second-largest number of endangered whooping cranes. Volunteers can get involved in most of the areas of the Foundation, including the chick yard, field ecology, or as a tour guide.

Parental Stress Center
2120 Fordham Avenue
Madison, WI 53704
(608) 241-4888

Contact: Dale Leibowitz

The Center holds Parents Anonymous meetings and has a program for families in which sexual abuse has taken place. Child care is provided for all families using the Center, and volunteers interested in babysitting are needed. Volunteers are also needed in the office.

Wyoming

Association of Retarded Citizens
P.O. Box 1812
Cheyenne, WY 82003
(307) 632-1209

Contact: Paula Lindsey

Sponsors recreational and social activities for retarded individuals. Volunteers help with parties, such activities as bowling and swimming, and other fun activities. Volunteers are assigned to be buddies with no more than 4 or 5 clients during the activities, depending upon how

many other volunteers are available.

Big Brothers/Big Sisters of Sweet Water
809 Thompson Street
Suite B
Rock Springs, WY 82901
(307) 382-4357

Contact: Anita Hornsby

Seeks to match young boys and girls from single-parent homes with positive role models. Volunteers act as mentors and role models for their younger "siblings."

Bridger-Teton National Forest
Pinedale Ranger District
P.O. Box 220
Pinedale, WY 82941
(307) 367-4326

Contact: Ingra Draper

The national forest maintains a volunteer trail crew that reconstructs trails through the Bridger Wilderness. Volunteers do everything from office work to maintenance of trails and campgrounds, depending on the volunteer's interests.

Powder River Basin Resource Council
23 North Scott
Sheridan, WY 82801
(307) 672-5809

Contact: Jill Morrison

Works to promote wild and scenic designation for the Little Bighorn River and Dry Fork. Volunteers help with everything from mailings, research, and phone calls to community events such as cleanups and other special projects.

Wolf Fund
P.O. Box 471
Moose, WY 83012
(307) 733-0740

Contact: Libby Crews

Works to enhance public awareness of the important role the wolf plays in the ecosystems and to encourage wolf-recovery plans in many areas, including

Yellowstone National Park. Volunteers help with the dissemination of information to the public, putting together press packets and keeping track of the issue in the media.

Wyoming AIDS Project
Box 9353
Casper, WY 82609
(307) 237-7833

Contact: Dinah Utah

Provides services and a hotline number for persons needing information about AIDS. Volunteers can work in the offices or help on the hotline. Training is required and provided by the organization.

Wyoming Nature Conservancy
258 Main Street
Lander, WY 82520
(307) 332-2971

Contact: Paula Patton

Promotes habitat conservation, wildlife preserves, and wilderness preservation in the state of Wyoming. Volunteers can do any number of things, from dealing with the public to working on the wildlife preserves. Placement depends on interests and skills.

Wyoming Outdoor Council
201 Main Street
Lander, WY 82520
(307) 332-7031

Contact: Bonnie
  Hofbauer

Concerned with habitats, conservation, and recycling in the state of Wyoming. Has an internship program that entails research and special project work, but volunteers also work in the office, filing newspaper clippings and working on publicity.

Afterword
Taking Your Cause with You, Whatever Road You Follow

On days when you're cramming for a trig test or explaining to your friends why you *still* don't have a date for the prom, it may seem as though high school lasts forever. But it doesn't. The friends you've made may be around for a long time, and your memories will certainly linger, but your life after high school is bound to change. And changes in your lifestyle—such as a new work schedule or attending college away from home—may mean having to say goodbye to organizations and people with whom you've worked as a volunteer. But, by all means, don't let your commitment to your cause come to a halt.

Life after high school can be hectic, but you may actually find that your schedule is more conducive to volunteerism. In the words of Maribel Becker, a sophomore at Vassar College in Pough-keepsie, New York, "The problem with high school is that, though it seems like a lifetime, four years actually pass very quickly. Whether you've been volunteering since eighth or since the last semester of high school, before you know it, you'll be graduating. For most teens, this means changes in responsibilities, schedule, and location. Suddenly, you find you don't have the time to work at the soup kitchen, or you're leaving the state and, therefore, leaving your volunteer job. Does this mean your days of volunteering must come to an end? Hardly. At college, though classes, parties, sports, and other activities will certainly keep you busy, try to schedule some time for community service. Colleges can provide a lot of opportunities for volunteering, both on and off campus."

Purcell Parker, a junior at the University of North Carolina at Chapel Hill, says, "In high school, even though I was devoted to my cause, I was on a limited schedule. But once I got to college, I realized that there were so many volunteer opportunities to be had. Though it took me a while to get adjusted to my new schedule, I began during sophomore year to coach a soccer team of 5- and 6-year-olds and to tutor for a Project Literacy outfit near my school. I wouldn't have had the flexibility in high school to do either of those."

John Hamburg, a junior at Brown University in Providence, Rhode Island, says, "In high school, community service was a requirement. Basically, we were given a choice of activities and were told that we had to work for four or five semesters in order to fulfill our obligation. The first semester of my freshman year, I worked with a first-grade class, teaching certain slow students how to read. That was an excellent experience, but it was also the culmination of my high school community service work. In college, community service is in no way forced upon any of the students. They do work for the community not out of a desire to make their profiles more appealing but because they have a genuine interest in what they are doing. Fewer people might do community service, but those who do engage in such activity are much more dedicated to their work. I never really enjoyed my community service requirement in high school because I viewed it as just that—a requirement. In college, however, I have been making videos with kids from underprivileged schools. This project has been far more rewarding than the community service work I did in high school."

Whether you're in a college community or working 9 to 5, there are many ways to get involved as a volunteer after high school. You can join a club—yes, clubs actually exist in the "real" world—which is a great way to meet people with similar interests while you're doing good for something in which you believe. In most areas you can find clubs covering anything from women's rights to substance abuse to hunger and homelessness. Or you could volunteer to work for an organization, many of which have flexible evening and weekend hours. Some organizations don't even require that you leave your home. If you're interested in counseling, for example, you could opt to work for a hotline—the calls can be forwarded directly to your home telephone.

Maribel Becker says there are no limits to the volunteer opportunities available to college students. "There are lots of ways to get involved," she says. "You can join a club or contact your school's fieldwork office. You can also ask the career development office about internships. Internships are available both during the school year and during the summer. This is a good way to explore different careers in which you may be interested. You may even be awarded credit for your community service. In addition, some colleges organize community service events. In this case, you don't have to make a huge time commitment; you can just sign up to work at a shelter for a few hours or take on a specific job, such as painting a house. You can also get your fraternity or sorority to become an active contributor to the community, by raising funds for a favorite charity or adopting an underprivileged child. Aside from assisting a group or cause, it's a good way to meet people and to explore the campus or surrounding community."

So wherever you're headed after graduation, make it a point to take your cause with you. You may even find that your work becomes more meaningful when you're not ticking off hours toward fulfilling a community service requirement or trying to impress a prospective employer or admissions committee. A commitment to volunteerism is one of the most valuable lessons one can learn in high school. Don't leave it behind.

About the Authors

Marian Salzman is the author of six books, including *War and Peace in the Persian Gulf: What Teenagers Want to Know* and *Greetings From High School,* both published by Peterson's Guides, and *Wanted: Liberal Arts Graduates* (Doubleday, 1987). She is managing director of the editorial services/marketing communications firm The Bedford Kent Group, of New York City and London. Salzman is a graduate of Brown University, class of 1981, and River Dell Regional High School in Oradell, New Jersey, and she has been editor in chief of *CV: The College Magazine.* She has also been editor of *Management Review* magazine, and her writing credits include *Forbes, Ms.,* and *Self.* She has been featured in dozens of newspapers and magazines, including *Business Week, Glamour,* the *New York Times,* the *New York Daily News, Savvy,* and *Women's Wear Daily,* and she is a regular guest on radio and television.

Teresa Reisgies is associate editor at The Bedford Kent Group and a graduate of Georgetown University, class of 1989. She is also coauthor of *Greetings From High School.* Teresa grew up in Alpine, New Jersey, and is a graduate of Tenafly High School in Tenafly, New Jersey. She lives in New York City.

Ann O'Reilly is a freelance editor and writer based in Washington State. She is coauthor of *War and Peace in the Persian Gulf: What Teenagers Want to Know* and has been senior editor and copy chief of *CV: The College Magazine*. Ann is a graduate of Bowdoin College, class of 1984, and the University of Denver Publishing Institute, class of 1986. She grew up in New York City and Pelham Manor, New York, and is a graduate of The Ethel Walker School in Simsbury, Connecticut.

Maribel Becker attends Vassar College in Poughkeepsie, New York.

Dan Altman attends Georgetown Preparatory School in Washington, DC.

Maya Beasley attends Bethesda–Chevy Chase High School in Chevy Chase, Maryland.

Sarah Beatty attends Princeton Day School in Princeton, New Jersey.

Jongnic Bontemps attends The Portledge School in Locust Valley, New York.

John Boris attends Brunswick School in Greenwich, Connecticut.

Suzanne Doran attends St. Lawrence University in Canton, New York.

John Gaghan attends Cherry Hill High School East in Cherry Hill, New Jersey.

Nicole Gaghan attends Cherry Hill High School East in Cherry Hill, New Jersey.

Sylvia Heredia attends Bronx High School of Science in Bronx, New York.

Jean Hoffman attends Tower Hill School in Wilmington, Delaware.

Jane Odiseos attends Greenwich High School in Greenwich, Connecticut.

Chris Pennisi attends Manhasset High School in Manhasset, New York.

David Portny attends Colgate University in Hamilton, New York.

Melissa Wagner attends Tower Hill School in Wilmington, Delaware.

MORE OUTSTANDING TITLES FROM PETERSON'S

GREETINGS FROM HIGH SCHOOL

Marian Salzman and Teresa Reisgies with several thousand teenager contributors

High school. Forty-eight months of living and learning. High school. A state of mind.

Adults aren't the only ones who get stressed out. Every day, teenagers deal with these concerns:

- schoolwork, teachers, and advisers
- college and careers
- parents and siblings
- friends
- romance
- money
- sports and fitness
- summer plans
- the media
- the world
- and, yes, how to ace high school

A book by, for, and about high school kids, *Greetings from High School* was written with the help of teenagers whose own words and insights appear throughout. Its upbeat question-and-answer format gives real-world advice . . . and the book is sure to become a "best friend" to teens who want to survive—and thrive—in high school.

$7.95 paperback

PETERSON'S SUMMER OPPORTUNITIES FOR KIDS AND TEENAGERS

An invaluable resource for families of the 4 million young people who participate in summer activities each year, this guide covers more than 1,300 summer programs.

Activities in the guide range from aerobics and aerospace engineering to wrestling and writing and include programs offered by private schools, colleges, camps, religious organizations, and travel and sports groups.

An easy-to-scan chart helps you quickly identify the programs that provide the activities you seek. Complete and up-to-date profiles on each program include:

- Address of the program
- Program offerings
- Type of participants for whom the program is designed
- Program costs
- Jobs offered to high school and college students
- Availability of financial aid

$18.95 paperback